While England Slept

The Theatre of the Absurd, Martin Esslin
Education for Critical Consciousness, Paulo Freire
Pedagogy of Hope, Paulo Freire
Marx's Concept of Man, Erich Fromm
To Have or To Be?, Erich Fromm
Truth and Method, Hans Georg Gadamer
All Men Are Brothers, Mohandas K. Gandhi
Violence and the Sacred, René Girard
Among the Dead Cities, A.C. Grayling
Towards the Light, A.C. Grayling
The Three Ecologies, Félix Guattari
The Essence of Truth, Martin Heidegger
The Odyssey, Homer
Eclipse of Reason, Max Horkheimer
Language of the Third Reich, Victor Klemperer
Rhythmanalysis, Henri Lefebvre
After Virtue, Alasdair MacIntyre
Time for Revolution, Antonio Negri
Apologia Pro Vita Sua, John Henry Newman
The Politics of Aesthetics, Jacques Ranciere
Course in General Linguistics, Ferdinand de Saussure
An Actor Prepares, Constantin Stanislavski
Building A Character, Constantin Stanislavski
Creating A Role, Constantin Stanislavski
Interrogating the Real, Slavoj Žižek
The Universal Exception, Slavoj Žižek

Some titles are not available in North America.

While England Slept

Political Writings: 1936–1939

Winston S. Churchill

Bloomsbury Academic
An imprint of Bloomsbury Publishing Plc

B L O O M S B U R Y
LONDON · NEW DELHI · NEW YORK · SYDNEY

Bloomsbury Academic

An imprint of Bloomsbury Publishing Plc

50 Bedford Square	1385 Broadway
London	New York
WC1B 3DP	NY 10018
UK	USA

www.bloomsbury.com

BLOOMSBURY and the Diana logo are trademarks of Bloomsbury Publishing Plc

First published in the UK as *Step By Step* by Thornton Butterworth Ltd., 1939

Bloomsbury Revelations edition first published in 2015 by Bloomsbury Academic

British Library Cataloguing-in-Publication Data
A catalogue record for this book is available from the British Library.

ISBN: HB: 978-1-4742-2353-9
PB: 978-1-4725-8751-0
ePDF: 978-1-4725-8753-4
ePub: 978-1-4725-8752-7

Library of Congress Cataloging-in-Publication Data
A catalog record for this book is available from the Library of Congress.

Series: Bloomsbury Revelations

Typeset by Deanta Global Publishing Services, Chennai, India
Printed and bound in India

Contents

Maps

PREFACE

During the last three years I have written a fortnightly letter mainly about Foreign Policy and Defence. When I came to read these letters through I was surprised to find that they seemed to tell the tale of these three eventful and disastrous years in a continuous flow. They are at once a running commentary upon events as they happened or were about to happen, and a narrative of what we have lived through. I therefore thought it would be right to present them to the readers of Great Britain, the United States, France and Scandinavia in this volume and its translations which I trust may be accepted as a faithful record.

I have not omitted a single letter nor have I altered what was written at the time in any essential. Where I have modified my opinion as the tale unfolded I have not concealed the change, the reasons for which emerge in the account. The reader may judge for himself how far these comments and forecasts, written in most cases before the events occurred, have been vindicated. It is a gratification to me that His Majesty's Government have at length by leisurely progress along their own paths of thought adopted even in detail the policy and theme set forth. I cannot conceal my sorrow that they did not reach these conclusions earlier. These contrary emotions lead me with all diffidence to present the story in a connected and permanent form.

Winston S. Churchill.
May 21st, 1939.

FOREWORD

In May 1935 Herr Hitler, having already outstripped Great Britain in the Air, repudiated the clauses of the Versailles Treaty which limited the size of the German Army to one hundred thousand long-service soldiers, and instituted universal compulsory military service. The Ministers of Great Britain, France and Italy met at Stresa and discussed common action to prevent the further one-sided denunciation of treaties. The Council of the League of Nations was invited to protest, and did so by formal resolution. Mr. Ramsay Macdonald yielded the Premiership to Mr. Baldwin, and Sir Samuel Hoare succeeded Sir John Simon as Foreign Secretary. On June 18 the Anglo-German Naval Agreement was signed which liberated Germany from the Naval stipulations of Versailles. This had the effect of condoning the breach of the Military clauses and was thus inconsistent with the action newly taken by Great Britain both at the Stresa Conference and at Geneva. All attempt to bring collective pressure upon Germany to prevent her rearmament was abandoned, and when, later in the year, a quarrel developed between Great Britain and Italy over the invasion of Abyssinia, the so-called 'Stresa front' was dissolved and the foundation of the Berlin-Rome Axis laid.

In November Mr. Baldwin appealed to the country upon the policy of sanctions against Italy in order to compel Signor Mussolini to relinquish his Abyssinian campaign. The result of the General Election confirmed Mr. Baldwin in power by an overwhelming majority.

On March 7, 1936, Herr Hitler reoccupied the Rhineland, denouncing the Treaties of Versailles and Locarno, but indicating that the occupation was purely symbolic. No steps were taken by the parties to the Treaty of Locarno to join in requiring the military evacuation of the Rhineland; nor was any attempt made to secure that it should not be fortified. The very great dangers resulting from the German occupation and fortification of the Rhineland were partially realised; and Mr. Eden, who had succeeded Sir Samuel Hoare as Foreign Secretary, announced to Parliament that Staff conversations with France would begin in order if necessary to carry out British obligations under the Treaty of Locarno. This step constituted in principle a military alliance between Great Britain and France; but for a long time very little was done to implement it. It is at this point that the story in these pages begins.

BRITAIN, GERMANY AND LOCARNO
MARCH 13, 1936

There has rarely been a crisis in which Hope and Peril have presented themselves so vividly and so simultaneously upon the world scene. When Herr Hitler on Saturday last repudiated the Treaty of Locarno and marched his troops into the Rhineland, he confronted the League of Nations with its supreme trial and also with its most splendid opportunity. If the League of Nations survives this ordeal there is no reason why the horrible, dull, remorseless drift to war in 1937 or 1938, and the preparatory piling up of enormous armaments in every country, should not be decisively arrested. A reign of law may be established in Europe, the sanctity of Treaties may be vindicated, and from that commanding eminence Germany may be welcomed back to the family of nations upon terms which will assure her a safe and honourable future. The risks to be run to gain this prize are, however, serious in the last degree. They must be faced with firm convictions and a steadfast gaze unfilmed by illusion.

France believes and declares that she has sustained a grievous injury at the hands of Germany. If *we* had been invaded four times in a hundred years, we should understand better how terrible that injury is. England has not seen the camp fires of an invading army for nearly a thousand years. To France and Belgium the avalanche of fire and steel which fell upon them twenty years ago, and the agony of the German occupation which followed, are an overpowering memory and obsession. The demilitarised zone which they gained by awful sacrifices is to them not only a bulwark, but the guarantee of a breathing space between them and mortal calamity. How should we feel if—to change the metaphor—we saw a tiger, the marks of whose teeth and claws had scarred every limb of our bodies, coming forward and crouching within exactly the distance of a single spring? Whether these fears are justified or not, is arguable. But it is particularly important for us to realise how the French and Belgians feel.

Instead of retaliating by armed force, as would have been done in a previous generation, France has taken the proper and prescribed course of appealing to the League of Nations. She has taken her case before the Court and she asks for justice there. If the Court finds that her case is just, but is unable to offer her any satisfaction, that will be a very serious blow to the Court. The Covenant of the League of Nations will have been proved a fraud and collective security a sham. If no means of patient, lawful redress can be offered to the aggrieved party, the whole doctrine of international law and co-operation, upon which the hopes of the future are based, would lapse ignominiously. It would be replaced immediately by a system of alliances, and groups of nations, deprived of all guarantees but their own right arm, which might take the law into their own hands and strike for their vital safety at whatever moment offered them the best chance.

On the other hand, if the League of Nations were able to enforce its decree upon one of the most powerful countries in the world found to be an aggressor, then the authority of the League is set up upon so majestic a pedestal that it must henceforth be the accepted sovereign authority by which all the quarrels of peoples can be determined and controlled. Thus we might upon this occasion reach by one single bound the realisation of our most cherished dreams.

But the risk! No one must ignore it. How can it be minimised? There is a simple method: the assembly of overwhelming force, moral and physical, in support of international law. If the relative strengths are narrowly balanced, war may break out in a few weeks, and no one can measure what the course of war may be, or who will be drawn into its whirlpools, or how, if ever, they will emerge. But if the forces at the disposal of the League of Nations are four or five times as strong as those which the Aggressor can as yet command, the chances of a peaceful and friendly solution are very good. Therefore every nation, great or small, should play its part according to the Covenant of the League.

Upon what force can the League of Nations count at this cardinal moment? Has she sheriffs and constables with whom to sustain her judgments, or is she left alone, impotent, a hollow mockery amid the lip-serving platitudes of irresolute or cynical devotees? Strangely enough for the destiny of the world, there never was a moment or occasion when the League of Nations could command such overwhelming force. The Constabulary of the world is at hand. On every side of Geneva stand great nations, armed and ready, whose interests as well as whose obligations bind them to uphold, and, in the last resort, enforce, the public law. This may never come to pass again. The fateful moment has arrived for choice between the New Age and the Old.

But there is one nation of all others which has the opportunity of rendering a noble service to the world. Herr Hitler and the great disconsolate Germany he leads have now the chance to place themselves in the very forefront of civilization. By a proud and voluntary submission, not to any single country or group of countries, but to the sanctity of Treaties and the authority of public law, by an immediate withdrawal from the Rhineland, they may open a new era for all mankind and create conditions in which German genius may gain its highest glory. So much upon the main issue.

I have not mentioned the obligations of Great Britain under the Treaty of Locarno. They are absolute. There is no escape from them. There is much goodwill in England towards Germany, and a deep desire for the day when the clouds may be dispersed and the three great peoples of Western Europe may join hands in lasting friendship. But it ought not even to be necessary to state that Great Britain, if ultimately called upon, will honour her obligations both under the Covenant of the League and under the Treaty of Locarno.

STOP IT NOW!
APRIL 3, 1936

It is a mistake to suppose that the problem of averting another European or probably a world war depends to any important extent either upon the reply which Herr Hitler has made to the Locarno Powers, or to staff conversations now decided upon between Great Britain and France or Belgium. Herr Hitler is continuing his efforts to separate Great Britain from France, and also to separate British public opinion from the British Government and House of Commons. The British Government, on the other hand, is anxious to comfort France in view of the great restraint which France, largely in deference to British wishes, has observed in presence of the German breach of treaties and military reoccupation of the Rhine zone. The realities are far larger and more profound than either of these moves upon the diplomatic chessboard.

First stands the rapid and tremendous rearmament of Germany, which is proceeding night and day and is steadily converting nearly seventy millions of the most efficient race in Europe into one gigantic, hungry war-machine. The second is that the recent actions of Germany have destroyed all confidence in her respect for treaties, whether imposed as the result of defeat in war or freely entered into by post-War Germany and confirmed by the Nazi regime. The third is that practically the whole of the German nation has been taught to regard the incorporation in the Reich of the Germanic population of neighbouring states as a natural, rightful and inevitable aim of German policy. The fourth is that the financial and economic pressures in Germany are rising to such a pitch that Herr Hitler's government will in a comparatively short time have only to choose between an internal and an external explosion.

Anyone who bears these terrible and sombre realities constantly in mind will acquire that sense of proportion without which the daily gestures and speeches of rulers, politicians and diplomatists are liable to be merely misleading. All who have acquired this indispensable standard of judgment will see that the issue which is open is not really one between Germany and France, nor between Germany and the Locarno Powers. It is an issue between Germany and the League of Nations. Indeed, expressed in its most searching terms, it is a life and death struggle between the Nazi regime in Germany and the principles of the Covenant of the League of Nations reiterated by the Kellogg Pact.

It therefore concerns all nations, including the German people themselves: but it concerns them all in very different degrees. The countries which lie upon or near the borders of Germany are in the front line. They see the wonderful roads along which four columns of troops or motor vehicles can move abreast, brought to their own frontier terminals. They dwell under the flickering shadow of the most fearful sword ever wrought by human agency, now uplifted in flashing menace, now held anew to the grindstone. Those that are more remote from the German arsenals and training-centres have naturally a greater sense of detachment. But none, even though protected by the oceans can, as experience of the last war proved, afford to view with indifference the processes which are already in motion.

The dear desire of all the peoples, not perhaps even excluding a substantial portion of the German people themselves, is to avoid another horrible war in which their lives and homes will be destroyed or ruined and such civilisation as we have been able to achieve reduced to primordial pulp and squalor. Never till now were great communities afforded such ample means of measuring their approaching agony. Never have they seemed less capable of taking effective measures to prevent it. Chattering, busy, sporting, toiling, amused from day to day by headlines and from night to night by cinemas, they yet can feel themselves slipping, sinking, rolling backward to the age when 'the earth was void and darkness moved upon the face of the waters.' Surely it is worth a supreme effort—the laying aside of every impediment, the clear-eyed facing of fundamental facts, the noble acceptance of risks inseparable from heroic endeavour—to control the hideous drift of events and arrest calamity upon the threshold. Stop it! Stop it!! Stop it now!!! NOW is the appointed time.

When, on that Friday night three weeks ago, Herr Hitler, against the advice of his generals, ordered his redoubtable troops to march through the 'scraps of paper' to occupy and entrench the Rhineland, he set in motion a trend of events which offered nothing less than blessing or cursing to mankind. Which fate shall befall us rests no longer with him, but with the world. The world, nay, Europe alone, is overwhelmingly strong compared to any single member of its family. But there must be Concert and Design guided by far-sighted unselfishness and sustained by inexorable resolve. This is no task for France; no task for Britain; no task for the Locarno Powers or any group of Powers; no task for small Powers nor for great; it is a task for all. The means are at hand; the occasion has come. There may still be time.

Let the States and peoples who lie in fear of Germany carry their alarms to the League of Nations at Geneva. Let the greatest among them lead the way and marshal the assembly. Let none be a laggard or a doubter. Let the League, if satisfied that their fears are well-founded, authorise, nay, adjure them, to take forthwith all necessary measures for mutual protection, and require them to stand in readiness alike to submit themselves to, or, if need be, enforce the reign of international law. Let us have, in the words of a writer in *The Times*: 'A block of peaceable but resolute nations determined to make a stand against aggression in any form.' Let the League then address Germany *collectively*, not only upon her treaty breaches but also upon her own grievances and anxieties, and, above all, upon her armaments. Let Germany receive from united nations a guarantee of the inviolability of her own soil unless she invades the soil of others. Let unchallengeable power and fair play march hand in hand. Let us move forward by measured steps, without haste and without rest, to a faithful and a lasting settlement in accordance with the general need.

WHERE DO WE STAND?
APRIL 17, 1936

Where do we stand about Italy and Abyssinia?

The past unfolds a lamentable tale. When, last June, Mr. Baldwin became Prime Minister in name as well as in fact, his first step was to remove Sir John Simon from the Foreign Office and install in his stead one of his closest adherents, Sir Samuel Hoare. This accomplished Minister had at length succeeded in carrying into law the India Constitution Bill, upon which Mr. Baldwin's heart was set. His promotion to the Foreign Office meant not only a reward for his achievement, but a special mark of the confidence which his chief felt in him. In order, however, to preserve a most intimate control over foreign policy, Mr. Baldwin adopted the extraordinary experiment of having a second Foreign Office representative in the Cabinet. He appointed the youthful and able Mr. Anthony Eden to be Minister for League of Nations affairs. Such an arrangement was clearly unworkable except upon the basis that the Prime Minister himself would give constant personal guidance. Having practically made two Foreign Ministers, he was in a position to hold the balance between them and to control both. We are bound, therefore, to attribute to the Prime Minister a degree of responsibility even beyond what is inseparable from his high office. All the power was in his hands. Let us, then, recall the main features of his policy.

A General Election was approaching in which foreign affairs must play an abnormal part. Earlier in the year the League of Nations Union had taken a ballot at which no fewer than eleven million persons in Great Britain had voted in favour of active adherence to the Covenant of the League, and a large proportion in favour of making serious and even military exertions to enforce it. Upon this strong national impulse both Mr. Baldwin's Foreign Ministers pressed the case for sanctions against Italy to their utmost. Great Britain took the lead at Geneva. Mr. Eden fought a vigorous battle for sanctions upon the committees there, and whipped up the nations in support of the British view as if they were to vote in a lobby. Early in September, when the ground was thus prepared, Sir Samuel Hoare flew to Geneva and delivered an oration in favour of the enforcement of the Covenant, which was accepted not only throughout Europe, but all over the world, as one of the greatest declarations upon international affairs ever made since the days of President Wilson. He received the rapturous applause of all the small States at Geneva, and the support not only of all parties at home but of all the Dominions of the British Empire.

Mr. Baldwin's policy and Mr. Baldwin's Ministers were thus raised to the highest pinnacle, and British foreign policy became the cynosure of world attention. The prominent part Britain was taking against Italy galvanised the League of Nations into action, and more than fifty States imposed their censures and their sanctions upon the Italian aggressor. The Abyssinians were encouraged to a desperate resistance by the feeling that almost the whole world, and, above all, Great Britain, were behind them.

These steps excited the vehement resentment of Italy. Threats filled the Government-controlled Italian Press. It became urgently necessary to reinforce the British Fleet in the Mediterranean and to place all our important establishments in and around that inland sea upon a war-footing. As these movements of ships, troops and aeroplanes became apparent, the possibility of war between Great Britain and Italy suddenly broke upon the British public. The Labour Party and the trade unions by a large majority threw their weight behind the Government and its cause. They dismissed their pacifist leader, Mr. Lansbury, and were in fact split from end to end. In these circumstances the General Election was fought under the most favourable conditions for Mr. Baldwin. The electors returned an enormous majority in favour of his policy, and he reached a position of personal power unequalled by any Prime Minister since the close of the Great War.

It was therefore with an intense spasm of surprise and disgust that Parliament and the public found themselves confronted with the Hoare-Laval proposals to reward the Italian aggressor with a great part of Abyssinia. These emotions were stimulated by the fact that at that time the Italian campaign seemed to be at a standstill. Mr. Baldwin approved, and led his Cabinet in approving, the Hoare-Laval scheme, and he told the House of Commons that if his lips were unsealed, no man would vote against him. However, when several days later he felt the full tide of the public indignation, he forced his Foreign Secretary to resign and solemnly admitted he had made a mistake. He sought to placate the League of Nations Union and their eleven million ballotteers by placing Mr. Eden in sole control of the Foreign Office. He repudiated the Hoare-Laval proposals, and resumed the policy of limited sanctions from which he and Sir Samuel Hoare had recoiled on account of its great danger. From that moment we saw Mr. Baldwin and his Cabinet carrying out a policy which their better judgment told them was too dangerous.

Meanwhile France had been dragged so far by Great Britain upon the sanctions path that her good relations with Italy were sensibly injured. The so-called Stresa front was broken. Herr Hitler saw his opportunity, and ordered the German legions to reoccupy the Rhineland. A crisis of supreme magnitude thereupon developed, and henceforward dominates European affairs. Great Britain is forced by her treaties to range herself if necessary in defence of France and Belgium, and staff conversations are now being held upon the war plan. At the same time, by pursuing the policy of sanctions against Italy which had proved so popular in the autumn, she condemns herself to weaken France and strengthen the force and prestige of the German Nazi regime. We have thus been led during the last nine months into a contradiction of purpose as hazardous as it is grotesque. To persist in sanctions is certainly perilous and probably futile. To recede exposes Mr. Baldwin and his Ministers to a humiliation before all the world ludicrous if it were not tragical.

Meanwhile what has happened to the Negus and his barbaric Highland warriors? I shall not attempt to prophesy, but obviously the Italian armies have made immense unexpected progress in their campaign. Seared and suffocated by poison gas, mown down by machine-guns, battered by artillery, bombed from the air, the primitive military organisation of the Ethiopians is in fearful disarray. Can they last till the torrential rains begin? If so, can they maintain a guerrilla until the autumn? If they can, will Mussolini and his gold reserve stand the strain? And, in any case, what other events are going to happen in Europe during these months of ever-growing tension? Ought we to encourage Abyssinia by feeble and half-hearted sanctions to further resistance? Ought we, on the other hand, to become parties to a settlement on terms incomparably worse than those which excited British wrath in the Hoare-Laval agreement?

One thing stands out squarely from this disastrous tangle. The Government must not delay the conclusion of a peace, if the Negus is forced to it, even though its terms are profoundly repugnant and mortifying to British public opinion. They must not think of themselves or of their political position. Unless Mr. Baldwin is prepared to take some effective action which will actually help the Ethiopian people, and face the consequences of that action, whatever they may be, he and his Ministers should not presume to offer guidance to Europe.

HOW GERMANY IS ARMING
MAY 1, 1936

One looks at the people going about their daily round, crowding the streets on their business, earning their livelihood, filling the football grounds and cinemas. One reads their newspapers, always full of entertaining headlines whether the happenings are great or small. Do they realise the way events are trending? And how external forces may effect all their work and pleasure, all their happiness, all their freedom, all their property and all whom they love? I can only see one thing. I see it sharper and harsher day by day. Germany is arming more strenuously, more scientifically and upon a larger scale, than any nation has ever armed before. I make my contribution to the public thought. I give my warnings, as I have given some before. I do not deal in vague statements. I offer facts and figures which I believe to be true.

How much is the Hitler regime spending upon armaments? It is difficult to learn. All their accounts are wrapped in mystery. No estimates are submitted to any Parliament. There are no longer any budgets. There is no criticism, no debate. We have to find out for ourselves. I declared several months ago that Germany spent upwards of £800,000,000 sterling on warlike preparation in the calendar year 1935 alone. Challenged to produce my justification of this truly astounding assertion, I offer for public consideration four distinct lines of approach, at the end of which lies my conclusion, or something very like it.

According to official and semi-official German statements between March 1933 and June 1935 the public debt of Germany increased by £600 millions and German taxation by £400 millions, a total of £1,000 millions (RM. 12,227 millions). That this prodigious figure is far below the truth the second line of approach will show. Every inland bill in Germany pays a stamp duty equal to one thousandth of its face value. In addition bills usually run for three months, and even when they run for longer periods, they are drawn in the form of three-months bills and prolonged and restamped at the end of the period as if they were new. From these stamp issues we see that in February 1933 the outstanding bills amounted to 8.5 milliard marks, but in May 1935 they had grown by 18.3 milliard marks, or approximately £1,500,000,000 spent in the main by the German government in the three years apart from their normal expenditure as previously existing.

The third approach is this: under the Hitler regime German economy as a whole is subject to close supervision and regulation by the Government. Capital expenditure on private enterprise in particular is subject to specific approval by the German Government. Owing to the limited supply of essential raw materials the German Government permits large capital expenditure on private enterprise only in so far as the expenditure is directly or indirectly devoted to armament purposes. In its bulletin issued at the end of 1935 the Reichskredit Gesellschaft states that the extension of non-residential buildings, which began in 1933, is only to a very small extent due to building operations for purely private enterprise. The following figures are taken from the Bulletin of the Reichskredit Gesellschaft issued at the end of 1935:

		In millions of RM.
Total capital expenditure for buildings, equipment and stores, less amounts spent on residential buildings	1933	4,740
	1934	7,700
(provisional)	1935	10,700
		23,140

Or nearly £2,000 millions.

The fourth line of approach is the increase in the normal income of Germany during the last three years. This can only be due to expenditure by the German nation for capital purposes. That none of this increased income has gone into consumption is shown by the fact that both wages and the cost of living have remained stationary during the period under review. Moreover, the level of wholesale prices for all finished goods other than consumption goods has fallen during the period, while consumption goods have risen rather substantially. The inevitable conclusion is that the increased German national income represents money spent by the Government on warlike preparation.

The following figures are taken from the *Statistical Year Book of the German Reich*, 1935, page 485. The figure for 1935 is an estimate based on figures given in the Bulletin of the Reichskredit Gesellschaft issued at the end of 1935, page 33.

		In millions of RM.
Increase in National income as compared with 1932	1933	1,200
	1934	7,200
(provisional)	1935	11,500
		19,900

Or nearly £1,700 millions.

Now let the reader look at the figures of German capital expenditure and increase of German national income set out above. They are practically in the same progression. The capital expenditure is in round numbers, five, eight and eleven milliards in the three years 1933–34–35, and the increase of the German national income is 1,200, 7,200 and 11,500 in the same period. What does this mean? It means the natural expansion of a munitions programme which, apart from keeping body and soul together, covers and absorbs the whole of German industry. And let the reader note that the figure of 11,000 million marks is substantially the same in both cases. Eleven milliard marks at twelve to the exchange is over £900,000,000. I have committed myself to £800,000,000; but if you like, say it is £700,000,000 or £600,000,000. It makes no difference except in gravity to the significance of the facts. Be it observed that when I challenged the Chancellor of the Exchequer to deny these figures, he in no way suggested that they were not broadly representative of the truth.

As a cross-check we may note the German net imports of armament material. Since 1932 German imports of iron ore have increased 309 per cent., kieselguhr by 145 per cent., bauxite by 153 per cent., asbestos by 197 per cent., nickel by 64 per cent., manganese by 273 per cent., wolfram ore by 345 per cent., chrome ore by 127 per cent., rubber by 64 per cent., and graphite by 220 per cent.

All this has gone into making the most destructive war weapons and war arrangements that have ever been known: and there are four or five millions of active, intelligent, valiant Germans engaged in these processes, working, as General Goering has told us, night and day. Surely these are facts which ought to bulk as large in ordinary peaceful peoples' minds as horse racing, a prize fight, a murder trial or nineteen-twentieths of the current newspaper bill of fare. What is it all for? Certainly it is not all for fun. Something quite extraordinary is afoot. All the signals are set for danger. The red lights flash through the gloom. Let peaceful folk beware. It is a time to pay attention and to be well prepared.

OUR NAVY MUST BE STRONGER
MAY 15, 1936

Bewilderment, not unmingled with dismay, has been caused by the announcement of the Government that, in order to comply with the Treaty of London, no fewer than seven 'C' class cruisers[1] are to be scrapped before the end of this year; that one of the Hawkins class is to be demilitarised at a cost of over £270,000; that the other three are to be reduced from 7.5-in. guns to 6-in. guns. We have been told by the Government that the Admiralty require a minimum of 70 cruisers to protect our food supply. We now have only 56, and the first step taken to raise them to 70 is to reduce them to 48, or even lower if the period when the Hawkins class are being reduced to smaller guns is taken into account. While, on the one hand, the taxpayer will have to pay an immense sum to construct new vessels, he is to watch these quite serviceable ships being destroyed or demilitarised. We are thus disarming and rearming at the same time. To this glaring and irrational climax have we been led by Mr. Ramsay MacDonald's 1931 Treaty of London.

One would have thought, considering that Japan has quitted the Treaty area and that our relations with the United States in naval matters are so good, it would have been possible at the recent Naval Conference to have invoked the Escalator clause by agreement upon all sides. No such steps were taken, and of course if the Government persist in their view that no excessive cruiser building has taken place by other Powers, we must keep our word. What an object lesson this is of the injury done to the Royal Navy and to the taxpayer by the Treaty of London!

It is not the only treaty from which we suffer. The Anglo-German Naval Agreement of 1935 constituted a condonation of German treaty-breaking which to foreign eyes seemed largely to stultify our insistence on the sanctity of international agreements and our main position upon the League of Nations. By it we authorised Germany to build a submarine fleet equal to our own. By it we put it out of our power to retain in Material Reserve old ships, without at the same time authorising Germany to build one-third of their tonnage in new construction. Germany is now building a powerful navy as fast as possible. It will naturally take her several years to build even one-third of our total tonnage, after which we may be told that the weather has changed and that the limitation to one-third is no longer applicable.[2] The Hitler regime therefore gained at our expense considerable prestige, and German naval activities were not in the slightest degree impeded.

It is certain that Germany has developed, to a pitch unprecedented, the process of constructing submarines in components and assembling them with extraordinary rapidity, almost by drill. There is no means of checking the construction of these

---

[1]These cruisers were eventually preserved.
[2]The Treaty was denounced by Herr Hitler on April 28, 1939.

components. In the war German submarine building reached a point where a new U-boat was completed on the average every five days. There is no reason why a similar speed of construction, or even a greater speed, should not manifest itself on the rivers and in the arsenals of Germany in the near future.

The Admiralty are now resolved to rebuild the Battle Fleet. The inquiry instituted under the Minister for the Co-ordination of Defence is not even to be completed, as it might have been in a few weeks, before this important decision is taken. The capacity of Germany in armour, great gun-plants and gun-mountings of the largest kind, is probably at the present moment greatly in excess of ours. No one can tell what use they will make of it in the future. The same kind of awkward surprises may be met with in the rebuilding of the German Navy, and especially the German U-boats, as have proved so disconcerting in the case of their air programme. It will be rejoined that, 'Treaty or no Treaty, nothing can stop them doing whatever they choose.' We ought, then, to have used every breach of Naval clauses of the Peace Treaty as another means of uniting together for purposes of mutual defence those nations which lie in fear of the immense Teutonic rearmament.

The latest of the naval agreements certainly seems to impose disabilities only on those Powers who are parties to it. It restricts in essential ways our freedom of design, the recovery of which is one of the most important aims of British naval policy. In the trammels of the treaties we have been forced to build at great expense unsuitable types of ships not based on any true conception of naval warfare. Both Great Britain and the United States have large numbers of these ten-thousand-ton Treaty cruisers, the bulk of which are thoroughly bad specimens of naval architecture. Japan or Germany, lying outside the new Treaty, enjoy perfect liberty and can easily call into being types which will decisively surpass the best vessels in our existing cruiser fleet. It is of the utmost consequence that the plainest assurances should be given to Parliament that we can escape from this position if at any time such steps are taken by States not parties to the new agreement. But even so it is very likely that a couple of years would elapse before any such danger became apparent. A stern chase is a long chase.

What a story of folly is unfolded in the efforts of the United States and Britain to tie each other down in naval matters! We have deferred out of goodwill to American wishes. The two great peaceful sea-Powers have hobbled each other, tied each other's hands, cramped each other's style, with the result that warlike Powers have gained enormous advantages against them both in the Far East and in Europe. Probably no conscious act of those who seek peace, and who have everything to lose by war, has brought war nearer and rendered aggression more possible than the naval limitations which the two English-speaking nations have imposed upon each other. There is no naval rivalry between us and the United States. No one in this island feels endangered by any additions which America may make to her Fleet. If she liked to build a bigger fleet than ours, most people would feel the safer. But we ought to be free to deal with our own special dangers, which are far more serious than those of the United States and far more near.

The only safe and sensible agreement between our two countries would be one enforcing not a maximum but a minimum of sea-power. And it may be that a day will come when such a principle will be accepted.

ORGANISE OUR SUPPLIES
MAY 29, 1936

In discussing the urgent need for creating a Ministry of Munitions [or Ministry of Supply], with a new Cabinet officer at its head, it is necessary first of all to emphasize the fact that the British Navy stands in an entirely different position from the Army and the Air Force. The Navy is already upon a world scale, enjoying parity with the United States, and incomparably superior in size and quality to the navies of any two European Powers. The Admiralty have their own arsenals and dockyards, and have maintained permanent relations with the armament firms upon which they have been accustomed to rely. There is thus no difficulty in maintaining the Navy, and even in expanding it very considerably, without doing more than open out its existing sources of supply. The maintenance or increase of British naval power is therefore solely a question of money, and the House of Commons is eager to vote for this purpose any sum, however vast, that His Majesty's Government may ask of them. This main bulwark of our strength being thus in a condition to withstand whatever perils the present and immediate future may bring, we are able to discuss with more freedom the totally different and far less satisfactory conditions which prevail in the Army and the Air Force.

The Army requires a very large emergency supply of all kinds of munitions and equipment in order that its reserves may be ample. The Air Force is in the process of being approximately tripled. Here is an enormous expansion which throws the greatest strain upon our manufacturing resources. But quite apart from these immediate needs lies the far greater task of organising British domestic industry so that it will be capable of casting the whole of its immense and flexible power into the channels of war production, assuming that a grave need should arise. In this third case it is not a question of interrupting to any large extent our very active peace-time trade. We have to make our industries what may be called 'ambidextrous,' so that almost every workshop is prepared not merely on paper, but with the proper appliances, to be turned over to war production in the last resort. This task has already been achieved with wonderful efficiency throughout Germany and the German example has been, and is being, followed to a very large extent in France, Italy, Russia, and many smaller countries.

There is no lack of money. The British finances so carefully restored by the Chancellor of the Exchequer are certainly capable of bearing a far greater strain than those of any other country in the world except the United States. The Government have committed themselves to a programme of rearmament which may well cost several hundred millions sterling in the next few years, and Parliament stands ready to vote these sums the moment they are required. The difficulty is not to get but to spend the money. Owing to the great neglect shortsightedness, and procrastination of the last two or three years, it is only possible to broaden the supplies for the Army and the Air Force gradually and slowly. Increasing paper programmes is useless; for the contractors can only earn a fraction of the payments on the existing Government orders. How can this be speeded up? How, besides, can the industries be adapted to meet a war need? Here are the two problems which await the exertions of a Ministry of Munitions.

In a long peace, when the needs of our small Army and modest Air Force were static and largely a matter of routine, their supplies might well be entrusted to the branches of the War Office and Air Ministry concerned. But when expansion on the present scale is urgently required, when a process of adapting the whole industry of Britain to an alternative purpose is imperative, then the problem is no longer one which Service Departments, with their officials, however faithful and zealous, can be expected to cope. Nor is it a problem which should burden the Secretaries of State for War and Air. They should concern themselves with the efficiency and improvement of their respective forces. They must entrust to business men and manufacturers the huge, complicated operation of production. It is no longer a departmental question, but national, industrial and economic.

This is not a process which can be achieved piecemeal. To throw the burden upon the newly appointed Minister for Co-Ordination of Defence [Sir Thomas Inskip] in addition to his prime duties, would be unfair to the man and disastrous to the job. For this Minister to rush around presiding over a series of disconnected inquiries into the hundred and one thorny problems which demand attention in the strategic and supply spheres would result in nothing but confusion and futility. The first lesson of the war, and even indeed of all very large transactions is, that a proper organisation must be created at the summit which covers the whole ground and gradually extends its control in all necessary directions. No human brain, not that of Napoleon himself, could deal directly with the innumerable complications of modern munitions production.

The first step is to bring into being a composite brain twenty times as comprehensive and untiring as that of the most gifted and experienced man. A dozen, perhaps, of the best business men, manufacturers of the new generation in the country, should be formed without delay into a Munitions Council. Each one should have his sphere assigned—design, guns, projectiles, explosives, raw materials, steel, etc.; each denoted by a letter of the alphabet. By ringing the changes upon these letters committees can be formed exactly adapted to handle any particular matter, while the general movement of business is held firmly together by means of a 'clamping committee' and sustained by a strong cadre of Civil Servants. Such a body once brought into being would be able to take over rapidly and by instalments all the existing supply staffs and duties of the War Office and Air Ministry; and developing as it progressed its own machinery, would very soon impart a general movement to the whole process of re-equipping our expanding forces and adapting industry to its war alternatives.

Up to the present the Government have refused to take these steps. They find innumerable excuses for delay. They admit that the necessity may be forced upon them. Meanwhile they remain in a state of indecision. This cannot last. In six months or less when it is realised that all their existing programmes, except the naval programme, are falling hopelessly into arrears, and as the public anxiety grows, they will be forced to do what they should do now, what indeed they should have done a year ago. The more time they waste, the worse our plight will be, and the more violent will be the transition from one system to another. The ordinary peace-time methods cannot accomplish the work declared to be necessary. There is no need to pass at a bound to wartime conditions—it is neither necessary nor indeed possible. But what is needed is not only a new organisation, but a new atmosphere. Many intermediate states are possible between the humdrum of peace and the fearful frenzy of war. There is no need to disturb the vast mass of British industry. We should set up a new organisation of a Ministry of Munitions and declare a period of Emergency Preparation.[1]

---

[1] The Government announced the creation of a Ministry of Supply in April 1939.

HOW TO STOP WAR
JUNE 12, 1936

Surely this is the supreme question which should engage the thoughts of mankind. Compared with it all other human interests are petty and other topics trivial. Nearly all the countries and most of the people in every country desire above all things to prevent war. And no wonder, since except for a few handfuls of ferocious romanticists, or sordid would-be profiteers, war spells nothing but toil, waste, sorrow and torment to the vast mass of ordinary folk in every land. Why should this horror, which they dread and loathe, be forced upon them? How is it that they have not got the sense and the manhood to stop it? Nowadays the masses have the power in all democratic countries. Even under dictatorships they could easily resume the power, if any large proportion of the individuals of whom these masses are composed singled this issue out among all others and thought, spoke and acted about it in a resolute, and if need be, a self-sacrificing manner.

The modern world presents the extraordinary spectacle of almost everybody wishing to prevent or avoid war, and yet war coming remorselessly nearer to almost everybody. Surely this will be the great mystery which future generations will find among the records, and perhaps the ruins, of our age. 'How was it,' the historians of the future will ask, 'that these vast, fairly intelligent, educated, and on the whole virtuous communities were so helpless and futile as to allow themselves to become the victims of their own processes, and of what they most abhorred?' The answer will be, 'They had no plan.' The thinking people in the different countries could not agree upon a plan; the rest continued to gape and chatter vacuously at the approaching peril until they were devoured by it. They were amused from day to day by an endless flow of headlines about trifles amid which they could not, or did not take the trouble to, discern the root of the matter. We have now gone so far down the slope towards the abyss that very blunt, stern measures will be required. Already the ground is beginning to crumble under our sliding feet. An intense effort must indeed be made. Above all, that effort must be practical. Sentiment by itself is no good; fine speeches are worse than useless; short-sighted optimism is a mischief; smooth, soothing platitudes are a crime.

And here at the outset is a mocking paradox, which seems to rob our collective thought of its logic. No plan for stopping war at this present late hour is of any value unless it has behind it force, and the resolve to use that force. Mere passive resistance by some nations would only precipitate the disaster if others, or their leaders, stood ready to take advantage of it. It is easy to deride the pacifist who is ready to fight for peace. None the less, safety will only come through a combination of pacific nations armed with overwhelming power, and capable of the same infinity of sacrifice, and indeed of the ruthlessness, which hitherto have been the attributes of the warrior mind. The scales of

Justice are vain without her sword. Peace in her present plight must have her constables. To bring the matter to an agate point, there must be a Grand Alliance of all the nations who wish for peace against the Potential Aggressor, whoever he may be.[1] Let us, therefore, without delay make this Grand Alliance.

Let all the nations and States be invited to band themselves together upon a simple, single principle: 'Who touches one, touches all.' Who attacks any, will be resisted by all, and resisted with such wrath and apparatus, with such comradeship and hearty zeal, that the very prospect may by its formidable majesty perhaps avert the crime.

Surely there is no other saving thought in the world but this. But how to convert it into reality? 'There's the rub!' What happened to the Negus of Abyssinia when he invoked the sanctity of treaties, and the faith of governments who had admitted him to their pacts? What moral is to be drawn from his melancholy fate? Surely not the moral that the principle of mutual aid was wrong, but rather that the will to enforce it was lacking. To abandon the principle in despair of its efficacy in other circumstances may well be to condemn ourselves to a similar but immeasurably magnified doom. The moral is surely to take steps forthwith to ensure that next time neither the will nor the means will be lacking.

It must be observed that the Potential Aggressor presents himself in different forms to different countries—some fear one, some fear another; that some in each case are near to danger, others some distance from it, others again far off. Theorists would claim that all shall be equally bound in principle and in degree in every case. To ask this is to demand more than mankind in its present development can sustain. To press the theme so far is to divorce it from reality. There must not only be regional pacts, but zones of different though defined responsibility. In the front line, pledged to all the necessary measures, well-equipped, strictly combined, stand those who dwell nearest to the Potential Aggressor; in the second line those likely to be next affected, or indirectly affected, by his aggression. Farther off, and least heavily committed, will be the States who, while they do not fear this particular Potential Aggressor, nevertheless realise that some day, in a different set of circumstances, their turn may come.

To weave together the various regional pacts into one world-wide organism, with the engagement of each nation prescribed according to the occasion, with all the necessary preparations made by each faithful member, presents itself as an immediate, inexorable task. Difficulties must not affright us. If some stand out, all the more must the others be banded together. All the more thoroughly must they be prepared. For what is the alternative? The alternative is being destroyed one by one. When war breaks out who shall say when and where it will stop? Therefore a speedy and genuine organisation of the maximum force against Potential Aggressors by a series of regional pacts included in a Grand Alliance or League offers us the sole hope of preventing war or of preventing, if war should come, the ruin of those who have done no wrong.

---

[1] This policy was at length adopted in substance by Mr. Chamberlain in March, 1939.

WHY SANCTIONS FAILED
JUNE 26, 1936

Sanctions have been dropped with a dull thud. An inglorious chapter in British foreign policy has closed. There was very little doubt among all parties of the House of Commons that this particular step had become inevitable. Even Mr. Lloyd George, while blaming the Government, has declared that in the form in which they were applied, sanctions were contemptible. The Government had therefore no difficulty in proving that the policy they had pursued so long, about which they had delivered so many inspiring speeches, in the name of which they had gained notable advantages at the election, was vain and futile. But before it drifts away down the stream let us just look at Mr. Baldwin's Sanctions policy. Was it ever likely to be effective; was it real or sham?

I began to understand the details of these sanctions only at the beginning of this year, when I discovered the principle upon which they were founded. Parliament ought to have found this out at the beginning. From first to last the sanctions policy stood upon a non-rational basis. First the Prime Minister had declared that sanctions meant war; secondly he was resolved that there must be no war; and thirdly, he decided upon sanctions. It was evidently impossible to comply with these three conditions. We can see now that they were bound to result in fiasco. At an early stage Signor Mussolini let it be known that he would submit to sanctions which merely inflicted hardship upon the Italian people, but that if they hampered the operations of his armies against Abyssinia, he would regard them as an act of war. He thought that any privations or inconvenience, inflicted upon the Italian people would have the effect of rallying them more strongly around him. He thought he could use the pressure of sanctions to make Italy a more completely self-contained and war-mobilised country. The result has vindicated his judgment. What he would not stand was anything that prevented his armies from conquering Abyssinia.

Consciously or unconsciously, unconsciously we must hope, the League of Nations Committee charged with devising sanctions conformed docilely to the limitations prescribed by the Aggressor. They proceeded to the rescue of Abyssinia on the basis that nothing must be done to hamper the invading Italian armies. Let me give some instances. We all know how important aluminium is for war purposes. The export of aluminium into Italy was strictly forbidden by the League of Nations. But aluminium is almost the only metal that Italy produces in quantities beyond her own needs. The importation of scrap iron and iron ore into Italy was sternly vetoed, in the name of public justice. But the Italian metallurgical industry makes but little use of these, and as steel billets and pig iron were not interfered with, Italy suffered no hindrance. It would be easy to multiply these examples. Thus the sanctions which we have been pressing with so great a parade were not real sanctions to paralyse the invader, but merely such half-hearted sanctions as the invader would tolerate, because in fact they stimulated Italian war spirit.

It is true that included in the sanctions were many measures, especially financial measures, which in the long run would have destroyed the Italian financial power to purchase necessities in foreign countries, and that these would have eventually affected their war-making capacity. But the chief of these, the financial sanctions, did not require Geneva to impose them. The credit of Italy had already fallen, and was bound to fall, so low that the ordinary market factors would have been as valid as the League decision. The League of Nations, therefore, embarked upon a policy of sanctions which were largely illusory, many of which arose naturally in any case, and the effects of all of which must require a long time. The general policy at Geneva was 'Sanctions with no teeth in them.' I must frankly confess that I was not aware of this until a few months ago.

It is therefore not true to say that economic sanctions have failed. It was the will power to enforce them in a real and biting manner which failed. It failed because of the mental reservation of the principal Powers concerned that nothing must be done which would provoke a war. If economic sanctions had been imposed with ruthless vigour from the outset, they would have crippled the invading armies. But before this happened Signor Mussolini would have attacked the British Fleet, or let it be known that he would, and therefore, as war was not to be contemplated, it was not possible to press them in an effective manner. Let it, however, be clearly understood that of all the Sanction-imposing Powers Great Britain was the most honest. She executed her part with punctilio; hers was the greatest loss, and had war resulted through an international over-stepping of Mussolini's line, it was Great Britain which would have borne practically the whole brunt.

The morals which result are these. First, do not deal in shams. Second, if it is known that you do not mean to fight, and will do nothing which forces the other side to attack you, it is better not to take a leading part in fierce quarrels. Leadership cannot exist upon the principle of limited liability. Let us hope that these lessons will be digested, not only by the British people but by all the other nations. Not one of them can point a finger of scorn at us, except for our leadership, without at the same time in a greater measure condemning themselves. There is overwhelming reason to condemn the weak and bluffing course, which, no doubt from the best motives, has been followed. There is no reason to despair of collective action against the Aggressor. If a sufficient number of powerfully armed nations were ready to enforce economic sanctions, the Aggressor would in many cases have to submit or attack the combination.

The League has made its first feeble essay in action. Let us hope that next time it will either go in with overwhelming force, or stand clear.

DUSK APPROACHES
JULY 13, 1936

The first Session of the new Parliament is drawing to its close. May it not also be the close of a chapter in modern history?

Ever since the fall of the Lloyd-George Coalition thirteen years ago we have dwelt under what may be known as the 'Baldwin-MacDonald Regime.' At first in alternation, but for the last five years in political brotherhood, these two statesmen have governed the country. Nominally the representatives of opposing parties, of contrary doctrines, of antagonistic interests, they proved in fact to be more nearly akin in outlook, temperament and method than any other two statesmen who have been Prime Ministers since that office was known to the Constitution. Curiously enough the sympathies of each extended far into the territory of the other. Ramsay MacDonald nursed many of the sentiments of the old Tory. Stanley Baldwin, apart from a manufacturer's ingrained approval of Protecttion, was by disposition a truer representative of mild Socialism than any to be found in the Labour ranks. Especially upon Imperial questions like India, Egypt, the mandated territories, and above all National Defence, his temper and feelings corresponded to what used to be called 'Lib.-Lab.' standards.

Both men excelled in the art of minimising political issues, of frustrating large schemes of change, of depressing the national temperature, and reducing Parliament to a humdrum level. Their ideal of government appears to be well expressed by the noble lord in the Gilbert and Sullivan opera who 'did nothing in particular, but did it very well.' No wonder they agreed so happily when, instead of throwing the ball to one another across the Parliamentary table, they settled down as colleagues side by side. How this remarkable regime will be viewed in history depends upon whether the epoch through which they have guided us was a time for great causes and intense effort by all classes, and for striking and lively action by the State; or whether after the exhaustion of the war Great Britain required a solid period of somnolence and tranquillity. If the supreme need of John Bull after the war and its aftermath was a rest-cure, no two nurses were better fitted to keep silence around a darkened room and protect the patient from anything in the nature of mental stress or strong emotion.

No one should disparage such functions. On the contrary, history may well declare that they met the real need and expressed the undoubted wish of the British people after the frightful experiences they had undergone. The suppression of party spirit, the simultaneous frustration of Toryism and Socialism, the formation of Governments of compromise and of amiable futility, the relaxation of National and Imperial morale, which were part of the treatment, may well have enabled the natural processes of healing and recuperation to work upon a constitution so strong as John Bull's. Indeed, if our island were planted a thousand miles out in the Atlantic Ocean, there is no reason why the rest-cure should not have been indefinitely prolonged, and large majorities of the British electorate have proclaimed the dictum, 'Happy are the nations whose annals are blank in the pages of History.'

Unfortunately, we are only ten minutes by air from the stormy Continent, and the jarring clang of external events has broken up this sleepy, though not necessarily unpleasant or unhappy, scene. When four years ago it began to be apparent that the Teutonic giant was stealthily regathering the weapons with which he had almost conquered the world, a dire change affected the whole situation. This unwelcome—nay, hateful—intrusion of the external upon our two poor eminent friends was received by them at first with inveterate incredulity. So unwilling were they to accept the plainest evidence of danger that they covered themselves contentedly with a cloud of well-meaning platitudes. They closed their eyes to what they did not wish to see. Thus the seasons passed swiftly away, and all the time the sombre processes which were to undermine the peace of Europe hurried forward amain.

By the spring of 1934 incredulity was worn threadbare. It was succeeded by half-measures and dismay. No attempt was made to grapple courageously with the European situation while it could have been controlled. Nor were even those simple precautions taken which would have enabled Great Britain to be placed swiftly in a state of security. A year ago Mr. MacDonald transferred the growing burden with exhausted strength to his co-partner. Mr. Baldwin became for the third time Prime Minister. He appealed to the country most urgently to rearm; but at the same time he stipulated that there should be no large rearmament. It may well be that he sustained the impression at the General Election that he won it himself. In fact it was won by the clear resolve of the British people not, amid multiplying dangers, to entrust their affairs to the weak and discredited Socialist Party.

The new Parliament met at Westminster under the impact of realities. Almost every month it has been smitten by fresh hammer-blows. The country is slowly but undoubtedly awakening to the fact that world peace is menaced, and that our island safety is no longer unquestioned. Gradually it is being understood that whereas four years ago all was sure and easy, all has now become dark, doubtful and hazardous in the extreme. It is this growing comprehension that the times have changed, that woeful miscalculations have been made, that a violent period is drawing near, and that we ourselves are neither ready for it nor even making the exertions which are now possible, that has weakened so profoundly the position of the Prime Minister. No one is more affected by this general feeling than himself. National leaders flourish or fade, and ought to do so, only in proportion as they express and meet the public need. Bold captains are required for perilous seas. However unpalatable it may be to docile adherents of the powers that be, the Baldwin-MacDonald regime is passing out of life into history. There may still be time to turn the affairs of the British Empire to a different fortune.

At the end of July 1936 the increasing degeneration of the Parliamentary regime in Spain, and the strength of the movements for a Communist, or alternatively an Anarchist, Revolution, led to a military revolt which had also been long preparing. A ferocious civil war immediately began, with mass executions, class murders, and proportionate reprisals. The French Government proposed a plan of Non-intervention, whereby both sides would be left to fight it out without any external aid. The British Government accepted this view. The German, Italian and Russian Governments also subscribed to it. In consequence the Spanish Government, now in the hands of the most violent revolutionaries, found itself deprived of the right even to buy the arms it had ordered with the gold which it possessed. It would have been more reasonable to follow the normal course, and to have recognised the belligerency of both sides as was done in the American Civil War (1860–5). Instead, however, the policy of Non-intervention was adopted and solemnly agreed to by all the great powers. Italy and Germany on the one side, and Russia on the other made little pretence of breaking continually their agreement. Great Britain alone observed a strict and impartial neutrality throughout.

THE SPANISH TRAGEDY
AUGUST 10, 1936

We must regard the civil war in Spain as a sinister and, perhaps, a fatal milestone on the downward path of Europe. The worst quarrels only arise when both sides are equally in the right and in the wrong. Here on the one hand the passions of a poverty-stricken and backward proletariat demand the overthrow of Church, State and property, and the inauguration of a Communist regime. On the other hand the patriotic, religious and bourgeois forces, under the leadership of the army, and sustained by the countryside in many provinces, are marching to re-establish order by setting up a military dictatorship. The cruelties and ruthless executions extorted by the desperation of both sides, the appalling hatreds unloosed, the clash of creed and interest, make it only too probable that victory will be followed by the merciless extermination of the active elements of the vanquished and by a prolonged period of iron rule.

How did it happen? It happened 'according to plan.' Lenin laid it down that Communists should aid all movements towards the Left and help into office weak constitutional, Radical or Socialist, governments. These they should undermine, and from their failing hands snatch absolute power, and found the Marxist State. This procedure is well known and well proved. It is part of the Communist doctrine; it is part of the Communist drill book. It has been followed almost literally by the Communists of Spain. The constitutional and would-be Liberal and democratic Republic found itself sliding steadily towards the Left. Its ministers soothed the middle classes by the appearances of a Parliamentary system. They weakened or paralysed the resisting power of Conservatives and Monarchists; but they found themselves falling into the grip of dark, violent forces coming ever more plainly into the open, and operating by murder, pillage and industrial disturbance. They continued to play the Parliamentary game long after it had ceased to have any contact with reality. Since the election in the early part of this year, we have witnessed in Spain an almost perfect reproduction, *mutatis mutandis*, of the Kerensky period in Russia.

However, the strength of Spain had not been shattered by a foreign war. The army still retained a measure of cohesion. Side by side with the Communist conspiracy, there was elaborated in secret a deep military counterplot. It is idle to claim that a constitutional and Parliamentary regime is legally or morally entitled to the obedience of all classes, when it is actually being subverted and devoured from day to day by Communism. A constitutional government, to be worthy of the name, must prove itself capable of preserving law and order, and protecting life, freedom and property. If it fails to enforce these fundamental guarantees, no parliamentary system can endure. The murders and outrages which culminated in the assassination of Señor Sotelo produced a situation in which neither side could justly claim the title-deeds of legality, and in which citizens of all classes were bound to consider the life of Spain.

As far as one can judge from the news, which has reached the outside world at this stage, the two sides seem equally balanced and in possession of equal parts of Spain. If it were a question of the Old Spain against a New Spain, between the faith, traditions and culture of the past and the appetites and hopes of the future, it would probably go hard with the so-called 'rebels.' But this is not the issue. *Two* new Spains are struggling for mastery. Two antagonistic modern systems are in mortal grapple. Fascism confronts Communism. The spirit and prowess of Mussolini and of Hitler strive with those of Trotsky and of Bela Kun. Here is no class conflict, no ordinary division of the poor and the rich, of the have-nots against the haves. All the national and martial forces in Spain have been profoundly stirred by the rise of Italy under Mussolini to Imperial power in the Mediterranean. Italian methods are a guide. Italian achievements are a spur. Shall Spain, the greatest empire in the world when Italy was a mere bunch of disunited petty princedoms, now sink into the equalitarian squalor of a Communist State, or shall it resume its place among the great Powers of the world? Here is a living appeal to the youth and manhood of a proud people. The Old Spain fell with the monarchy. The Parliamentary constitution has led to a chaos of blood and fire. Who will make the New Spain, and in what form? There is the issue which it seems must be fought to an indubitable decision.

The reverberations of the Spanish upheaval extend far beyond the boundaries of the Peninsula. Causes are at stake which in varying degrees disturb the people of every land, and sharply divide the governments of Europe. The wars of Religion, we were told, have ended. Perhaps the wars of rival Irreligions have begun. Fascism and Communism each vaunt their themes, and neither will lack champions or martyrs. Can we wonder that Fascist Italy and Nazi Germany hail or aid Spanish insurgents, or that Bolshevist Russia backs the Communist effort? How, then, do the two liberal and Parliamentary nations of the West stand? What is to be the course of France and Britain? Whoever wins in Spain, freedom and free democracy must be the losers. A revivified Fascist Spain in closest sympathy with Italy and Germany is one kind of disaster. A Communist Spain spreading its snaky tentacles through Portugal and France is another, and many will think the worse. The obvious interest of France and Britain is a liberal Spain restoring under a stable and tolerant Government freedom and prosperity to all its people. That we can scarcely hope will come in our time.

Meanwhile it is of the utmost consequence that France and Britain should act together in observing the strictest neutrality themselves and endeavouring to induce it in others. Even if Russian money is thrown in on the one side, or Italian and German encouragement is given to the other, the safety of France and England requires absolute neutrality and non-intervention by them. French partisanship for the Spanish Communists, or British partisanship for the Spanish rebels, might injure profoundly the bonds which unite the British Empire and the French Republic. This Spanish welter is not the business of either of us. Neither of these Spanish factions expresses our conception of civilisation. We cannot afford in our perilous position to indulge a sentimental or a sporting view. All that is happening increases the power of those evil forces which from both extremes menace the existence of Parliamentary democracy and individual liberty in Great Britain and France. Let us stand aloof with redoubled vigilance and ever-increasing defences.

KEEP OUT OF SPAIN
AUGUST 21, 1936

I make no apology for returning to the Spanish scene. The ferocious drama, of which the newspapers give us such lurid accounts, is rolling steadily forward to its climax. It must increasingly grip the attention and emotions of the world. There is no doubt it is being followed with avid interest by the British people. The situation is more clearly defined than it was a fortnight ago. Anyone can see that it is not a revolt, but a civil war, and that the strictest neutrality and impartiality is enjoined—whatever happens—upon Great Britain. The struggle is evenly balanced and may be prolonged. On the whole, at the moment, the advantage seems to be turning against the Government. It is true that they hold Madrid. In almost every war of this kind the side which has held the national Capital has won. London settled the Great Rebellion against Charles I. Again and again Paris has dominated revolts in the French provinces. Washington withstood the onslaught of the confederacy. Moscow proved itself capable of ruling Russia. Many other instances will suggest themselves. Time is on the side of the Government and Madrid. Their Workers' Militia must be gaining in discipline and military knowledge every week. Unless the rebels, anti-reds, patriots or whatever they may be called, according to taste and sympathy, can establish themselves in Madrid in the near future, no one can predict their victory.

On the other hand it seems certain that a majority of Spaniards are on the rebel side. Four and a half millions of them voted only last spring for the various Conservative parties of the Right and Centre against four and a quarter millions who voted for the parties of the Left. One must suppose that those people who were then opposed to constitutional Socialism, are to-day all the more hostile to the Communist, Anarchist and Syndicalist forces which are now openly warring for absolute dominance in Spain. There are large areas of Spain which returned whole blocks of Conservative members to the recent Cortes. Around Burgos and Valladolid, around Cadiz and Seville, dwell communities as solidly Conservative as our Home Counties. In these regions the army leaders find themselves upheld by a friendly population with a wealthy middle class and a daring martial youth. In the Carlist provinces there are other reserves of strength which provide, as long ago in La Vendée, the spectacle of a countryside passionately united in support of Church and Monarchy. Here are strong foundations and bases for the rebel armies. All history shows that armies without civil populations behind them are prone to collapse. No such weakness afflicts the Anti-Red movement.

On the purely military side the insurgents have certainly great advantages. They have trained troops, competent officers and the whole system of an army command. We witnessed at Badajoz their storm of a fortified town and the extermination of defenders who possessed a large supply of modern weapons and outnumbered the attackers by two thousand fighting men. The handiness and discipline of the troops has proved itself in a hundred skirmishes. Foreign opinion has been shocked at the employment of Moorish soldiers in Spain. But the issue is now one of pure, ruthless, lethal force, and questions of sentiment do not count for much between mortal foes in desperation. Bayonets and bullets are the arbiters.

The Anti-Red leaders have in their hands almost all the regular arsenals and munition factories of the Peninsula. They have no doubt received important supplies of munitions and aeroplanes from German and Italian sources. They have the resolute friendship of Portugal, which lies behind them all along their western border. They are now in possession of a naval power in the North certainly equal to the fleet which murdered its officers in the South. Every Spanish colony is enthusiastically on their side. In spite of the military aeroplanes sent by France to the help of Madrid, the Anti-Red Air Force is gaining the ascendancy. The Anti-Reds appear to be steadily closing in upon the Government strongholds, San Sebastian at one end of the country and Malaga at the other. The military cadets and their partisans are still maintaining their epic defence of the Alcazar in Toledo. We must suppose that experienced generals like Franco and Mola, with their professional staffs, have a well-thought-out plan for the capture or reduction by starvation of Madrid, where large numbers of their now terrorised sympathisers await them.

This cold survey of a scene of merciless strife has excluded all emotional considera-tion. The butcheries of the well-to-do classes and of Conservative politicians in Madrid and Barcelona and of the priests wherever the violent Reds can catch them, continue. The Madrid Government, acting under the dictation of the extremists, still feel them-selves strong enough to conduct the formal trials and executions of well-known Rebel generals. On the other side these cruelties are matched by equally bloody and senseless retaliation. In the almost ceaseless wars of mankind the practice of giving quarter did not arise from feelings of humanity. Quarter was given because it paid to give it; because desperate men cost too much life to kill. It is astonishing that General Franco has not realised how great is the advantage to the winning side of offering fair terms of surrender to beaten foes. Such a course would markedly help the winning side.

It looks as if political hatred had blinded military sagacity. Here is the darkest feature in the Spanish civil war. Both sides have the deep conviction that the future of Spain can only be built upon the extermination by thousands, and perhaps by scores of thousands, of their opponents. This sub-human rage manifests itself in every action down to the pettiest village scrimmage. Hatred of the Communists for the existing order of society, hatred of the existing order for the Communists, has effaced all laws, every tie between man and man, every rule of civilised society and even the calculations of common prudence. Two opposite creeds, from both of which Christianity recoils, are at each other's throats. Spain was not bled white by the Great War. It profited from neutrality. The vials of wrath were filled with fermenting poison. We now witness its hideous outpourings. We can only pray that this delirium will subside or that the result will soon declare itself.

Great allowance must be made for the difficulties of M. Blum. It is earnestly to be hoped that even if Germany and Italy, on the one hand, and Soviet Russia, on the other, send help to their respective factions and fence disingenuously with proposals for a collective neutrality, France will none the less adopt the same attitude of detachment as Great Britain. A serious divergence between the two powerful Parliamentary countries of the Western World would be the last disaster. However the Spanish convulsion may end, Great Britain and France will be seriously weakened and the growing ascendancy of Nazism will be proportionately accelerated. It may well be that events are pending in Europe which will relegate the news from Spain to a subordinate position. However hard it may be, there is only one rule for the liberal Parliamentary countries: Send charitable aid under the Red Cross to both sides, and for the rest, Keep out of it and arm.

A dramatic public trial took place in Moscow of the surviving members of Lenin and Trotsky's Bolshevik associates. They pleaded guilty to astonishing acts of treason against the Soviet Republic. Most of them were shot. Thus the Russian, as was said of the French Revolution, 'like Saturn devours its own children.'

ENEMIES TO THE LEFT
SEPTEMBER 4, 1936

Hardly a week passes without some dark, sinister event marking the downward movement of Europe, or revealing the intense pressures at work beneath its surface. The Spanish Horror broadens and deepens as the days pass. A sense of indefinable uneasiness, alike about external and internal affairs, broods over France. Hitler decrees the doubling in numbers and quality of the German army. Mussolini boasts that he has armed 8,000,000 Italians. The smaller States reflect these fears and preparations in strange local variants. Everywhere the manufacture of munitions proceeds apace, and science burrows its insulted head in the filth of slaughterous inventions. Only unarmed, unthinking Britain nurses the illusion of security.

What is the meaning and effect in this oppressive scene of the Moscow executions? The modern world is becoming very familiar with the spectacle, aforetime deemed atrocious, of the shooting of political opponents. It has become almost an everyday occurrence to read of public men in powerful, historic countries being set against the wall by scores and dozens to face the firing squads. Certainly if ever human tears were rightly lacking upon such occasions, it would be at the fate of the Bolshevist Old Guard. Here are the fathers of the Russian Communist Revolution; the architects of the logical Utopia to which, we are assured, the whole world will one day conform; the pioneers of progress to the Left; men whose names and crimes are bywords throughout the world— all put to death by their comrade Stalin, the General Secretary of their party.

Did I say all?—well, all but one. Trotsky still survives to embarrass the well-meaning Norwegians, and Lenin's widow waves him signals of despair faintly distinguishable in the Russian twilight. Gone are the heroes of the British Socialist Party. Kameneff, the maker of the first Anglo-Soviet trade agreement, Zinoviev, of the famous election letter, shot to rags by Soviet rifles. Tomsky, with his gold watch from our Trade Union Congress, blows out his brains to escape his sentence. What does it all convey? What does it all portend?

Many people unable to be shocked at the long-delayed expiation of these miscreants who have blithely sent uncounted thousands of good men to their doom, were nevertheless sickened at the elaborate farce of their trial. Its technique throws a gleam of intimate light upon the mysterious nature of a communist State. We see some glimpses of the unknowable; we feel for a moment the weight of the imponderable. A few points are vividly illuminated. First the abnormal behaviour of the accused. They all avow their guilt. They descant upon the enormity of their crimes. They applaud the justice of their punishment. Each in his turn recites the words put in his mouth by processes we cannot pretend to define. Evidently in this grisly charade each has been well coached in his part.

The obvious conclusion is, of course, that they were promised their lives at the price of their abjection, and then cheated of that sorry guerdon. The odd tiling is that such an exhibition should be expected to make a good impression outside Russia. We see the gulf between the Communist mentality and the wider world.

The second point to notice is that these victims were nearly all Jews. Evidently the Nationalist elements represented by Stalin and the Soviet armies are developing the same prejudices against the Chosen People as are so painfully evident in Germany. Here again extremes meet, and meet on a common platform of hate and cruelty. But it is the third aspect which has most to do with the Western democracies. What is the effect of this butchery upon Russia as a military factor in the balance of Europe? Clearly Soviet Russia has moved decidedly away from Communism. This is a lurch to the Right. The theme of a world revolution which animated the Trotskyists is cracked if not broken. Russian nationalism and discrowned Imperialism present themselves more crudely but also more solidly. It may well be that Russia in her old guise of a personal despotism may have more points of contact with the West than the evangelists of the Third International. At any rate it will be less hard to understand. This is in fact less a manifestation of world propaganda than an act of self-preservation by a community which fears, and has reason to fear, the sharp German sword.

A TESTING TIME FOR FRANCE
SEPTEMBER 18, 1936

There is a great deal of loose alarming talk about what is going to happen in France in October. Everyone can see that very great difficulties and even dangers are closing in upon the French nation. The parties of the Left are in power. There is a renewed epidemic of stay-in strikes. The Communists, of whom seventy were returned at the election, press themselves upon the public attention, now advertising their views on foreign policy and defence, now breathing dark threats about the future.

The decision not to devaluate the franc appears to foreign eyes almost incomprehensible. It is said that the Communists wish to uphold the franc because that is the most likely way to bring about a great exacerbation of economic conditions in France, and so provoke a violent crisis. The new Government of the Popular Front has made many costly concessions to the artisan workers at the expense of the employers, without regard to the economic and financial consequences.

It must be very difficult to carry on a productive business at a profit under the new conditions and especially in view of the extremely quarrelsome, bullying mood of the trade unions and other workers' organisations. No employer is in a position to make forward contracts when at any time he may be exposed to a sudden strike on political grounds alone. Trade is slack under the severe deflationary policy. Prices are going up. Bread and meat, especially the former, have risen remarkably. The extra wages granted incontinently by the Government are already being sensibly reduced by the increasing cost of living. The tragedy of the Spanish civil war continues to play every day directly under the eyes of the French people, and its varying fortunes and invariable brutality stir profoundly every section of politics, and range in hateful and perilous antagonism not only parties but classes. Meanwhile Germany continues to arm night and day, and her giant power rises in clanking panoply month by month on both banks of the Rhine.

It must be admitted that this is a formidable catalogue upon which the prophets of disaster may feast their minds. What wonder that the well-to-do should be thoroughly frightened! What wonder that a horrible bitterness infects the brilliant journalism of France! Is it strange that the allies and friends of France in eastern and southern Europe should feel profoundly uneasy, or that small Powers, and not only small Powers, which have a move either way, should be considering with which European system their safety lies? Is it strange that we should hear it said in many interested quarters that the Communists are going to plunge France into the same ferocious welter as they have plunged Spain; or that German propaganda should so hopefully and stridently invite all conservative nations to form up behind the inimitable Führer in his grand and indispensable anti-Bolshevist and anti-Communist campaign?

However, I am very decidedly of opinion that France is going to come through her troubles this autumn and winter, not only without any fatal catastrophe, but with an actual accretion of moral and material strength. No doubt parliamentary countries cannot present the same show of unity as can be commanded by Nazi or Communist regimes. Not to criticise the government of the day is, in a parliamentary country, to be out of the fashion. To criticise it in a Nazi or Communist State is to be sent to the concentration camp, the gaol or the grave. It must not, however, be supposed that because no expression is allowed to Russian and German feelings, everyone in those countries are entirely satisfied with their lot. In France as in England every form of discontent can manifest itself. Troubles rise to the surface, and at the same time also there often rise forces to control or remedy them.

There is no resemblance between France and Spain. Spain is the most backward country in Europe; her people miserably poor, long cramped by the Church, and with a fierce subterranean life of their own. France had her revolution nearly one hundred and fifty years ago when she led all Europe by terrible paths into the modern age. The peasants have the land. The aristocracy are broken. The Church is quelled. For good or for ill the French people have been effectively masters in their own house, and have built as they chose upon the ruins of the old regime. They have done what they like. Their difficulty is to like what they have done. Nevertheless, the whole character of French society is incomparably superior to that of Spain in moral quality, in military power, in urbanity, experience and intelligence.

But there is another difference no less decisive between France and Spain. No country in Europe has been so detached from external affairs as Spain. No country is more exposed to foreign pressure than France. The outbreak of a civil war in France, or even a marked degeneration of French national life, would be the signal not only for the destruction of French authority and world power, but for the immediate pillage of French territory in Alsace-Lorraine and in the Mediterranean. Foreign invasion prowls like a wolf around every French cottage home. There is only one safeguard. It has hitherto proved effective—the French army. Since the fall of the monarchy the French army has been the highest expression of the soul of France. No one can doubt its fine enduring qualities. English people who speak slightingly of the strength of the French Republic should remember that it is common ground between all parties in France at the present moment that at least two years' compulsory military service should be required of every Frenchman in time of peace. The sense of national comradeship and unity which calls forth this immense and ungrudged sacrifice gives us the measure of patriotism with which French people in the mass confront their dangers.

Since the fall of the Roman Empire the Gallic race have maintained themselves against all comers in possession of what is upon the whole the fairest tract of the earth's surface. It will take a lot to convince me that the qualities and devotion which have made and preserved the greatness of France have suddenly departed from the French people.

But this is the testing time.

AN OBJECT LESSON FROM SPAIN
OCTOBER 2, 1936

The civil war in Spain now presents a picture which is very clearly defined. The dread scales have tilted decidedly, if not indeed decisively, against the Government. For the last six weeks all initiative has rested with the so-called rebels or Nationalists, as they prefer to be called. They alone possess forces capable of attacking effectively. The storming of Badajoz was the first sign of their mettle. The long and hard fighting for Irun proved their cohesion and pertinacity. The heroic defence of the Alcazar revealed qualities not often equalled in the annals of war.

At the beginning the generals expected an easy and even a bloodless victory. They laid their plans with deliberation. General Franco's letter to the Minister of War, written three weeks before the revolt, shows how earnestly he was warning the Government of the perils into which they were drifting. It may well be that he and the leading soldiers, all of whom had faithfully served the Republic, expected that the Government, when it found itself losing grip, would call upon the army for aid. Perhaps this would have happened if the moment had been delayed; but the murder of Señor Sotelo was the spark that fired the mine.

The whole army obeyed the orders of their generals—the officers with ardour, the soldiers dubiously. Nevertheless, every garrison mutinied dutifully. Only in Barcelona, Madrid and San Sebastian were there miscarriages. There the fierce rally of Socialists, Communists and Anarchists affected the soldiers. The officers were disarmed and arrested, and have been shot by scores, and even hundreds, as the weeks have passed. Elsewhere throughout the whole peninsula the military have gained or held control. Their advance has been continuous. Every objective they have set before themselves has so far been achieved. Nowhere have they yielded territory. They have been strong enough to pursue a spirited campaign in the north at the same time as their main advance upon Toledo and Madrid. They have beaten the Government militia in almost every single action, and they are now closing in from every quarter on Madrid, which they threaten either with assault or famine or both.

Meanwhile horrible degeneration has taken place upon the Government side. The position of President Azaña and those who led Spain to the precipice is agonising. They committed a grievous crime by allowing the Parliamentary system to cover the advance of Communism and Anarchy. They undermined every stabilising force. They drifted each week into more hopeless impotence. They clung to the responsibilities of office while all the means of discharging them were fast slipping from their hands. And then suddenly hell broke loose all round them. In a single morning they were engulfed in a ferocious bloody tumult. The helpless Parliamentarians found their only defenders in the dark extreme forces which had revolted against the Republic in 1934. All real authority passed at once from the Ministers. Some were allowed or often compelled to remain as puppets to make a show of constitutionalism. In this situation they presided over the hideous series of nightly butcheries which have robbed the Madrid Government of the lineaments of a civilised power. After a few weeks of farce their presence could be dispensed with, and the direct rule of Communists and Anarchists was openly established. Señor Largo Caballero, the 'Lenin of Spain,' is now engaged in the double task of carrying forward the Marxian revolution and defending the contracting circular front around Madrid.

A civil war of this character, where hatreds and reciprocal injuries rise to an incredible pitch, was almost bound to be disgraced by military severities on both sides. Some discernment is necessary in judging these. It is a barbarian act to deny quarter to wounded and to fighting men taken in arms, unless they are proved to have committed outrages against the customs of war. But of this there are endless examples in the history of many nations. The massacre of hostages falls to a definitely lower plane; and the systematic slaughter night after night of helpless and defenceless political opponents, dragged from their homes to execution for no other crime than that they belong to the classes opposed to Communism, and have enjoyed property and distinction under the Republican constitution, ranks with tortures and fiendish outrages in the lowest pit of human degradation.

Although it seems to be the practice of the Nationalist forces to shoot a proportion of their prisoners taken in arms, they cannot be accused of having fallen to the level of committing the atrocities which are the daily handiwork of the Communists, Anarchists, and the P.O.U.M., as the new and most extreme Trotskyist organisation is called. It would be a mistake alike in truth and wisdom for British public opinion to rate both sides at the same level.

It is always rash to predict the course of violent events. But it is not easy to discern any forces on the Government side capable of preventing the capture by the Junta troops of Madrid, Malaga and Bilbao within a comparatively short time. Once the Junta is established in Madrid, all Spain, except Catalonia, will pass under the complete and sovereign control of a Government and army which will certainly have behind them not only overwhelming military forces, but the ardent support of the majority of the nation, including all its strongest elements. Such a regime will be immediately recognised by Germany and Italy and hailed with enthusiasm by neighbouring Portugal. It may well be that the final phase of the struggle will be a new Nationalist war waged by the whole of Spain for the reconquest of Separatist Catalonia. Such is the grim and sombre outlook.

A strange mood of fatalism reigns over these Spanish combatants. Men of all classes on both sides accept their fate with dignity and composure, entranced by some lyrism of Death. If it be true that grass grows quickly over battlefields but slowly over execution grounds, there will be many bare spots in Spain. No one can impugn the courage of the untrained Communist and Anarchist militias who rush impetuously upon their more competent foes. On the other side, the defence of the Alcazar by its unconquerable cadets will live for ever in the history of Spain. If to a fibre so tense and a devotion so boundless the victors can add the quality of mercy, they may at the end of their journey make Spain a home for all its people.

But of this there is at present no sign.

THE COMMUNIST SCHISM
OCTOBER 16, 1936

We live in a very queer time. The rival political religions of the Communists and the Nazis grate upon one another. Their devotees evidently wish to fly at each other's throats. They wish to make the world the arena of their struggle, and urge us to join one side or the other. But the vast central mass of mankind, including no doubt a majority of the populations of Communist and Nazi countries, would like to be let alone to live in peace and bring up their children and make a little money, and have some pleasure in life. The question which distresses us is whether these ardent passionate fanatics at either end of the political scale are going to have the power to plunge us all into their dark and peculiar quarrels.

It becomes most necessary to understand, if that be possible, the position and policy of the Russian Bolshevist Government. What Rome is to Catholics, Moscow is to the Communists of every country: with the important difference that whereas devout Catholics contribute to the centre of their faith, it is Moscow which distributes money to its adherents in foreign lands. A remarkable dualism, amounting to a veritable schism, has grown up in Moscow. For ten years it has been mainly confined to the higher organisation of the Soviet Republic. Put shortly, it is the quarrel between Stalin and Trotsky. Stalin has now come to represent Russian nationalism in somewhat threadbare Communist trappings. Trotsky stands for the orthodox theory of international world revolution. Stalin has acquired Lenin's authority. Trotsky, banished, hunted, a world-pariah, has Lenin's message. Inside Russia Stalin is supreme. He broods and presides over a change which has shifted the axis of Russia. Russia, under the pressure of Germany and Japan, is being focussed around the Russian army. The predominance formerly exerted by the Communist priesthood, is now passing with the full assent of the Dictator to the high military command, upon whom the life-defence of the nation may at any moment fall. It would be premature and far too sweeping to say that Russia is a military dictatorship rather than a Communistic State. In fact, Russia enjoys the blessings of both dispensations at the present time; but there is no doubt which is on the wane.

It follows from all this that a very noticeable division has broken out among the Communists in all the different countries outside Russia. Those who are paid by the Soviet Government, or are still under the Moscow spell, conceive as their first duty the furtherance of Russian foreign policy and the maintenance of Russian national safety. The orthodox doctrinaires in whom resides the pure venom of the Leninic word regard these tendencies with fury and disgust. There is thus a rift throughout the whole Communist underworld.

The external action of Moscow proceeds along two contradictory paths: the first tries to bring about the world revolution. It has played an all-important part in giving birth to the Spanish Horror. The second seeks to become a serviceable factor in European relationships, and is, whatever we may feel about it, an essential element in the balance of power.

These antagonistic forces now manifest themselves remarkably in France. There the official Communists, Moscow pattern, Stalin brand, present themselves as active, competent agents for the strength of France. They are the declared supporters of M. Blum. They do their best to make things as easy as possible for him. They not only vote all the credits for defence; they urge that even more intense efforts should be made. They do nothing to hamper the preparations of the French army, and would to-morrow support and smooth out its mobilisation in the face of a Nazi menace. Communist conscripts present themselves with the utmost punctuality at the depots, and in many cases prove model soldiers. Communist agitators use their influence against serious interruption in the production of munitions of all kinds in the factories. I am not at the moment commenting on these facts. I am merely stating them. The perverted intelligences of these sectaries make them willing, though Frenchmen, to fight not for France, but for Russia, or to fight for France only if France will fight for Russia.

On the other hand, the Trotskyites, now almost entirely cut off from the Moscow finance, are emerging as a separate force. Even in the Spanish welter we discern their appearance as the P.O.U.M., a sect achieving the quintessence of fœtidity, and surpassing all others in hate. The so-called Communist disturbances in France are mainly attributable to the Trotskyite section. It is credibly and openly stated in France that the finance on which the Trotskyites depend comes not from Moscow, but from Berlin. I find it difficult to believe myself that the Nazi Government, while volunteering to lead a world crusade against Communism, should at the same moment be fostering its most subversive form. But the point ought to be discussed in public and cleared up one way or the other.

Such then, is the strange scene so far as the normal eye can comprehend it. It would certainly explain the recent farcical trials and well-staged executions of the Communist Old Guard in Moscow. The demonstration was intended for the Communists abroad. It was meant to be a signal proof that the Russian Government was master in its own house and would have no truck with the Trotskyite schismatics. We have to ponder carefully over all these matters now that the world has become so dangerous, because otherwise we might be very suddenly surprised by the way things happen.

There are two morals to be drawn from this cursory survey of a strange and terrible sub-society. The first should appeal to all classes of the British people. We ought to arm night and day in conjunction with other friendly countries and make ourselves independent of all these monstrous and fathomless intrigues. The stronger we are, the more upright and free-spoken, the less danger will there be of the civilised and normal nations being drawn into the quarrels of cruel and wicked forces at either extreme of the political gamut.

The second conclusion brings us home. An eddy of this Continental whirlpool has had its ebullition in the East End of London. An attempt has been made, joined in with equal zest by both factions, to reproduce before our decent, kindly English audience the dark passions which torment Europe. The proper course for British Communists and Nazis, if they feel so strongly their reciprocal hatreds, is to go over to the Continent and fight out their quarrels there. We do not want to have any of these displays over here. We do not mean to have them. The impartial hand of the law should fall with heavy weight upon all disturbers of the King's peace. The Government will be supported by Parliament in measures which may be judged apt and necessary to prevent our streets being used as a cockpit. Everything should be done to isolate these factionaries, and thus reveal how small their numbers are. The great steady masses of British Conservatives and Labour men have many real conflicts to fight out, and we have a free Parliament to fight them out in. We neither fear the malice of one side, nor do we require the aid of the other.

It is especially important that British Jewry should keep itself absolutely clear from this brawling. In Great Britain the law-abiding Jew need not look to the Communist for protection. He will get that as his right from the Constable.

GATHERING STORM
OCTOBER 30, 1936

If we look back only across the year that has nearly passed since the General Election, the most thoughtless person will be shocked at the ceaseless degeneration abroad, and also of our own interests on the Continent. Abyssinia has been conquered. The League of Nations and all that it stands for has been grievously stricken. The old friendship between Great Britain and Italy is sundered. In its place there has arisen a dangerous association between the martial dictators. France is passing through a phase of apparent weakness and acute anxiety. Upon all this there has supervened the hideous Spanish Civil War, now raging towards its climax.

Meanwhile, Germany, whose annual quota of manhood reaching the military age is already double that of France, has increased her period of service from one year to two. She has taken armed possession of the demilitarised zone in the Rhineland. Her fortification of it is far advanced and growing every week. Her armoured divisions, each comprising thousands of vehicles, present themselves as a vast new definite source of aggressive strength. Her terrific expenditure upon war preparations goes forward to the full limit of national capacity and regardless of financial embarrassment and food stringency.

Under the impression of this mighty, if haggard apparition, the smaller countries of Europe hasten to put themselves on good terms with the stronger Power. M. Titulescu has been overthrown in Rumania. Violent internal struggles are visible in the Little Entente. The Belgian King in the face of Rexist pressure has made a declaration profoundly disquieting to France and Britain. Soviet Russia has taken not a few steps likely to render difficult, if not impossible, her association with the western democracies, and with the League of Nations. What a catalogue of disaster for all of those who wish to see the reign of Law in Europe supported by overwhelming force and the prevention of war by concerted resistance to the potential aggressor!

All the while Great Britain has drifted along her fatuous feckless course, the sport of every wind that blows. Chatter to uphold the League of Nations and defend the rights of Abyssinia; chatter for the Hoare-Laval pact; chatter for its reversal; cheers for Mr. Eden and the policy of more vigorous sanctions; cheers and chatter for their total abandonment; chatter about reforming the League of Nations without decision whether to strengthen it or weaken it; chatter for a new Locarno in the West—all in a year; only a year! Thus did the people of Madrid sit in their cafés, visit their cinemas, shout in their demonstrations, while day after day some strong point of their defences was torn away and the iron ring of consequences contracted remorselessly upon them. But why worry? The Ministers have had good holidays. Except for the derelict areas, the country is fat, prosperous and contented, and every eye is fixed upon the joyous festivities of the approaching Coronation.

What has happened to our defences in the meanwhile? Three years ago there was time. Two years ago there was danger. One year ago great new programmes of rearmament, and especially of expansion in the Air, were announced. What has happened to them? Are they being fulfilled? Are we making up for lost time? Are we overtaking foreign countries? Will the goods be delivered at the dates promised? How long must we wait in a condition, apart from the Navy, of lamentable weakness and confusion?

Public attention has been vigorously attracted to our Air Defence by the dispute between Lord Nuffield and Lord Swinton.[1] The importance of this is not its personal aspect or even the particular incidents upon which it centres. It is a lightning flash which has illuminated momentarily, partially, but vividly the whole scene of British rearmament. For more than a year past I and others have sedulously pressed for the creation of a full-grown Ministry of Supply. Such an organisation would have surveyed the whole field of British industry and all the facilities of purchase which are open to us in foreign countries. Broad plans would then have been made to employ all resources to the full, and to parcel out the work to the best advantage. Repeatedly this has been pressed upon the Government; repeatedly we have been assured that it was wholly unnecessary, that all was proceeding in the most satisfactory manner, and that the programmes would be punctually executed without the need of disturbing in any way the normal life and trade of Britain. But what is the truth?

Surely Parliament should take some effective interest in a matter which so vitally affects the safety of the State. Surely Members of the House of Commons have a responsibility towards their constituents to find out where we stand, and to make sure that everything possible is being done to remedy our admitted weakness. The Parliaments of the past would never have been content with smooth generalities or partial illustrations. They would have been ashamed to dwell in supine ignorance of the true state of our affairs. They would have insisted upon searching inquiry, conducted in secret where necessary, and on receiving a report upon the facts from persons independent of Ministerial control. A new session is about to open. Is it to be marked only by a series of fitful, disjointed and inconclusive debates where nothing is brought to a head and a few new Ministerial announcements are sufficient to tide over the afternoon, or are the Houses of Parliament going to satisfy themselves definitely that everything that is possible is being done, and done in the best way; that the organisation for the production of munitions of all kinds is really harmonious, symmetrical and comprehensive? Are the members going to discharge their responsibilities to the Empire and to the nation, and earnestly associate themselves with the business of national defence? Or will they simply shrug their shoulders, admit their impotency, and await in docile resignation the impending teachings of events?

---

[1] About the organisation of 'shadow' factories for war time expansion.

IN MEDITERRANEAN WATERS
NOVEMBER 13, 1936

In this year, so fateful for the future of Europe, the relations of Great Britain and Italy in the Mediterranean play an important part.

For over two hundred years, with only brief intervals, the British Navy has held the command of the Inland Sea. When, in the middle of the nineteenth century, United Italy began to rise upon the genius of Cavour and the valour of Garibaldi from the disjointed congeries of Italian and Papal States, the process was watched with enthusiasm by the democracies of England and France. It was shielded by the British Fleet. It was aided by the French army. In the original Treaty of the Triple Alliance made by Italy more than fifty years ago, a secret clause stipulated that never must Italy be brought into war against Great Britain. In the Great War itself the armies of the two western democracies by land and sea, and the wealth of Britain, sustained the vigorous Italian effort against her former Teutonic allies. After the war, jealousies arose between France and Italy, but until the summer of 1935 no cloud had ever overcast the broad plateau of Anglo-Italian friendship. Even Italian disputes with France had been satisfactorily adjusted at the beginning of 1935, and it seemed that the peace and accord of the Mediterranean Powers was a definite feature in European life.

How different is the scene to-day! Great Britain, in fulfilment of her obligations under the Covenant of the League, was drawn into a tense antagonism with Italy over the conquest of Abyssinia. Italian threats to destroy Malta and drive the British fleet out of the Mediterranean were matched and excited by formidable suggestions that Britain would sever the communications between Italy and her large army in Abyssinia, either in the Mediterranean or in the Suez Canal. For some anxious months the possibility of war was steadily faced by both countries. The danger passed away. No action was taken by the British Fleet, and Italy achieved the conquest of Abyssinia. For good or for ill, that episode in Anglo-Italian relations has closed. It has left an evil and dangerous sequel behind.

Neither Britain nor Italy feels safe in the Mediterranean. Each evidently has the power to work the other very grave ills. Signor Mussolini has indulged in a series of well-advertised flirtations with German Nazidom, and no one can say with assurance whether these are part of a settled policy of hostility to Britain and France, or a preliminary movement towards a renewed friendly understanding. But more deep-reaching than anything else is the growing and carefully fostered view in Italy that Great Britain is a worn-out, dying power, enfeebled by democracy, rotted by pacifists, a power whose great possessions and foremost place in the Mediterranean are the future inheritance of Fascist Italy. If this becomes the settled Italian view, it seems unlikely that a serious disagreement will be avoided.

This unpleasant prospect is necessarily aggravated by the development of air power as a prime arm of war. The old naval arrangements are evidently insufficient to guard the existing position of Great Britain in the Mediterranean. The British Fleet, unsupported by very strong air forces, and without bases effectually defended against air attack, would be exposed to most serious dangers. In order merely to maintain its former security, great exertions must be made in this new element. These exertions naturally give rise to fresh irritation and misgiving on the part of Italy and tend to estrange her policy both in the Mediterranean and upon the general European stage. All the more is it desirable that the Mediterranean Powers should strive to reassure one another, and to make the Mediterranean a sheltered sea unscourged by the storms of war, from which no cause of quarrel can arise. The land dangers of Europe are surely serious enough without that additional complication.

I like to think of the Mediterranean as a free and sure highway for all the nations great and small that have interests in its waters. It seems to me that Signor Mussolini is not asking for more than this in his last speech. But no progress can be made to this desirable end while the Italian public is taught by its government to regard Great Britain as a spent force, as a state whose greatness is ended, and whose decline will become more pronounced as the years pass by. In such an atmosphere Italian ambition and British distrust would inevitably grow together. Nor can we altogether wonder that such dangerous ideas should have grown in Italy. Our well-meant efforts and example at disarmament in the years before 1936, the tame and feeble character of our Government, the strident propaganda of Pacifism in our midst, the relaxation of our authority in India, the unwillingness of our young men to join the Army except in time of war—all contribute to conclusions which may not be found to accord with truth.

But those days are passing. Britain has begun to rearm on a great scale. Her wealth and credit, the solidity of her institutions, her vast resources and connections, all sustain this revival. The British Fleet is still incomparably the most powerful in Europe. Enormous expenditure is contemplated upon it year by year in the future. It must be several years before the new German navy can have any scope, except with submarines, outside the Baltic. Certainly for the next four or five years the British naval power capable of being moved from home waters will be very large indeed. Compared to the pre-war situation, when I found it necessary in 1912 to withdraw the battle-squadron from the Mediterranean and to hold those waters in tacit combination with the French only with a battle-cruiser squadron and a cruiser force, and also in relation to existing fleets, we are certainly far stronger in disposable naval power. The submarine menace has been sensibly diminished by new inventions, and the deep clear waters of the Mediterranean afford a far less hopeful sphere for submarine operations than the murky shallows of the North Sea or English Channel. There remains always the air. But here again the great expenditure now developing should eventually produce results.

Moreover, Britain is not alone in the Mediterranean. She has powerful and valuable friends. The tide of events in Europe will necessarily bring Great Britain and France into ever closer association. The friendly relations of Greece and Turkey with Great Britain are well known. No one should now predict what will be the future complexion of Spain. At any rate, here is a goodly company of States possessing various and extensive resources and all interested in maintaining peace in the Mediterranean. Let Italy join in this new regional pact of confidence and goodwill and make these historic waters a wide and beneficent area of free movement and tranquillity.

An Anti-Comintern pact was declared between Germany and Japan, to which Italy became a part.

GERMANY AND JAPAN
NOVEMBER 27, 1936

The German-Japanese agreement is another formidable step upon the downward road along which mankind is allowing itself to be led or forced. So many disastrous things happen nowadays that it has become customary for Parliament and the Press to minimise their gravity, or dismiss them with a shrug. Thus we read that 'the announcement adds little to our previous knowledge,' and 'the actual terms seem less serious than was supposed.' The public, puzzled and baffled by the complexity of events, is glad to accept these lulling assurances. After all there will be something new to read about to-morrow. Thus we drift and slide, and while away the time. But this German-Japanese pact so-called 'against Communism' can only be in fact, however expressed in form, a military alliance against Russia. I have often written and spoken about Germany arming, as Herr Hitler himself tells us, 'night and day.'

Let us gaze for a moment at Japan. Here again is a martial race of more than sixty millions straining every nerve to arm in spite of serious financial difficulties. Here again is a nation imbued with dreams of war and conquest. Here again is a State where the military mind is supreme; where the export trade is used not so much for profit as to acquire the means of bringing in necessary war materials; where every voice of moderation is silenced by death; where the murder of political opponents has been for some years the accepted practice: where even trusted commanders may be slaughtered by their supporters for suspected luke-warmness. Communism in Japan as in Germany is held fast in the grip of a highly efficient, all-pervading police force, eagerly waiting to smite the smallest manifestation. Yet these two great powers in opposite quarters of the globe use the pretext of their fears of Communism to proclaim an association the purpose of which, and the consequences of which, can only be the furtherance of their national designs.

It is not suggested that either has any present intention of going to war; that depends upon other considerations. But should Germany at any time make war in Europe, we may be sure that Japan will immediately light a second conflagration in the Far East.

The position of all countries having important interests in China and in the China Seas is called in question. Great Britain and the United States cannot but feel an added anxiety for the fate which overshadows all their establishments, commercial, cultural or religious, in China. The brutal ill-usage of British sailors at a Formosan port is but a foretaste of what may befall all white men in and around the China Seas should Europe be convulsed by war.

But after all it is upon Russia that the glare of Japan and Germany is primarily and directly turned. I have already tried to explain the extraordinary dualism which the

Russian State displays. On the one hand we see the Comintern, organ of world-wide revolution acting through its devotees, busy in a score of countries. We see the Spanish tragedy unrolling day by day, and the champions of Nazism and Bolshevism hastening to prove their prowess in the bullring at Madrid. We are in presence of an Italian declaration that no new Communist state will be tolerated in the Mediterranean; and anyone can see how much more grave this declaration becomes on the morrow of the German-Japanese pact. On the other hand there arises the great mass of the Russian power with its national spirit, its large, vigorous, well-equipped armies, its desire to be left alone, its resolve to resist invasion or dismemberment. Now surely the time has come when Russia should choose once and for all her path to safety. Stalin, with the chiefs of the Russian army and the leaders of Russian foreign policy, should disperse and eradicate the Comintern. They should present themselves to Europe as a Soviet Socialist state strongly armed to maintain its national independence, and absolutely divorced from any idea of spreading its doctrines abroad otherwise than by example.

Such a step, taken now, and proved to the satisfaction of every country which desires to preserve peace and bears goodwill to the Russian people, would enormously reduce world tension and increase the prospects of Russian safety. It would immediately force Germany and Japan to reveal their true aims. It would enable Geneva to pursue its prophylactic work with far greater harmony; it would clear the air for that union of defensive strength against unprovoked aggression which is the sole hope of averting general ruin. It would remove the greatest impediment to the co-operation of the United States and Russia in maintaining peace in the Pacific. Surely this is the moment for Soviet Russia to reduce her risks and augment her national strength. Moreover, the policy of Stalin has for many years moved in this direction. What propaganda could be more potent from his point of view than the spectacle, if ever it be achieved, of a really prosperous Russia organised on a Socialistic basis? As in all great decisions, there are no doubt fierce urgings to the contrary; but I for one shall not abandon hopes that this great opportunity for Russia will be seized.

There is one other reaction of a favourable character which should not escape notice. Germany has made her choice. It is definitely hostile to Russia. Germany has bound herself to Japan for these five momentous impending years. The differences between Germany and Russia may be partly about Communism and partly about territory. The differences between Russia and Japan are wholly concerned with the clash of territorial and Imperialistic claims. For some years past the relations of these two neighbours in the Far East have rested solely upon a constant measurement and remeasurement of brute forces, cannon and aeroplanes. Germany has now involved herself in the profound and enduring antagonism of interests between Russia and Japan in the Far East, and has anchored herself firmly to the Japanese side. The danger of a Russo-German arrangement at the expense of the western democracies has definitely receded. All the more then should the Russian Soviet Republic define its position with unmistakable clarity. Here their choice, too, has narrowed sharply.

THE PLEDGE OF FRANCE
DECEMBER 11, 1936

The armies and air fleets are preparing; in the arsenals and dockyards of Europe the great hammers descend with ceaseless clang. The heels of millions of soldiers crunch the gravel of the drill grounds. In the aerodromes new machines and new pilots take the air; squadrons form in rapid succession. Enormous stacks of bombs and shells pile up in the magazines. The dictators add the weekly outputs to their mounting tally. In Germany fats and cash run short; faces grow grimmer. In Spain, blood, fire, merciless destruction and the blotting out of defenceless men and women insult the light of day.

But it would indeed be a pity if one great and hopeful event should not be discerned in this sombre scene, should not be set on its pedestal and acclaimed by the British nation. On Friday last Monsieur Delbos, the Foreign Minister of France, rose in the French Parliament to reply to Mr. Anthony Eden.

The British Foreign Secretary had said a fortnight before that England was bound to fight in defence of France and Belgium. Although this obligation was made public at the time of the March agreement, this was the first time that it had been stated in so plain and decisive a form. It was for France to give the answer. 'If,' said Monsieur Delbos, 'England is the victim of unprovoked aggression, France will immediately and spontaneously proceed to her aid with all her forces by land, sea and air.' This statement is remarkable for two reasons. First, it is the declaration of a people who subject themselves to the grinding burden of two years universal compulsory military service, that they will make common cause with a people who spurn all idea of conscription, who cannot even maintain the numbers of their small voluntary armies, and whose Government, even in the sphere of belated munitions production, is not prepared to interfere with the normal course of trade and industry.

The second impressive feature was the absolute unanimity with which M. Delbos's declaration was received. From the Communists on the extreme left of the French semicircular chamber to the Royalists on the extreme right, its unanimous acceptance was at once apparent. It may fairly be said that no more striking gesture of comradeship and goodwill has ever been made by a well-armed and hard-strained nation to a more comfortable and far less well-defended neighbour. Nor could anything have been done more likely to maintain the peace of Europe in the precarious year 1937 which is about to dawn.

Of course the inherent power of Britain and her Empire is immense. We have no Army worth mentioning, but so far as Europe is concerned Britannia still rules the waves. Our Air Force, though as yet only a fraction of that of Germany, is respectable in quality, and expanding with speed. Our financial strength, credit and resources, carefully tended, are unequalled. The command of the seas carries with it enormous facilities for obtaining food and raw material, all realisable through the mercantile connections of Great Britain in all quarters of the globe. One has the feeling that the magnificent French Army with its innate, supple, flexible efficiency and profound knowledge of the art of war, shielded in part by its fortifications, will be a factor which, joined to the resources of Britain, should constitute a deterrent upon the aggressor. It does not seem a vain hope that the 85 millions of English and French people who desire only peace and seek no quarrel, will together present so solid and respectable a front that they will be let alone.

But then strikes in as a cold corrective the suddenness with which the strokes of modern war may be delivered, and we ask ourselves whether, under new conditions, time will be given to us to realise the vast latent resources of the British Empire. At any rate this dual insurance reduces the risk of war. It reduces also our own danger. It may conceivably give us time to place ourselves in a reasonable state of defence. But two spectral years lie ahead. These are the ghosts of the years 1934 and 1935 which, to quote Sir Thomas Inskip's revealing phrase, 'the locust hath eaten.' Here they are again, those years which passed so lightly, so agreeably away, amid loud cheers and large majorities; years when the people must not be disturbed from their contentment and complacency, nor aroused from idle dreams by ugly truths. These were the years when Ministers assured us that all was well, when all warnings were rejected, when those who uttered them were mocked at as jingoes and scaremongers, when the docile Parliamentary battalions trudged through the Lobbies in that faithful 'footwork' which Mr. Baldwin has eulogised as among the first of political virtues.

No one has attempted in Parliament to analyse the astounding apologia in which the Prime Minister indulged himself three weeks ago.[1] [When he explained that 'democracy must always be two years behind Dictators.'] When I first went into Parliament, now nearly forty years ago, it was inculcated upon me that the most insulting charge which could be made against a Minister of the Crown, short of actual malfeasance, was that he had endangered the safety of the country and neglected its defences for electioneering considerations. Yet such are the surprising qualities of Mr. Baldwin that what all had been taught to shun has now been elevated into a canon of political virtue.

If any mischance should result from a failure of duty or a concealment of facts, we are assured that this is the inherent fault of democracy, and that democracy must always be two years behind the Dictators.

These are the 'two years behind the Dictators' that we have now to live through.

---

[1]"Supposing I had gone to the country and said that Germany was rearming, and that we must rearm, does anybody think that this pacific democracy would have rallied to that cry at that moment. I cannot think of anything that would have made the loss of the election from my point of view more certain.' (Mr. Baldwin, House of Commons, November 12, 1936.)

MR. BALDWIN'S REVIVAL
DECEMBER 28, 1936

The strange, eventful year now drawing to its end began with the death of one beloved British Sovereign and closes upon the abdication of another.

A singular completeness and harmony characterised the reign of George V. That of his successor was ill-starred from the outset; brief, cut off untimely, amid the destruction of hopes which had soared so high. The abdication, although assented to by the whole Empire, and by majorities in every part of it, has brought grievous internal injuries which will take years to repair. Every effort should be made by those whose will has prevailed, to conciliate those whose sentiments have received a profound shock. We have a good King and Queen around whom all must rally. The institution of limited monarchy was never more necessary to the British Empire and the British peoples wherever they may dwell: never more precious to those ideals of freedom and resistance to dictatorship which shine so clearly before us between the renewing storms.

At home the progress of trade revival has been rapid and unceasing. The wealth and prosperity of the nation, the numbers employed, the wages earned, the power of the masses to consume necessaries and comforts, were never higher in time of peace. The addition of an enormous defence programme drives forward the expansion of trade and industry as high winds swell high tides. Nor is there any reason, apart from a world war, that these conditions should not continue for several years. All the more then ought it to be possible to concentrate a portion of these vast resources upon the derelict areas and either bring new employment to their distressed population, or move that population to the new employments. Probably both processes should be pressed forward together.

In the centre of this stands Mr. Baldwin. For him indeed it has been an amazing year. No Prime Minister's political repute has ever stood lower than when it opened, or higher than as it ends. The Hoare-Laval convulsion only a year ago had almost shaken him from his seat. The unexplained statement about 'sealed lips,' the jettisoning of the Foreign Secretary for executing a policy agreed to by the Cabinet, and especially by the Prime Minister, were facts in the teeth of which recovery seemed improbable. But the Christmas of 1936 cast its merciful cloak between Mr. Baldwin and his difficulties. The death of King George turned the current of men's minds into channels of mildness and mourning. Mr. Baldwin, greatly weakened in national esteem, and—as it seemed from his demeanour—in his natural self-confidence, was able to meet Parliament and struggle through the session at the head of his ample, indulgent but none the less anxious majority.

To the ordinary cares of administration were added personal questions of a distressing character. The two Mac-Donalds, father and son, had lost their seats at the

General Election by exceptional manifestations of the public wish. Their presence in the Government was by a strange political fiction deemed indispensable to its National character, while in all England no constituency could be found which would return them to the House of Commons. The extraordinary exertions of the Conservative Party in Scotland succeeded in January and February 1936, in restoring these two key representatives of Labour and Socialism to their places upon the Front Bench upon the condition that they omitted the words Labour and Socialist from their platforms.

This difficult task was no sooner accomplished than rumours of a Budget leakage began to lap around the next most prominent figure in the small band of Socialist Ministers who had joined the National Government in 1931. After long and most painful investigations the Colonial Secretary was condemned by a Special Tribunal upon evidence which probably no jury would have entertained, and saw himself forced to resign his Seals and his seat. His engaging human qualities and his proved patriotism enabled him to carry into retirement no small measure of public sympathy, even from those who had felt themselves most concerned to question and censure his indiscretion.

These personal cares and the aftermath of the Hoare-Laval crisis, including the displacement of the Secretary of State for Foreign Affairs, fell in a manner peculiarly intimate and direct upon the Prime Minister. As the session advanced he bent visibly beneath them. The question upon all lips, especially among his own colleagues, was whether he could carry on till after the Coronation, or even last out the session. In August he found it necessary to take a complete rest. For nearly three months under medical advice he laid aside his duties, and the whole vast process of British affairs at home and abroad floated majestically forward unguided by human hand, eye or brain. It was unfortunate that at this time, when vigilance and foresight were never more needed at the summit, that the Lord Chancellor, the Keeper of the King's Conscience, was also struck down by serious illness, and that the third figure in the Government, the Lord President of the Council, was not in a condition to undertake any strenuous political work. Upon Mr. Neville Chamberlain descended the practical conduct of affairs. His financial administration continued to be successful in the highest degree, and he found himself presiding over an increasing revenue and soaring credit at the very time when these were most needed for the purpose of defence. But no understudy, however able, can wield the authority inseparable from the highest offices in the State.

In no sphere was this more apparent than in that concerned with the personal affairs of the Sovereign. It was not in October, but in August or earlier, that the first serious advice should have been tendered to King Edward VIII. Events moved forward remorselessly. When the captain, restored, rejuvenated indeed, by his much-needed and well-earned repose, returned to the bridge the ship already lay among most dangerous reefs, and the strange light which portends a hurricane glared in the western sky. By his resolute and dexterous management of the abdication Mr. Baldwin regained at a bound the authority and regard that he had lost since the General Election. Indeed, a new vigour seemed to animate him. Physically as well as politically, he walked with decided step. He has never spoken with more force or more Parliamentary skill than in the speech which announced the abdication to the House. It is now clearly his duty, whatever his inclination to watch over the inauguration of the new reign and the Coronation of a King and Queen upon whose success British hopes are centred and British fortunes in no small measure depend.

Meanwhile, abroad, all dangers to peace have grown, mounted and woven themselves together with a frightful persistency. Nazi Germany has certainly spent the equivalent of one thousand million pounds on warlike preparation during 1936. Her leaders have decreed conditions of war in times of peace. 'Cannon before butter' is the maxim preached to a proletariat already overstrained and underfed, already the most heavily armed in history. Under the pressure of this grave alarm Britain and France have made declarations of mutual protection of the most explicit character. It is hoped that the antagonism created between the two Western democracies and Italy by the Abyssinian conquest, may gradually be mitigated; and that so great a gathering of powerful States and groups of States, both in the West and in the East, may be united at Geneva in support of the Covenant of the League of Nations, that Europe, and indeed the world, may be rescued from the catastrophe with which the future is loaded.

NO INTERVENTION IN SPAIN
JANUARY 8, 1937

When the Spanish Civil War began six months ago, the British Government, with general approval, declared a neutrality which they have ever since strictly observed. Everything that has happened since justifies and strengthens that policy. First, we have seen how evenly Spain is divided both in territory and fighting force. Secondly, both sides have sullied their conflicting causes with unspeakable cruelties. Thirdly, neither side in any way represents the British point of view. Victory for either at the present time may mean a horrid revengeful massacre of the defeated. The Spaniards have shown themselves to be poisoned by hatred.

It is probable that whoever wins, Spain will be, perhaps for years, a weak, flaccid State absorbed in its own recovery. What have the British people got to do with this? Have we not enough trouble on our hands in other directions? Is the state of our defences so remarkably good that we can afford to involve ourselves in this quarrel? Could we as a united nation take either one side or the other? If by any action of ours we helped one side to win, should we not bear a moral responsibility for the ruthless severities which the victor might inflict?

But it is said, 'Look at all the volunteer soldiers, weapons and munitions which Germany and Italy are sending to General Franco, and which Russia and also France are sending or allowing to go to Señor Caballero. Does this not show that the conflict in Spain has become European? Can Britain afford to remain outside? If the issue being fought out in Spain is whether Nazi dictators or Bolshevist dictators are to triumph, must not Britain take a view?' The answer is that we are equally opposed both to Nazism and Communism. We desire to see the return of a liberal age where Parliaments will guard freedom, where science will open the banqueting halls to the millions, and where what Bismarck once called 'practical Christianity' will mitigate suffering and misfortunes.

When I read of large numbers of German Nazis and Italian Fascists travelling to the Spanish arena to slay large numbers of Russian Bolshevists and French Communists, I deplore these savage excursions. But when I search my heart I cannot feel, that if all these armed tourists to Spain were to transfix each other with the simultaneous efficiency of Ivan and the Bulbul Amir till there was no one left, except the Press representatives to tell the tale, the interests and safety of Britain would be in any way endangered.

It is further argued by advocates of British intervention that if General Franco wins with the help of the Nazi and Italian dictators, Spain will be a new focus of Nazi tyranny and power. A Germanised and German-run Spain will, we are assured, menace Gibraltar and also force the hard-pressed French to develop a new southern front along the Pyrenees. It does not, however, follow that if General Franco wins he will be grateful to his Nazi and Fascist allies. On the contrary, the probability is that the first thought of all patriotic Spaniards, once delivered from their awful plight, will be to escort their rescuers to the nearest seaport. It is possible that once the decision of arms has declared itself, the strong desire to rid the Peninsula of the foreign meddlers will be general throughout Spain. Also there may be the feeling, whoever wins in Spain, that Great Britain, which has intervened only upon errands of mercy, and which possesses at the time overwhelming seapower without coveting anything, is probably a country with which Spain would like to live on exceptionally friendly terms. This at any rate is a reasonable hope.

Is Germany likely to send any large portion of her regular army into Spain? Hannibal, it is true, began the second Punic war by making Spain his base. But it is most unlikely that the German General Staff would care to lock up in Spain a dozen or even half a dozen of their rapidly forming regular divisions. Unless these troops could subdue the whole Spanish nation and compel it to work in German interests—which is highly improbable—all German troops in Spain would be hostages of superior sea-power. As for an attack on Gibraltar, war with the British Empire is a serious matter. It would certainly not be only one Mediterranean naval base which would be in danger in such an eventuality.

On all grounds, therefore, we should adhere obstinately to our neutrality and do our utmost to persuade M. Blum's government to conform to our attitude. Neutrality does not only mean abstention from active aid for one side or the other. It means a cool detached habit of mind, an avoidance, however tempting, of partisanship. It also implies so far as Great Britain is concerned, a readiness to accept a minor role, not to pose as leader or principal actor. We must be careful not to repeat in Spain the same kind of ridiculous conduct of which we were guilty a year ago over Abyssinia. We must not act beyond our duty and beyond our stake. It is no use once again leading other nations up the garden and then running away when the dog growls. It is this memory which disturbs me when I read that we have sent 'sharp notes' and have delivered 'emphatic protests.' It is at Geneva rather than in Spain that the peace of the world may best be secured in 1937.

Meanwhile, let us press forward our rearmament, for the world danger grows.

HOW TO MEET THE BILL
JANUARY 22, 1937

During the financial year 1936–7 the Government have been trying to spend as much money as possible on re-armament, but as they began very late and did not make the preparations long enough beforehand, they have not been able to spend as much as they would wish and as is certainly necessary. The defence estimates for the year that is closing amount to £160 millions, of which only £40 millions is for air defence. There will probably be a series of supplementary estimates which may increase these figures. But still I doubt very much whether they will be able to spend more than £180 millions on defence before March 31. This compares with between £800 to £1,000 millions expenditure in Germany, of which probably £120 millions at least is being spent on aviation. It is substantially less than the £200 millions which President Roosevelt is spending in the United States, although that fortunate Republic is protected on each side by thousands of miles of ocean.

Nevertheless, as time passes our re-armament programme gets under way, and the expense will broaden very markedly during 1937. The preliminary stage will be approaching completion; and increasingly large instalments will be earned by all the contractors. I cannot form any estimate of how much they will require. It depends on how far the Government think it necessary to speed up the programme at the expense of interfering with civil industry. In any case, however, it must be a very large additional sum. The Admiralty have a fine programme of ships, all of which will be building at full blast during the whole year. The two great battleships will come into full expense during this year, and no doubt two or three more will be begun; while the numerous fleet of cruisers and destroyers will make a heavy bill. The outputs of heavy shell and torpedoes and all the ancillary supplies of the Navy will all increase rapidly and simultaneously. The Admiralty, having preserved during all these years large armament-producing plants is, as I pointed out last year, able to get into its stride much quicker than the Air or the Army.

Still more difficult is it to guess how much the Air Ministry will be able to spend. The more they can spend the better. If they could spend three times as much as this year we should be far safer and happier, and there would be more chance of Britain being able to play an effective part in preserving peace. There will also be heavy expenditure on guns and shell for the army and for the anti-air defence, also tanks and mechanical equipment of all kinds. Though all our programmes are, and will remain during 1937, very much in arrear, and it is not until 1938 that the big results will begin to show, still the actual figures will certainly be considerable.

The Chancellor of the Exchequer has happily by his prudent management of our finances restored our credit and raised it to an exceptionally high level. The increased prosperity stimulated by the defence programme will most surely bring a very large increase in the yield of each shilling of the income tax. There must be an enormous number of firms all over the country, and especially in the heavy industries, which in late years have made only small profits or no profits at all, which will now come back into the revenue-producing area; and the Government will get back through the tax collector a large proportion of the money it is spending through the fighting departments.

It would certainly be a great mistake to hamper the trade of the country and check the tide of prosperity by piling on new taxes on any large scale. It will, of course, be utterly impossible to meet the expenditure of 1937 without heavy borrowing. The condition of the money market and of the public finances is most favourable to this. There is no doubt that a defence loan of medium term could be floated at so low a rate of interest that the very fact would redound to the public credit. However low the interest rate, it must always be remembered that the Government by taxation recover from the interest as they pay it, nearly a quarter. Therefore the annual burden of interest plus a special sinking fund would not be heavy. It would seem, however, that the taxation ought to be increased to cover these new charges for interest and sinking fund.

Mr. Chamberlain last year increased his Income Tax by 3*d*. to 4*s*. 9*d*. in the £. It would seem very natural if he this year advanced it by another 3*d*. to the full five shillings. The yield of the extra three pence would more than cover the service of the new loan. If the Chancellor should feel it his duty to make such a demand, the House of Commons would support him with alacrity and the taxpayers would respond with their traditional fidelity.

We cannot contemplate a prolonged period during which the armed forces of Europe will continue to develop and subsequently be maintained at their hideous maximum level. Events are certainly moving forward towards a climax. Judged by every standard Germany is bankrupt. In the next two or three years, perhaps in a much shorter period, she will either be forced to reduce sensibly her outlay upon armament, or be tempted to some desperate venture. If the decision of Germany is to plunge the whole world into war, no one can tell what the future may discharge upon us. We can, however, be sure that such a war would spell the ruin of such civilisation as Europe has been able to build up and preserve. No limits can be assigned to the miseries of mankind during the period of struggle, or to their long impoverishment and degradation at its close. If, however, the Nazi regime in Germany should turn away from such fearful delirium and soberly and sincerely tread the paths of peace and prosperity, they will certainly find on every side not only guarantees for the inviolability of German soil, but the good will of friendly nations, now arming resolutely, rapidly and unitedly in common defence.

I personally grasp the larger hope; but, however this grim issue in world destiny may be decided, it is evident that Great Britain should finance the expansion of her defence programmes to the fullest possible extent by loan, and thereby maintain her economic and financial life at the highest level of power and activity.

EUROPE'S PEACE
FEBRUARY 5, 1937

We live in precarious times. How astonishing it is that present-day civilisation should be exposed to dangers from which it was believed the labours of the seventeenth, eighteenth and nineteenth centuries had permanently rid the world; and that we, with all our vast delicate scientific structure of economics and finance upon which so many new millions get their bread, lie exposed to potential strokes far more sudden and immediately decisive than any which could be dealt by the Cimbri and the Teutons, the Parthians, the Visigoths and the Gauls. Owing to the helplessness and subservience of democracy in the hands of ambitious and commanding men, added to the facilities of modern locomotion and propaganda, many communities have been plunged back into a state of insecurity hitherto only associated with barbarism. Moreover, the appetites and hatreds of the dark ages are now expressed in terms of the most frightful death-dealing machinery.

Take a State like Czechoslovakia, which under popular government embodies the old traditions of Bohemia, where 'Good King Wenceslas looked out upon the feast of Stephen.' This community of fifteen million more or less educated Christian people dwells from day to day under the fear of violent invasion with iron conquest in its wake. At any moment a quarrel may be picked with them by a mighty neighbour. Already they see the directions given to the enregimented German Press to write them down, to accuse them of being Communists, and, in particular, of preparing their airports for a Russian assault upon Germany. Vain to protest their innocence, vain to offer every facility for German or neutral inspection of their arrangements. The hate-culture continues, fostered by printing-press and broadcast—the very instruments, in fact, which philosophers might have hoped would liberate mankind from such perils. Thus we see the Czechs in the nineteen-hundred-and-thirty-seventh year of our Lord frantically fortifying their frontiers, and for the rest sombrely resigned as in the Stone Age to the possible deprivation of life, home and freedom. To this point, then, has the public law of Europe sunk. To this lamentable pit of degradation has Christendom and the circle of the European family drifted or strayed.

But observe: the will of a single man with a handful of deeply involved confederates and a host of valiant obedient agents might in a few weeks turn this blast of propaganda against Belgium or Holland, against Sweden or Switzerland, or, last and by no means least, against the British Islands and the peaceful Empire of which they are part. Truly it is a horrifying position in which all the nations lie through the elevation of military despots to the summit of mighty races armed by science.

It is because of these conditions that the latest speech of Herr Hitler was awaited with anxiety not unmingled with hope by all who dwell within his reach. Fair offers of friendship and of economic aid to cover a German transition from war-preparation to peaceful industry, from isolation to world commerce, were made both by France and Britain. It was hoped that these overtures from two powerful and obviously peace-seeking States would meet with some response, and that great words of peace and reassurance would have been spoken by this gifted man raised so high. But what was the outcome? It is our duty to face the bald, hard fact that the super-arming of Germany is to continue, no matter how severe be the material sacrifices imposed upon the German people, nor how straitened the raw material, food and money situations become. Every day that process continues the tension in Europe must grow.

Secondly, Herr Hitler's ominous silence about Czechoslovakia and the usual anti-Bolshevist tirades keep all Eastern Europe aquake or agog. Thirdly, Belgium and Holland are assured by the Nazi chief that their neutrality is for ever inviolable. The Dutch have always formed their own opinion about such guarantees. The Belgians, unhappily, cannot be expected to forget that this same inviolability was guaranteed to them, not by the declaration of an individual, but by solemn treaty with the Prussian Government in 1839; and that the treaty was still binding when the unfortunate events of 1914 occurred. France is assured that no German quarrel with her is possible. She gains an added assurance from her fine army and immensely fortified frontier. Even so, she does not seem to be entirely free from preoccupation about her safety.

And how lies Britain in this darkling scene? The main point of Herr Hitler's argument is directed against Mr. Eden and his speeches. The word 'ignorant' is applied in full peace by the head of the German State to the British Foreign Secretary. The open Nazi demand is for the surrender of the former German colonies. This question, so fraught with difficulties and dangers, comes to the front as a prime objective of German policy; and already we read that the process of marshalling a departmental case against Britain has begun. Any day the German Press may be ordered to point the denunciatory finger at England. The discomforts, privations, lower wages, and now to some extent hampered workshops of Germany may at any time be attributed to the fact that 'England' has stolen the German colonies with all the immense supplies of food and raw materials which they are supposed to be capable of providing. We are told we ought to be pleased with the tone of Herr Hitler's utterance. The Dictator has spoken, and no new evil has come upon us. The gates to a peaceful settlement have not been opened, but neither have the gates of war. 'At worst,' it is said, 'if the speech does not make things better, it does not make them worse. It is a speech of "marking time."'

But perhaps it is time that is needed by Germany. On all sides we hear that the General Staff have declared that the German army is not immediately ready for a major war, that they have refused to become responsible for any large military detachment to Spain; that they require more time to develop their officer class. Naturally the German army chiefs would expect of their political directors that the German people should not be led into another struggle in which the whole world—in opinion at least—would be against them and into which several powerful nations would probably come. There is perhaps a breathing-space.

But where is the security for the peace of Europe? It can only be found by the combination of many well-armed States, great and small, upon the basis of the Covenant of the League. Perhaps it can only be found by an association, upon the basis of the Covenant, of the defensive groups of alarmed countries which have been formed and are forming in the East and in the West of Europe. If ever there was a moment when a League of mutual defence against unprovoked aggression should be formed it is now during this present year, 1937. Then any possible German explosion might well take place internally, instead of devastating the surrounding lands.

FRANCE FACES A NEW CRISIS
FEBRUARY 19, 1937

When in the early autumn of 1936 I last wrote about the French situation, we were everywhere confronted with whispers and rumours that there would be a revolution in France in October. A wave of industrial disturbances swept the country. It was believed that the Blum Government, supported as it was by the newly elected Communists, would be quite incapable of procuring or maintaining peace and order, that France would 'go the same way as Spain,' and that some violent counter-movement from the Right would perhaps be set on foot. I ventured at that time to contradict this alarmism, to point to the great stability of France, and to the general loyalty of Frenchmen to their Republican institutions and to predict 'that France would emerge from the winter stronger than she entered it.' In the main all this has proved true.

The violent manifestations of working-class discontent and their demand for improved conditions, their clashes with the employers, the immense series of strikes and lock-outs, have all passed without any serious physical strife or destruction of life or property. France is at work to-day. The violent Communists have lost ground in a marked manner. The red balloon which was inflated and ascending last August is shrivelling and drooping down in February. The suppression of Communism which is taking place in Spain, the savage rifts in the Communist party between the followers of Stalin and Trotsky, have both contributed to this weakening process. Moreover, the French Communists have, it must be frankly admitted, placed many restraints upon themselves and their more violent followers in the interests, not indeed of France for her own sake, but of France as the opponent of German Nazism. The Government of M. Blum, composed of very able men, has succeeded in appeasing to a large extent the internal stresses, and at the same time has shown itself capable of rallying the whole strength of France to the cause of National defence. It may be doubted whether under any other political grouping so many satisfactory measures for the strengthening of the armed forces could have been carried through—certainly not with such overwhelming assent. The relations between the fighting services and the Government are exemplary. The army salutes and obeys whatever chiefs Parliament gives it, and those chiefs, whatever their party political record, discharge their administrative duties wholeheartedly.

Thirdly, in the sphere of foreign politics, the action and influence of the Blum Government has been successful, or at least beneficial. There never was a time since the war when closer and better relations existed between the French and British Governments. Nor was there ever a time when the two western democracies worked more smoothly together in the common cause of peace and freedom. Most noteworthy of all, of course, have been the public declarations unchallenged on both sides of the

Channel that in the face of unprovoked aggression upon either, Britain and France must be regarded as one.

These remarkable events have spread favourable reactions throughout Europe, and there is a renewed readiness on the part of many States, both great and small, to unite themselves against an unprovoked aggression, to take effective measures of defence and association beforehand, and to try to make the Covenant of the League a reality. To pretend for one moment that the danger in which Europe stands is not increasing would be absurd. But so also are the measures to cope with it. If the scene has darkened, the atmosphere has become more clear, and the shape of objects more sharply defined. In all this rallying of the forces which stand for peaceful and tolerant solutions of world problems, M. Blum has rendered a high personal service. Indeed, it was not in the power of any other Frenchman at this particular juncture in the life of France or Europe to do so much for the common good.

But now he has to face a crisis of a different order from those that have been surmounted. The concessions made to the urban wage-earners in hours and pay are imperfectly related to economic realities. The immediate institution wholesale of a 40-hours week coupled with the increases of wages involved all industries, the railways in particular, in very heavy additional deficits. As many as 60,000 additional men had to be engaged. Small employers working themselves with their two or three men, of whom there are a large number scattered about France, have been plunged in the greatest difficulties. In some cases the single workman protected by law, absorbs nearly the whole yield of a two-man business and forces the so-called 'patron' to part company with his assistant and do the best he can on a smaller scale himself. The immense class of officials at small salaries which plays so marked a role in French life all find their way of life affected by the inevitable rise in the cost of living. The balance between town and country has been deranged. The artisan with only 40 hours' work a week and his increased wages is no longer rendering a service to the community proportionate to the exertions required from the peasant and the farmer. On top of all this social expenditure has come the paramount needs of defence, which have simultaneously to be met upon a lavish scale.

Hitherto the spending of money has been found a panacea for all difficulties, foreign and domestic, with which the Government was confronted. But now the financial factor asserts itself in an imperious way. I do not wish to compare the highly competent, courageous and patriotic Government over which M. Blum presides with the feckless chatterboxes and spendthrifts at whose head Mr. MacDonald led Great Britain into the crisis of 1931. But a crisis not very different in character from what was then ours threatens France today. Prices are leaping up to a point where they affect the export trade as well as the small rentier. Behind them may come demands for further wage increases merely to maintain a portion of those gains which the French workpeople thought they had won in the autumn.

There appear to be two courses open. The first is one of extreme danger, namely, that the Government should attempt to fix prices—and in consequence everything else—at arbitrary levels. This would entail little less than the introduction of the present German system, and would rob French trade and industry of all that fertile flexibility by which economic truth is ascertained, and from which the wealth of nations flows. The second course, also indicated by British experience, would be the formation of a still more powerful and broadly based Government in France, similar to the national Coalition by which Great Britain was so swiftly led from her misfortunes.

In view of the war danger which any weakening of France would bring appreciably nearer, it would seem the duty of French statesmen of all parties to make large sacrifices of personal opinion and party affiliation in order to secure the greatest objects for which States exist. In the background there lies the possibility, so novel to Frenchmen and so familiar to us, of a premature curtailment of Parliament and a fresh appeal to the electorate. Meanwhile, by whatever means these financial and economic stresses may be met, we may be confident that the safety and underlying unities of France will not suffer fundamental injury.

GERMANY'S CLAIM FOR COLONIES
MARCH 5, 1937

I was one of those who welcomed Herr von Ribbentrop's appointment as Ambassador to London. Although relations between Great Britain and Germany are governed by the tides of European and world events, the exertions of a distinguished man in the closest confidence of the ruling powers of Germany might well add those clarifying and emollient influences which help to maintain goodwill. But it must be admitted that difficulties are caused when an Ambassador to a foreign country also plays the part of an active party and political leader in his own. These difficulties become more precisely defined when the reply to his confidential interview with the British Foreign Secretary is made by the Ambassador in a public speech in Germany. These, however, are matters of usage and procedure, and stand on an altogether subordinate plane to the actual issue with which Herr von Ribbentrop was dealing.

The decision by Germany to bring the Colonial question to the fore and to press it peculiarly against Great Britain will certainly not make things easier between the two countries. Mr. Eden last July said: 'The question of any transfer of mandated territories would inevitably raise grave difficulties, moral, political and legal, of which his Majesty's Government have been unable to find any solution.' This was in no way a personal statement by the Foreign Secretary. It was the result of a series of prolonged deliberations by the Cabinet. There is no doubt that it represents their view to-day. If there has been any change it will have probably been of a hardening character. Mr. Eden's latest statement after Herr von Ribbentrop's speech should be noted: 'His Majesty's Government has not considered, nor are they considering, the transfer of any territory.' At any rate, opinions in the Conservative Party and in Parliament as a whole have crystallised themselves in a sense markedly adverse to the German suggestion. The overwhelming feeling of the Party Conference at Bournemouth should not pass unnoticed. In the House of Commons, the German request would not commend itself to any of the parties, fresh as they are from contact with the constituencies.

All the strongest forces in the Conservative Party have expressed themselves decidedly against any transference of territory or subjects from a British to a foreign flag. The Socialist Opposition, although they might toy with the idea of making the colonies of every country as it were wards of the League of Nations, would certainly be inveterately opposed to the handing over of millions of natives to that Nazi rule which they regard as obnoxious in the last degree to democracy and freedom. The small band of Liberals would no doubt be willing to discuss the question in the general interests of European appeasement. But this would only be one of three or four factors which they would consider indispensable to any general settlement. The kind of conditions they might be expected to urge would be, first an immediate halt in German war preparations and a substantial measure of disarmament; secondly, the return of Germany to the League of Nations and full co-operation in the cause of world peace; thirdly, the effective modification, in common with other countries, of the German policy of commercial isolation and the reduction of barriers to freer trade and intercourse. It will probably be thought that willingness to discuss the return of colonies to Germany upon this basis would not at the present time differ in results from unwillingness to return them at all.

Thus the House of Commons is for all practical purposes solid against any concession, and it is most unlikely that the Government, even if they differed from the House—which they do not—would depart in any respect from the general declarations of the Foreign Secretary. All these adverse forces would, of course, be augmented and welded together by anything in the nature of pressure and still more of menace. For this reason the Ambassador's reference in his speech at Leipzig to 'the German people's own strength' has attracted attention. I do not read it however in its context as in the nature of a threat. It is not used as an alternative to the return of the Colonies, but as an additional means by which the German people may develop their own domestic prosperity. In that aspect it would command general sympathy throughout the British Empire.[1] One of our most important interests is a contented and prosperous Germany, and the declared desire of the British Government and nation is to work side by side with Germany, France and other great Powers for their mutual benefit and security.

It is, however, gravely to be doubted whether Germany would be well advised to raise and press the Colonial question at this juncture. If a flamboyant and machine-made propaganda is set on foot among the German people upon this issue, it cannot fail to foster the same kind of slow latent antagonism as was created by the growth of the German Navy before the Great War. It would certainly prove a fatal obstacle to the personal success of Herr von Ribbentrop's mission. It would tend to draw more closely together upon the basis of the Covenant of the League those nations who, for one reason or another, dwell in increasing anxiety about the eventual aims of the Nazi Government. It is therefore greatly to be hoped that Herr Hitler will, like a good diplomatist, not press the question to a point where it would encounter blunt refusal.

Those who wish to see how strong is the case which could be marshalled behind such a refusal should read the admirable pamphlet, 'The British Colonial Empire and the German Claim,' just published by the Empire Economic Union. It cannot be doubted that all other Powers who are mandatories for ex-German colonies will in their own way adopt a similar attitude. It would be a thousand pities if German opinion were misled by the extreme pro-German elements in our island. These have been utterly unable to prevent the establishment of what is virtually a defensive alliance between Britain and France against unprovoked aggression upon either of them. They will be increasingly ineffectual should this Colonial controversy be unfortunately allowed to become too prominent.

---

[1] Herr von Ribbentrop expressed his thanks to me for making this point clear, and fully confirmed the view expressed.

REBUILDING THE BATTLE FLEET
MARCH 22, 1937

The decision of his Majesty's Government to rebuild the battle fleet at the rate of two or three battleships a year, and also to modernise and preserve the existing battle fleet, together with the very large programme of cruisers, destroyers, submarines and smaller craft, constitutes an event of first magnitude to Europe and the world. The announcement, following upon the rest of the British rearmament programme, has been greeted with out-spoken welcome in almost every country not under dictatorship, and in some countries which are. States as different as Sweden and Turkey, as Holland and Switzerland, as Czechoslovakia and Greece, have joined with the Great Powers in the League of Nations in expressing their satisfaction and relief. The Swedish Foreign Minister, Mr. Sandler, on reaching London this week, used remarkable words about the British rearmament programme when he described it as 'a bastion of peace.' Considering that Sweden was neutral, and often considered by us pro-German in the late war, and is a Baltic State in close commercial and cultural relations with Germany, and that the Swedes are evincing a strong interest in the Covenant of the League, such a declaration should go far to reassure the people in this country that the motives which animate the British Government are not misunderstood by the peace-seeking Powers on the Continent.

The reactions in the United States have also been most favourable. President Roosevelt's administration will no doubt exercise their undoubted right to build up to parity with Great Britain, and a series of formidable naval programmes will come into construction on the other side of the Atlantic Ocean. The two English-speaking peoples will have under construction at the same time ten of the newest and strongest battleships ever built. There has not been any complaint by the United States that the British naval programme puts them to undue expense in maintaining parity. On the contrary, there are many signs that they welcome the opportunity of adding to their own margin of security in these dangerous years.

It certainly was very fortunate that the Government of Japan released Great Britain and the United States from all limitations in the numbers of ships. The Japanese did not like the ratio of 5.5.3. But it will be very difficult for them in practice to maintain even that ratio against the rapid building and immense resources of either of the two English-speaking democracies. Even a resort by Japan to larger guns and tonnage would not remedy this. On the other hand, there is not the slightest need for Japan to feel alarm, for the United States and Great Britain have long been the traditional friends and helpers of modern Japan. Moreover, by joining the League of Nations Japan could secure the growing amenities and securities which will follow from its renewed strength.

So far as Germany is concerned, everything remains upon the basis of the Anglo-German Naval Agreement of 1935. By this instrument Germany is free to build up to 35 per cent. of the British tonnage. The very great increases now being made in that tonnage will give Germany ample scope in fleet-building for some years to come. It is very satisfactory to hear that the Nazi Government is strictly observing the Naval Treaty, and also to feel that for some time they would have difficulty in breaking it, even if they should be tempted to do so. The steel shortage and the tremendous rise of prices, particularly of war metals, do not facilitate the later developments of the immense German rearmament.

There remains the Mediterranean. I have applauded the Anglo-Italian Agreement of friendship and good will and respect for each other's lines of communication across the inland sea. It would be affectation to pretend that British public opinion has not been shocked by the cynical manner in which the Non-intervention Agreement in Spain has been violated by the large-scale invasion of Spain by several divisions of the Italian army. When the Duce seeks to be acclaimed as the Protector of Islam throughout the world it is, of course, natural for us to remember that the British Empire contains about a hundred millions of Mohammedans, and that the King-Emperor is the Sovereign of the greatest mass of those who profess the Moslem faith. Some anxiety may be caused in Egypt by the wonderful new road, 1,200 miles long, built 'for tourist purposes' from Libya to the Egyptian frontier. But none of these considerations ought in any way to weaken the force of the friendly reassurances which Great Britain and Italy have interchanged on the subject of the Mediterranean.

Before the war the rapid growth and great strength of the German navy made it necessary, as has been mentioned, for the Admiralty, of which I was then the head, to transfer the Mediterranean battle squadron to the great concentration then being effected in the North Sea. We were compelled to relegate the Mediterranean interests of Great Britain for the time being to the care only of a battle-cruiser squadron, and to our friendship with France. Happily no such difficulty confronts us to-day. It should be possible for Great Britain continuously to maintain in the Mediterranean or in easy reinforcing distance, not only a line of battle of incomparable power, but also the necessary strength in all other classes of warships. The technical discoveries since the war have placed the submarine in a position of far less strength and far greater danger than was apparent even at the moment when the U-boat warfare was decisively mastered. So far as any lessons can yet be drawn from the Spanish war, it would seem that the claims of air experts to destroy warships at their pleasure and discretion have, to put it mildly, not so far been made good. Broadly speaking, the command of the seas and of the oceans still rests with the great fleets which are in no way rendered obsolete by the new methods of attack. This fact also should make for stability and peace not only in the Mediterranean, but in wider spheres.

CAN THE POWERS BRING PEACE TO SPAIN?
APRIL 2, 1937

Neither the Spanish civil war nor its reactions in Europe diminish in gravity as the months pass by. The prolongation of the struggle is not favourable to Franco. Great dangers and many failures have forced the various ferocious sects of Communists, Socialists and Anarchists, who control the Valencia and Catalan Governments, to submit themselves to an increasing measure of military discipline. Forces are growing and developing behind the Government Fronts, which have already acquired the faculty of manœuvre and attack. The so-called International Brigade, composed of the most fanatical revolutionaries in Europe, and amounting to probably 25,000 men, aided by the powerful Russian aviation and tanks, has inflicted a grievous and humiliating defeat upon at least an equal number of Italian regular troops. There is no doubt that this rebuff to Italian pretensions has caused satisfaction and merriment throughout the greater part of the world, even in quarters where Franco's victory would be welcomed. The German military men, whose poor opinion of the Italians as soldiers has never been successfully concealed, have had all their misgivings about the value of Italy as an ally revived and even redoubled.

Nevertheless, it would be rash to assume that these Italian volunteers, hustled into the midst of this Spanish quarrel without any national cause behind them, and with their Blackshirt enthusiasm worn threadbare, are really representative of the qualifies of the immensely numerous Italian army. Private soldiers do not give their lives as easily as dictators make speeches. Those who know how bravely the Italians fought during the Great War in defence of hearth and home will certainly not consider that anything that has happened in Spain constitutes a reflection upon the honour of the Italian army, and Signor Mussolini is perfectly right in treating the episode coolly and as a check to policy rather than as a serious wound to the nation. A similar check to policy has been sustained by the German dictator, Herr-Hitler, who wished so ardently to brandish the bright sword of Prussia upon the Spanish scene, and has been effectually restrained by his own military chiefs. He has encountered, during these last months, a steady but resolute opposition from the army leaders to undue extensions of his intervention in Spain, and there is no doubt that the German people did not like their sons being sent to fight in a non-German quarrel, nor did the sons themselves, in any large number, evince an eagerness to do this.

In spite of all the fraud and humbug which has brought derision upon Mr. Eden's Non-intervention Committee, it has presided over a considerable limitation of foreign interference in Spain. Still more, it has preserved a semblance of concert, and more than a semblance, among the Great Powers whose sympathies are ranged on opposite sides. Everything shows how right Great Britain has been to be obtrusively neutral, and to dissuade our French friends from becoming too excited. Indeed, it may have been a comfort to M. Delbos to be able to deplore to his Left Wing hotheads the lack of passionate imagination in the British democracy and the total absence of partisanship in the British Government. There must be perseverance to reduce this Spanish tragedy to its true proportions, and to make sure as far as possible that only Spanish blood flows in it. That blood, alas, continues to flow, not only on the fighting fronts, but far behind them. The odious cruelties and murders by the Communists and the Anarchists of helpless people belonging to classes for whose extermination they thirst, still persist at Barcelona. The revelations of what occurred during the Red Terror at Malaga, where perhaps ten thousand unoffending persons were foully slaughtered, have recently been confirmed by a credible British witness, Major Yeats-Brown, well known as 'Bengal Lancer.' The bound corpses of butchered hostages, which the sea casts up upon the French coast, bring home to the French people the horrible realities of the Spanish conflict.

No one can doubt that grim retaliation has been practised by the Nationalist Government. Peace and order reign over the broad areas of Nationalist Spain, and industry and agriculture pursue their course. Trains run. Food and petrol can be freely purchased. All the decencies of civilised life appear upon the surface, but the slightest signs of disaffection are repressed with prompt and ruthless executions. It is surprising that after all these months of training Franco has not been able to bring into the field larger numbers of disciplined party troops. It was surely a great mistake to allow Italian divisions to bear the brunt of an attack upon Madrid, and one cannot believe that they would have been used if national forces were available.

It is certain that, if Franco wins, he will be in no position to interfere with British and French interests in the Mediterranean. He will be entirely absorbed in his own internal problems. The Germans and Italians will have little or no influence upon Spanish policy once the firing stops. Indeed, the world may then see an example of Spanish ingratitude on the largest scale, and of the most salutary character. Sea power will decide the future of the Mediterranean. The immense naval preponderance of Great Britain and France should relieve them from major strategic anxieties. The liberal nations should be able to mitigate the severities to the vanquished of a Nationalist victory—triumph it cannot be. On the other hand, the success of the Anarchist and Trotskyite forces, whose excesses Largo Caballero has sought in vain to control, would be followed by class and party atrocities which would for many years devastate and depopulate the whole Iberian Peninsula.

So far we should applaud the policy of his Majesty's Government. The fact that British, German, French, Russian and Italian vessels are co-operating in a kind of blockade, and that their Ambassadors wrangle volubly but still peaceably around a table in Whitehall, is remarkable and reassuring. The question that all must ask is whether they may not one day move forward together to induce some kind of concordat in Spain, which would prevent the triumph of either side, and urge, if not enforce, some compromise and regime under which the tortured Spanish people may find bread, peace, and merciful oblivion.

Such a settlement, if achieved by such a combination, would carry its blessings around the whole world.

THE NEW PHASE IN INDIA
APRIL 16, 1937

Indian events are beginning to cause anxiety through wide circles in Britain, and especially in those circles responsible for the India Constitution Act.

Those Conservative members, who during five years opposed the new adventure and were decisively voted down in both Houses of Parliament, have maintained a punctilious silence from the moment that the India Bill received the Royal Assent. Neither by word nor action have they intervened, or prejudiced the implementing of the vast, complicated scheme which they had so resolutely opposed. This period of restraint is by no means at an end.

Moreover, the action of His Majesty's Government has been strictly in accordance with the law which has been passed and with the undertakings and safeguards which were an essential part of its progress. There has been no failure upon the part of the Viceroy or of the India Office to carry out loyally and faithfully the intentions of Parliament and the pledges given both to the British and Indian peoples. It must also be remembered that the opponents of the India Act professed themselves—with great reluctance and many misgivings—ready to support the institution of provincial government apart from the Federal scheme; and it is the stage of provincial government alone that has now arrived. But though there is therefore no occasion for controversy or reproaches at the present time, it would only be prudent to take stock of what has happened.

A gigantic process of gathering the votes of an electorate of thirty million Indians spread over an immense sub-continent, many of them dwelling under primitive conditions, has passed off with smoothness and efficiency. The electoral machinery has worked better than many of its designers expected. The results have, however, seriously disconcerted them. Those who said during the passage of the Act that the Congress Party would be supreme, were disbelieved and brushed aside. But now we see that the Congress Party is powerful everywhere, and all-powerful in six of the eleven provinces of India. Even in Madras, which it was believed almost without dispute would return a moderate Liberal legislature, the Congress nominees have swept the board. They claim to speak in the name of an enormous majority of the Indian electorate. They can govern, at any time they choose, the greater part of India. The administration of justice and the control of the police will, at their request, be placed immediately in their hands. They can dispose of the revenues of half a dozen countries almost as large as leading European states. They can make or mar the welfare of masses, numbered by the hundred million, and they can vindicate or break the Constitution created for them.

They now refuse to take office without assurances from the Provincial Governors that the fundamental safeguards without which Parliament would never have passed the Act, will be set aside. The Governors and the Viceroy, acting in the closest concert with the home Government, have had no choice but to refuse such assurances. Departmental Ministries have been set up to carry on, pending the meeting of the Assemblies. As soon as these Assemblies meet we shall see the beginning in every Province of the same kind of constitutional conflict which scarred the history of England in the seventeenth and eighteenth centuries. On every side Governors, armed with the prerogatives of ancient kings, will be confronted with the agitation of modern Parliaments. The Congress has declared its united resolve to make the Constitution unworkable and to court, or even in some cases create, an absolute deadlock. The stop-gap Ministries will be humiliated, chased from power, or reduced to impotence or servility. On the other hand, the Government of every Province must be carried on from week to week, and the Governors have ample powers in law *and in fact* to enable them to discharge this prime responsibility. Such is the crude, harsh issue which is now emerging.

Read here the hard declaration of the Pandit Jawaharlal Nehru—Communist, Revolutionary, most capable and most implacable of the enemies of the British connection with India. 'It is as clear as the noonday sun that our paths lie in different directions. There is nothing in common between us, and we shall go along our path resolutely and with a will to put an end to this bogus Act which has been forced upon us.' But now comes forward Mr. Gandhi with smooth and specious words. 'Why imperil,' he pleads in effect, 'this great experiment of self-government for the sake of legal pedantry? Let us have a "gentleman's agreement" to explain away and remove from practical politics these galling statutory safeguards. Then you will reap your rich reward.' Congress will then, perhaps, it is suggested, consent to assume the Government of the provinces and take control of the police, and thus advantaged will be able to carry out its declared intention of destroying the Constitution and achieving Indian independence.

These barbed blandishments are reinforced from British-Indian quarters by arguments of practical expediency. The Congress, it is said, gained their majority by making large promises to the electors. To fulfil these promises would split their party. To refuse to take office and throw the blame for all disappointed hopes upon the wicked English and their 'bogus constitution,' keeps the party united and their electorate behind them, and thus builds up the forces which will be required in the impending struggle. To frustrate these schemes, it is said, the remedy is to force the Congress men, as they are now called, to assume the responsibility of office. The constitution therefore must be so interpreted that the reserve powers on which Parliament, even in its most facile mood, insisted, should be allowed to lapse.

But it is to a different England or Britain that these appeals are now directed. Here is an England which feels in all conscience that it has done its best for the Indian political classes. It will stand by its word in spirit and in letter; but it will go no farther. It will enter upon no new slippery slope. Britain has done her best. Others now must make their sincere contribution. Besides all this, we are in a different climate of opinion.

The dangerous sloth-fulness of two or three years ago has passed. The mood of pacifism is gone. Britain is arming on a gigantic scale. The gravity of the European situation presses upon men's minds. There is a sterner temper in the air.

Meanwhile, as if to strike a note of realism to Pandits, Mahatmas and those who now claim to speak for the helpless Indian masses, the Frontier is astir; and British officers and soldiers are giving their lives to hold back from the cities and peace-time wealth of India the storm of Pathan inroad and foray.

GERMANY AND THE LOW COUNTRIES
MAY 7, 1937

The position of the two small ancient countries lying on the North Sea shore, about the mouths of the Rhine and the Scheldt, has recently attracted serious attention. Both Holland and Belgium are the possessors of great and rich colonial domains, and are the neighbours of Germany. Both naturally feel anxiety at the unceasing progress of German armaments, at the breach of Treaty obligations which carried the German armed forces into the Rhineland, and also at the activities of Nazi propaganda among their own peoples. It is satisfactory that Herr Hitler should have offered 'to recognise and guarantee Belgium and Holland as inviolable neutral territories.' But this assurance has not removed their fears.

Such hesitation is easy to understand when we remember that the inviolability of Belgian neutrality was guaranteed by Germany before the late war, not merely in a speech or public declaration but by solemn formal Treaty; and that nevertheless the German General Staff for many years before the war perfected in full peace, in cold blood and minute detail, the Schlieffen plan, the essence of which was the violation of Belgian neutrality and the invasion of France through Belgium by that road; and that this was carried out unhesitatingly and with ruthless severity. It is believed that had the Great War been postponed for two years the right-handed sweep of the increasing German armies would have passed through Holland as well as through Belgium. But in 1914 Holland was spared. She preserved a strict neutrality, favourable in many ways to Germany, while all the time the entire Dutch male population stood to arms along their dykes.

The response which the Dutch Government, under the leadership of its remarkably prudent, resolute chief Dr. Colijn, made to Herr Hitler's assurance was a model of dignity. The Netherlands Government informed the German Government that, while gratified by this expression of goodwill, 'we should not be prepared to conclude an agreement with any country upon the inviolability of our territory. Such inviolability is for us axiomatic, and therefore cannot form the subject of any Treaty which we may conclude.' Both the Dutch and the Belgians are increasing their forces and fortifying their frontiers. They use for this purpose the modern resources of concrete blockhouses, of elaborate preparations to blow up roads and bridges, and above all the inundations which have played so large a part in their past history.

The fate of Belgium has long been judged of vital consequence for Great Britain. For four hundred years in four successive great wars we have prevented the Low Countries from falling under the control of a great military power; be it the Spain of Philip II or the France of Louis XIV or the France of Napoleon or the Germany of William II. A few days ago in conjunction with France we renewed our guarantee to Belgium in the most precise form. There is no doubt that a German invasion of Belgium would be the signal for a general European war involving from its very first moment the British Empire, and therefore in spite of the past everyone must welcome Herr Hitler's assurances.

Nevertheless the value of those assurances will be greatly enhanced by every preparation made by Belgium and her joint guarantors to impose the strongest deterrents upon the overrunning of Belgian territory. The Belgians have, however, in fear of their great and rapidly-arming neighbour, wished to confine their efforts strictly to the defence of their own soil. They no longer pledge themselves as under the Franco-Belgian agreement of 1920, or the Treaty of Locarno, to come to the assistance of France. They give no reciprocal guarantee of coming to the aid of the two protecting powers. This change of attitude has been induced not only by the armed advance of German forces and road terminals to the Belgian frontier, but also by the pro-Nazi spirit fostered, particularly among the Flemings, by the Rexist leader, lately rebuffed in Brussels. King Leopold and his able Prime Minister, Van Zeeland, felt that they could better unite the whole nation for the defence of Belgium upon the basis of a policy of strict independence, and that this would give them more safety even than prior arrangements with France and Great Britain. Their decision, however, is, of course, subject to the obligations of the Covenant of the League, which expressly forbids any signatory to remain impartial as between an aggressor and a victim.

It would be idle to pretend that this change in Belgian policy has not caused some regrets and misgivings to both of the guaranteeing Powers. It would be obviously impossible for Belgium or Holland to defend their frontiers unaided against the mighty tide of a German invasion. Should such evils come upon us, which God forfend, the only sure defence in present circumstances will be salt water and the French fortress line. That line is now being drawn along the French frontier *behind* Belgium. The endless succession of brilliantly conceived fortifications upon which and through which the mobile French armies will fight and manœuvre, will soon leave Belgium outside its rampart. On the other hand, the development of great roads, railway sidings and airfields is proceeding ceaselessly opposite Belgium along the German frontier.

Only the future can show whether the decision of Belgium has been right in the interests of her national independence, and whether they are not almost acquiescing beforehand in their absorption by an aggressive German empire. It does not seem, however, that France and Great Britain have lost very much by the change in Belgian policy. If, as the Belgians hope, their integrity is respected in a war by Germany, that will certainly be a great help to France. She will not have to hold in force the long stretch of her frontiers which abut on Belgium. This will sensibly lessen the strain upon the French defence. But this fact only makes one feel more doubtful whether in a life and death struggle these happy conditions will prevail.

DEFENDING THE EMPIRE
MAY 13, 1937

The statesmen of the British Empire assemble in conference to-morrow. They are men of wide experience and strong personality, who have risen in the self-governing Dominions by the use of those arts, and the play of those forces, which bring political leaders to the head of Parliamentary democracies. It is unlikely that Constitutional questions will play any part in their discussions. These have already been settled for good or for ill by the Statute of Westminster. This memorable Act leaves the self-governing Dominions linked to the Mother Country and to one another only by the golden circle of the Crown, and by their resolve to remain equal partners in the Commonwealth. Trade and economic questions will no doubt absorb much thought; but after all it is upon the question of Defence that the whole significance of this Conference turns.

After efforts to procure general disarmament, so unseasonably protracted as to bring us into grievous danger, the Mother Country has plunged into a gigantic scheme of national and Imperial defence involving the expenditure in five years of at least £1,500,000,000 as fast as this sum can be judiciously and effectively employed. There is no power in the Constitution of the Empire to call for any proportionate contribution from any of its members. They can do much or little or nothing, entirely as they choose. It is to be hoped that no one is going to ask them for any contribution. They are already well informed upon the general situation. The secret facts at the disposal of the British Government will be laid before them, and they will do what they think is right. Even if they decide to do nothing there will be no reproaches, other than those which their own Parliaments and peoples may make. When their decisions have been taken, the technical process of co-ordinating the available resources of this unexampled, loosely knit and yet highly sensitised confederacy will be undertaken by all its members in common. It is therefore worth while at this juncture to restate the broad principles and main forces upon which our unmilitarised Commonwealth of Nations relies for its continued existence in the midst of the armed and arming world which rises in clanking panoply around.

The life of the British Empire arises from sea power. Its maintenance depends upon the Royal Navy. The possession of the effective command of the seas and oceans alone converts these expanses of blue water from impassable gulfs into bonds of union. Under the treaties with the United States, the two main branches of the English-speaking peoples live together upon the basis of equal navies. A quarrel between them would paralyse and probably shatter the British Empire, and would be deeply injurious to the United States. For this reason, it has become increasingly the cardinal policy of both countries to maintain relations of unbreakable peace. Both have renounced war as an instrument of policy. Mutual confidence and friendship between them were never greater than now.

Therefore the British Parliament and the Admiralty have not for many generations made any provision against American naval power; and the British conviction to-day is that the stronger the United States navy becomes the better chance there is of world peace. Apart from the United States, the Royal Navy, in consequence of the immense measures now being taken, has every prospect of being able to extend to the whole Empire, in the future, its old unfailing naval protection.

Naval strength to-day cannot, however, be considered apart from air power. An efficient fleet must be provided with the most perfect air arm that can be devised; and must have secure harbours and fuelling points where it can rest and replenish, and whence it can operate. Modern developments will confront the Imperial Conference with very large new special problems in this sphere. Two great harbours at present attract attention. The first is Cape Town, which the Union Government of South Africa is bringing up to a standard capable of resisting what is called first-class attack. Cape Town, when fully equipped, will afford an alternative route into the Indian Ocean in addition to the main highway we intend to keep open through the Mediterranean. The second strategic harbour is Singapore. Upon this during nearly twenty years an immense amount of work and money has been spent. The fortress and dockyard will soon become capable of maintaining if necessary an important battle fleet with its ancillary craft. Singapore is as far from Japan as Portsmouth from New York, and it is, therefore, in no way a menace to our old friends the Japanese. It is, however, the stepping-stone by which alone we can make sure of being able to give that effective protection to Australia and New Zealand which the Mother Country regards as a trust doubly sacred after what happened in the Great War.

So far as the oceans are concerned, the arrival of aircraft as a prime factor in war can only be a help to the stronger Navy. A strong Navy requires above all things to find its antagonist, be it a hostile fleet or a single commerce raider. Whereas in 1914 a squadron of cruisers could only search on a front of perhaps a hundred miles, the same squadron equipped with aircraft and aircraft carriers could now cover a front of nearly a thousand miles. It took thirty ships and many weeks to find the Emden. When found, one ship could destroy it in less than an hour.

I do not myself believe that well-built modern warships properly defended by armour and anti-aircraft guns, especially when steaming in company, are likely to fall a prey to hostile aircraft. Battleships which are built to stand the plunging fire of the heaviest cannon should also be able to endure the bombs of aeroplanes. We were assured that the insurgent battleship España was sunk by an aviator dropping a bomb down its funnel. It now appears it was sunk by a mine. Such a weak old vessel, with only 1 1/2-inch plate upon its deck, might well have been destroyed if hit by a heavy aeroplane bomb. It is, however, easier to hit a town or even a village from the air than it is to hit a moving battleship. Moreover, in attacking a battleship, aircraft are attacking not defenceless houses, but a hostile battery. In attacking a British fleet they would be flying into a concentration of anti-aircraft gunnery unequalled in quality and in quantity. This and many other features have led the British Admiralty and all other Admiralties to believe that the battleship, and the power to draw out a superior line of battle, still constitute the only trustworthy foundation of sea power. This, if true, is of the highest importance to the British Empire and the United States, each of which possesses a battle fleet superior to the present battle fleet strength of all other Naval Powers combined.

The submarine also is not nowadays regarded as the menace it used to be. It is believed that the new methods which have been discovered and perfected make the submarine liable almost certainly to be found and thereafter hunted to death far more easily than was possible even in the days when the British Navy strangled the U-boats. It is not of course possible here to deal with all aspects of defence. Grave and grievous dangers threaten the heart of the Empire, its enormous cities, its feeding ports, and its manufacturing centres. But the members of the Imperial Conference may meet together with the conviction that the peace and unity of the Empire may still be preserved by sea power reinforced by air power, and that the Mother Country tardily but earnestly is taking vast measures directed to that end.

AMERICA LOOKS AT EUROPE
MAY 31, 1937

No fact in the world situation is more hopeful or important than the excellent relations and understanding which have developed between the United States and the two Western democracies, Great Britain and France. I cannot recall any period when the good will between the two main branches of the English-speaking peoples was so pronounced. This has not been the result of diplomacy or negotiation. It has arisen naturally and almost unconsciously from an identity of outlook in both peoples towards world problems in Europe and in the Far East. It is not true that this harmony is expressed only in smooth platitudes about the joys of peace and the horrors of war. On the contrary, it is sustained in the United States by a marked and reasoned approval of British and French institutions and policy, and an equally noticeable dislike of the tendencies of the Dictator-ruled countries.

One may say that throughout the United States there is a keen abhorrence of the doctrines and practices both of Nazism and Fascism, and a strong current of sympathy with the countries great and small who are faithfully endeavouring to preserve their parliamentary institutions, and to maintain the conditions of law, freedom and peace. It is remarkable that the new American Ambassador in Paris and Mr. Gerard, the envoy to the Coronation, should within a few weeks have given vent to these sentiments in public. For instance, on February 22 Mr. Bullitt said in Paris:

'We are not indifferent to the state of those countries which carry on the great tradition of Western civilisation.... As children of the old civilisation of Western Europe, we believe that there is such a thing as truth. It is only fair to point out that we did our utmost to stay out of the war which broke out in 1914, that we stayed out of it for three years, and that we shall stay out of any war which may break out in the future so long as God permits. We hope to stay out of war, but we are entirely aware that there is always some possibility that some nation might be sufficiently reckless to drive us into war.'

And last week Mr. Gerard said in London: 'When you are armed, then armed Britain will be the greatest guarantee of peace on earth.... We in America—I think in this one thing I can presume to speak for my country—are firmly determined on three things. First, we are against war; secondly, we are against any alliances; and, thirdly, we are against meddling in the muddled affairs of Europe. But we and you, the great British Empire, are bound by something more binding than alliances and treaties. We are bound together by mutual trust, by mutual understanding, by a common desire for stability and peace, and especially by the feeling that at this moment, with Fascism on one side and Communism on the other, the three great democracies, Great Britain, France and the United States, stand as the sole hope of liberalism and of the freedom of the world.'

There certainly has not been any occasion either before or since the Great War when the views of the United States Government have been so clearly and weightily expressed upon European affairs.

It would be a mistake, however, to assume that these friendly declarations imply any intention on the part of the United States to become involved in the quarrels and combinations of Europe. On the contrary, the main movement of opinion in America is more set on avoiding foreign entanglements and keeping out of another world war than ever before. No European statesman should be so foolish as to count upon the armed assistance of the United States even if his country were the victim of unprovoked aggression. It is much better to face the real facts. The intense desire of the United States to keep out of any European war is shown in the striking change in American opinion upon the so-called 'freedom of the seas.' Because this doctrine brought about a war between the United States and Great Britain in 1812 and a war with the German Empire in 1917, it is now widely discarded at Washington.

The various neutrality Bills which have been passed or discussed in Congress all seek to prevent by various methods a repetition of the past. Rather than be drawn into another Armageddon, it may be that the United States will forbid their citizens to traffic on the high seas with any belligerents at all. A kind of neutrality is now being considered which appears at first sight to be isolationist and impartial in the last degree. The doctrine of 'cash and carry' means that no American ships will carry supplies to the warring countries, but if these countries choose to present themselves in ships at the American doorstep with ready money in their hands they will be allowed to buy non-military supplies. This arrangement certainly has the merit of rendering to superior sea power its full deserts. It avoids for Great Britain, if engaged in war, the danger of any dispute with the United States such as caused so much anxiety in 1914 and 1915. It may be rather chilling comfort, but it is comfort none the less.

Ever since the United States built a Navy equal to that of Britain, and even before, it has been impossible for the British Navy to enforce any blockade contrary to the final will of the United States. Our resources would be altogether insufficient, and it is now a settled maxim of British policy that without the good will, or at least the acquiescence, of the United States the famous weapon of a blockade cannot be used. For this reason the growing moral association of ideas between the three great parliamentary democracies is above all to be welcomed. The only kind of struggle which can arise in Europe is one in which a Dictator country is declared to be an unprovoked aggressor against a victim State. One cannot conceive that in these circumstances the United States, while maintaining strict neutrality, would hamper in any way the victims of aggression.

There are two other questions which affect British and American relations. They stand upon a different plane to these great moral issues, but they are none the less important. The first is the question of the British war debt to the United States. No solution has yet been offered of that problem. It is quite certain that the economy of the whole world would be prejudiced by the sterile remittance from Great Britain of thirty-five million pounds sterling per year across the Atlantic. It would repeatedly rupture the exchanges and distract the entire finance of international trade. On the other hand, John Bull would always be anxious to have the quittance of Uncle Sam. This question should be perseveringly studied in the light of the obvious fact that matters cannot indefinitely remain as they are.

The second great question is one of co-operation in world finance. Is not an undue burden being borne at the present time by the United States in the maintenance of the gold price? We are witnessing the absurdity of gold being produced from the womb of the earth, in South Africa, in Russia, in Canada, and being purchased and reburied in the United States. Evidently we are approaching a point where the two great capitalist Powers must co-operate together in securing a stable world currency. It may even be that these two financial questions would be easier solved together than separately. If so, the atmosphere of comprehension and friendship which we now feel around us would be a stimulus to statesmen to act with hopeful energy.

would always be anxious to have the guidance of Uncle Sam. This question should be perseveringly studied in the light of the obvious fact that matters cannot indefinitely remain as they are.

The second great question is one of co-operation in world finance. Is not an undue burden thrown on at the present time by the United States in the maintenance of the gold price? We are witnessing the absurdity of gold being produced from the womb of the earth, in South Africa, in Russia, in Canada, and being purchased and admitted to the United States. Evidently we are approaching a point where the two great capitalist Powers must co-operate together in securing a stable world currency. It may even be that these two financial operations would be easier solved together than separately. If so, the atmosphere of neighbourliness and friendship which we have felt around us would be a stimulus to any action to which both should agree.

THE ROME-BERLIN AXIS
JUNE 11, 1937

The Coronation is over. A new King and Queen are seated upon their thrones amid the acclamations of the British people. The Abdication has been digested. The Duke of Windsor is married according to his resolve and with the good wishes of all that is decent in Britain. After a period of pageantry and of domestic stress the British public may be invited to turn their attention again to Europe.

How has it all gone in Europe while we have been thinking about our own affairs? I, personally, have never been able to forget Europe. It hangs over my mind like a vulture. How are we going to prevent our happy, peaceful, free, progressive life from being destroyed by what may happen in Europe? All the time the German armament hammers have been descending. All the time the great flow of destructive weapons has been passing from the factories to fighting units of brave, virile, competent men improving in their training month by month. All the time the German Army has been increasing its numbers above those of the French Army. All the time the efficiency and ripeness of the German Officer-Corps has been improving. All the time the German Air Force in quantity and in quality has been gaining on our British effort.

It is curious that Parliament, which a year ago showed itself genuinely concerned about our defences, has now forgotten even that there could be such a fact as danger. Some say, 'How right the Government were not to be alarmed by the scaremongers! How right they were not to have a Ministry of Supply, and not to upset the ordinary business prosperity of the country! A whole year has passed and nothing has happened. How stultified are those who cried "Alarm!"' But this complacent movement may soon be stirred by less comfortable reflections.

What is the precise character of the arrangements between Germany and Italy? Here are these two Dictators seated on their thrones high above the common mass of peaceful, well-disposed, heavily-burdened mankind. Both have plenty of obedient men. Both are hard pressed for money. Both have to ask their obedient men to tighten their belts. Both are confronted with the awkward sense that though Germany is all for Hitler, it wishes to be known as Germany; and though Italy is all for Mussolini, it would like to be known as Italy. Both are disquieted by the fact that large sections of their population would like to stand in with the general efflorescence of the world, and that quite large numbers of Fascists and Nazis would be very much inclined to vote 'that a good time should be had by all.' Grim Dictators glowering over gaunt populations! What are their personal relations to be?

At the hub of any Berlin-Rome axis there grits the Italian neutrality at the outbreak of the Great War and the Italian junction with the Allies nine months thereafter. There is a good deal to be said about this, and not all by any means on one side. The Triple Alliance bound Italy to make war in common with Germany and Austria. But by a secret article known only to the highest authorities in Germany and Austria, Italy had stipulated for the right in all circumstances to stand out of any war in which she would be the enemy of England. This article was unknown to the British Government, and only became public property after Italy had actually entered the ranks of the Allies. It is the supreme justification of Italian honour—certainly it covers entirely the Italian abstention from declaring war in unison with the other two powers of the Triplice. No German can preserve a quarrel with Italy on that account. Far more questionable to German eyes was the action of Italy in declaring war upon Austria and later upon Germany in the spring of 1915. This was regarded throughout Germany as a base betrayal of solemn obligation. Anyhow, one may say that Italian good faith in the hour of dire need is profoundly distrusted in Germany.

We cannot doubt the fact that British and Italian relations have not improved as was hoped in the early months of this year. Signor Mussolini affronted the Liberal and religious forces in Britain when he subjugated the Abyssinians. He infuriated the Socialist-Labour element as well as the Liberals when he made his intrusion into Spain. He disturbed the Conservatives, who are his only friends, when, seated on his white charger, he proclaimed himself the protector of Islam. Our King-Emperor reigns over more Mohammedans than can be found in the rest of the world. All the British military and Conservative classes have a profound historic liking for the Turk. They fought the Turk with extreme reluctance. But now the relations between Great Britain and Turkey are better than they have ever been before. Also in India the Mohammedans, confronted with the violent Communist politics of some elements of the Congress party, look to the Imperial power as their true foundation. Therefore great offence was caused, though little was said, when Signor Mussolini declared himself the protector of Islam, he having only a handful of Islam in his control, and that part by no means contented.

On the other hand, the invitation of the Negus to the Coronation, the steadfast refusal of Great Britain to concede any recognition of the Italian conquest of Abyssinia, and the repeated taunts of British Left-wing newspapers about the behaviour of the Italian troops in Spain, has formed the basis of a prolonged anti-British Italian press and broadcast campaign. But those who are friends of the Mediterranean accord between Great Britain and Italy seek continually for opportunities of dissipating these very noticeable antagonisms. Will they succeed, or shall we all be nakedly exposed to the challenge of the two harassed Dictators at the head of their two impoverished nations armed to the teeth?

Who shall presume to lift the veils of the future, and who would be believed if he reported what he saw? Evidently we are approaching the point in European history where the League of Nations, if properly supported, will have an immense and perhaps decisive part to play in the prevention of a brutal trial of strength. How else are we going to marshal adequate and if possible overwhelming forces against brazen, unprovoked aggression, except by a grand alliance of peace-seeking peoples under the authority of an august international body? One is astonished to hear the vain talk and chatter that proceeds in certain social and political circles in London against the League of Nations. Only by a European union spreading gradually to a world union against war can the dreaded catastrophe, which nevertheless approaches inch by inch and day by day, be warded off. I hold that at the present time an alliance of an offensive or even of a defensive character between Italy and Germany is far from being achieved. There is still time to build Europe into a better framework. There is still time to conciliate existing grievances. There is still time, if all friendly efforts for peace are futile, to forge and weld a grand alliance for international law and justice, which will arrest armaments, avert war and confound the wicked of every land.

In the middle of February the French Premier, M. Blum, announced a 'pause' in the programme of the Front Populaire in order to reduce the mounting public expenditure. Shortly afterwards the French Government raised a short term loan of forty million pounds in England.

On March 16th the police fired on the Communists at Clichy; five persons were killed and more than 200 injured.

Throughout May the Senate increased its opposition to the Blum Government and eventually rejected a Bill authorising the Government to take by decree measures to restore the public finances. This rejection led to the resignation of the Blum Cabinet on June 21.

"VIVE LA FRANCE!"
JUNE 25, 1937

In prejudiced quarters, the usual scare has been raised about France. The finances are in disorder; the currency is quaking; Blum has resigned; the Government has fallen; Bolshevik revolution is very near; and the Exhibition is not ready either. But, in truth, what happened last week in France only shows the extraordinary flexibility of the French Parliamentary apparatus.

In Great Britain, governments often change their policies without changing their men. In France, they usually change their men without changing their policy. In Great Britain, a Minister enters a department expecting to stay there three or four years. In France he makes his bow of greeting or farewell—here to-day and gone to-morrow—to the permanent official who keeps the whole thing going. In Great Britain, the Cabinet is the Government. In France, it is the Chamber; and all parts of the Chamber within certain limits co-operate for a perfectly understood common purpose. In the British Parliament, there is a marked and felt dearth of men of high ability. In France, there is a plethora. The whole beehive of the French Chamber and Senate buzzes about vehemently, but with a clear purpose in accordance with the spirit of the hive.

Many countries, not excluding our own, are apt to regard the French as a vain, volatile, fanciful, hysterical nation. As a matter of fact, they are one of the most grim, sober, unsentimental, calculating and tenacious races in the world. At this present moment, all Frenchmen, from militant Monarchists to militant Communists, are resolved that France shall be defended, and that the freedom which the French people gained in the Revolution shall not be invaded or restricted from without or from within. France has always been prodigal of the blood of her sons; but she has a great reluctance to pay taxes. The British are good at paying taxes, but detest drill. The French do not mind drill, but avoid taxes. Both nations can still fight, if they are convinced there is no other way of surviving; but in such a case France would have a small surplus and Britain a small army.

M. Blum has played a big part. He has been Prime Minister for more than a year. In France—where the leading men take it in turn to govern—this is already a considerable feat. Blum filled with distinction a period in the life of France, which but for him might have been a hiatus. The French wage-earners were not having as good a deal as the wealth of France and her civilization warranted. Their standards were definitely below those which we have established in our own moist, misty, and sometimes fog-bound island. They meant to make a push (in German, 'putsch') for a larger share in the Gallic commonwealth. M. Blum has given expression to this intention. At the same time, in foreign policy he has brought France nearer than she has ever been before to the two Western, liberal democracies who speak the English tongue. And always the greatest care and expense have been lavished upon the army and other defence forces. All have been agreed on this. Even the Communists have paraded the streets crying, 'Long Live the Army of the Republic.' The opponents of France would make a profound mistake if they were to undervalue her inherent national and moral strength at the present juncture.

There is, however, serious criticism open against the Blum Government. In facing their great difficulties at home, they were found far too ready to take the easy course in finance and social legislation. It may be that they had little choice in view of the temper of organised labour. The present financial situation of France is discreditable to any Administration. The Senate which, unlike our House of Lords, is confident of its own strength within the limits of the constitution, has been justified in its intervention. The reconstruction which has been so smoothly effected was a step at once imperative and salutary. The demand for powers of financial dictatorship by a Government and a Finance Minister who had such a sorry tale to tell was not one which ought to have been accepted.

When our Socialists brought us to the disreputable collapse of 1931, Great Britain could never have recovered without their being displaced from office. No party has the right to involve a country in financial confusion, and then ride off upon a claim for greater executive power to cope with 'speculators' and 'high finance.' Such methods would speedily achieve the ruin even of the wealthiest State. The establishment of credit, and the repatriation of fugitive capital, can only be achieved by confidence. Exported capital will not return to be confiscated or squandered. In all the circumstances the changes made are the least which the situation demanded.

The Government of the experienced M. Chautemps, in which M. Blum patriotically takes the second place, will fully maintain the strength of France and her place in the European peace system. It is too much to hope that the financial difficulties will now be solved. They will be tided over, and in a sense met, by further devaluation, by more taxes and more economies, *not affecting national defence*. This Government, like all French Governments, is one of transition. I am very careful not to prophesy. 'Never prophesy unless you know!' But it would certainly not surprise me if M. Chautemps' Government proved to be a stepping stone to something very like a National Government, even in the course of the present year.

France is not going to be the country to betray the cause of democracy. Nor will she be false to the inspiration of freedom and individualism which was the message—however falsified in practice—of the French Revolution. The 'will to live' is strong in the French people. They will not fail mankind in these years, when civilisation has to be defended at once from the armed menace of dictatorship and from the morbid degeneration of Trotskyite Communism. With the moral support of the French military strength, other free and anxious States, the democracies of Europe, may be aided to maintain a firm and steadfast front against tyranny. And if peace is preserved the European masses may gain their share of the shorter hours, improved standards of living, and larger opportunities which nature, guided by science, stands ready to bestow on all her children who serve with strong right arm the causes of justice and freedom.

THE EBBING TIDE OF SOCIALISM
JULY 9, 1937

Pessimists have always assumed that the extension of the franchise till it became universal would spell the dominance of Socialism, or of even more extreme Left-wing ideas. It was feared that the great mass of poorer people dwelling under the hard pressures of life would cast their votes for any party which promised a general overturn of the existing social and economic system. But this has not happened in Great Britain. On the contrary, the reverse has happened, and the largest possible electorates have repeatedly yielded the largest recorded Conservative majorities. Thus the calculations of wealthy, ambitious careerists and would-be demagogic leaders, have been falsified. The belief that violence in propaganda and extravagant logic in doctrine would appeal to any large body of the British nation is proved to be untrue.

So also have been reduced to impotence and ridicule the Nazi conceptions of Sir Oswald Mosley. He had built his hopes upon the Socialist or Communist menace, and in all probability he would have risen in opposition to it. But at the present time it does not exist. The failure of the red-hot men of the Left has involved a simultaneous failure of the white-hot men of the Right. The massive common sense of the only long-trained democracy—apart from the United States—has established a spacious and predominant middle zone within which the class adjustments of the nation can be fought out, and from which the extremists at both ends are excluded. At the present time, they can do little more than chalk mutually insulting slogans upon the enclosure within which the cricket match is being played. It is with affairs inside this enclosure, occupied by all the nation, that practical people are now concerned.

The long series of by-elections, following two general elections, and six years of power held by one set of men and forces, have all told the same tale.

The Socialist-Labour Party, not only in its extreme varieties, but in its most moderate forms, seems to have reached the limits of its expansion. This might well have been expected of a class party, refusing all contact with other parties and professing in theory absurd and, if applied, devastating doctrines. The programme of giving the State, that is to say the politicians who have obtained a majority at an election, autocratic control of all the means of production, distribution, and exchange, would never commend itself to the strong individualism of the British race. To have everybody made equal under boards of officials directed by Socialist politicians would be to destroy the whole sparkle and progress of life without in any way raising the average. To join in one fist the authority of the magistrate, of the employer, of the landlord, of the food purveyor, and of the legislator, must be to reduce the ordinary wage-earner and his family, equally with more fortunate people, to an absolute subjugation.

Such doctrines might make their way in some semibarbarous Asiatic country, or in a nation ruined by defeat in war; but here, in our island, they have only to be presented under conditions of free politics and free criticism to be ignominiously repudiated. The foremost to repudiate them—in fact, if not in form—are the great trade unions. Nothing can be more remarkable than the sober, resolute control of the theorists and doctrinaires which has been exercised by the responsible trade union leaders. These leaders feel themselves responsible for securing better wages and conditions for the mass of their members. They have no intention of allowing themselves, or their organisation, to be made a vehicle for ambitious politicians.

In the main, they accept the existing social system, and mean to get as much out of it as they can for the working classes. They have found it necessary to proclaim an absolute ban against Communism. Although Communists are not an immediate menace in our country, the trade union leaders have felt it their duty to take a hard line against them, on the grounds, chiefly, that they are the disturbers and hinderers of the material betterment of the wage-earning classes. This is an example full of instruction for the world. The Labour-Socialist party in the House of Commons is, of course, the reflection of the forces at work in the country. Lately, its Parliamentary leadership has been much criticised. But, with a weak minority, it is very difficult to be effective in the House of Commons. Against a large, solid and capable national phalanx, even if you have the best of the argument, you have the worst of the voting. But the Socialist party, hampered by its theories and heterogeneous composition, very rarely has the best even of the argument. It would, no doubt, be possible with better instructed and more aggressive leadership to score off the Government more frequently. But this would not in fact alter substantially the course of events. It would make the Parliamentary scene more lively, but it would not change the scene.

The truth is, that the building up of a class-based Socialist-Labour party in Great Britain involved a great setback for Left-wing politics. The Socialist movement devoured the Liberal party, with its immense traditional hold upon the nation, without being in any way capable of taking its place. Not only millions of Liberal voters, but the floating mass of sturdy citizens who care little or nothing for parties, were estranged; and most of them have found a haven at election time behind the broad breakwaters of the National Government. It has been most fortunate that our country, in this period of world-confusion and of war danger, should present a solid, stable front to all kinds of violence, whether from Communists or Nazis, and should show itself in so striking a manner united upon fundamentals.

The influence which the British nation exerts throughout the world is profound and persistent. Except in Russia, where the intelligentsia have been largely destroyed, it is practically impossible to prevent facts about other countries leaking in. In Germany in particular, no matter how many foreign newspapers are seized, enough go through, often a few days late, to enable the public opinion of a highly educated race to form itself. Some of us believe that if only peace can be maintained, the German people will derive very great encouragement from the progress of democracy in Britain, and from the kind of life we are able to organise for ourselves here. The day may easily come when they will be tired of being led by the nose from one parade to another, and make themselves into a really free, grown-up people. But the chance of this depends upon whether Britain is well enough defended, and whether she is closely enough united to other peace-loving countries, to deter the embarrassed dictators from plunging their own people, and all the rest of us, into the agony of war.

The fact that there is really no difference between the political parties, and among all classes, upon British rearmament, carries with it the best pledge for the future, and the surest hope that the noble ship of freedom will escape the rocks, round the point and sail into the open sea.

PALESTINE PARTITION
JULY 23, 1937

When a Royal Commission of very able, experienced men, with no party bias, and no axes to grind, takes more than a year to study a problem with every advantage of information, it would be at once foolish and churlish not to treat their recommendations with respect. Nevertheless, with the best will in the world, no one can disguise from himself that the plan of cutting Palestine into three parts is a counsel of despair. One wonders whether, in reality, the difficulties of carrying out the Zionist scheme are so great as they are portrayed, and whether in fact there has not been a very considerable measure of success.

In the sixteen years that have passed since the mandate, many troubles have been overcome, and great developments have taken place in Palestine. When I paid my last visit, only three years ago, I was delighted at the aspect of the countryside. The fine roads, the new buildings and plantations, the evidences of prosperity, both among Jews and Arabs, presented on every side, all gave a sense of real encouragement, made the more impressive by the tiny military and police force which preserved order at so little cost to the population. This fair prospect has been over-clouded, and even to some extent blasted, by the events of the last two years. A great experiment and mission was proceeding hopefully when, owing to outside events, an undue strain was thrown upon its organisation. This was certainly not our fault. The persecutions of the Jews in Germany, the exploitation of anti-Semitism as a means by which violent and reactionary forces seize, or attempt to seize, despotic power, afflicted the civilised world with a refugee problem similar to that of the Huguenots in the seventeenth century.

The brunt of this has fallen upon this very small country and administration of Palestine. Jewish immigration, suddenly raised to 30,000 or 40,000 a year, may not have exceeded the 'economic absorptive capacity' of the settled districts, but it naturally confronted the Arabs with the prospect, not of an evolutionary growth of the Jewish population, but of actual flooding and swamping which seemed to bring near to them the prospect of domination. Too much current was put on the cables. And the cables have fused. That may be a reason for mending the cables and reducing the current. It is surely no reason for declaring that electricity is a fluid too dangerous for civilisation to handle. While I hold myself free to study the whole situation anew, I do so under the strong impression that the case for perseverance holds the field. I am quite sure that the genius of a man like Lawrence of Arabia, if Fate untimely had not swept him from the human scene, would in a few months restore the situation, persuade one side to concede and the other to forbear, and lead both races to bathe their hands together in the ever-growing prosperity and culture of their native land.

But when we turn our eyes from the ills that be to those we know not of, it may be that a stimulus will be found for renewed exertion. The Commission has done no more than outline the policy. Apart from principles, no one can judge such a policy without the details upon which its execution depends. At this stage nothing appears to have been thought out. Certainly one must consider that the Partition plan, as now set forth, marks the end of the Zionist dream. The tract of land assigned to the Jews, no bigger than an English county, already bears a population of 140 to the square kilometre. It is as densely populated as Germany or England, and twice as densely as France. How then can there be any future for the idea of a national home of refuge and of inspiration for the hunted and hounded Jews of so many lands? Even in this limited area there are almost as many Arabs as Jews. If it be true that Jew and Arab cannot live side by side in the whole land of their birth, how can it be believed that they will dwell together in amity within the narrow compass of a fraction? Will not the same troubles reproduce themselves, in an intensified form, inside the tiny Jewish Sovereign State, as have thrown all Palestine into strife?

The military aspect does not seem to have been faced in any sense of realism. The wealthy, crowded, progressive Jewish State lies in the plains, and on the sea coasts. Around it, in the hills and the uplands, stretching far and wide into the illimitable deserts, the warlike Arabs of Syria, of Trans-Jordania, of Arabia, backed by the armed forces of Iraq, offer the ceaseless menace of war. And in between, holding the sacred places and some strategic points of British Imperial significance, are to stand such forces as Britain can spare. To maintain itself, the Jewish State must be armed to the teeth, and must bring in every able-bodied man to strengthen its army. But how long would this process be allowed to continue by the great Arab populations in Iraq and Palestine? Can it be expected that the Arabs would stand by impassively and watch the building up with Jewish world capital and resources of a Jewish army equipped with the most deadly weapons of war, until it was strong enough not to be afraid of them? And if ever the Jewish army reached that point, who can be sure that, cramped within their narrow limits, they would not plunge out into the new undeveloped lands that lie about them? In either case the dangers confronting the British garrison and administration in its neutral area would be vastly greater than those from which we are now assured we should recoil. One feels that the counsel now offered to us is like being urged to drink salt water when cast away on a raft.

The Government were unable to tell the House of Commons what guarantee of protection, if any, they would give to the Jewish State, or to the Arab State, or to the minorities in either, that they should not become the victims of aggression. Yet the nature of these guarantees is vital to both races, and still more to the British power. Obviously it would be an opening for Nazi and Fascist propaganda and intrigue to arouse and marshal the Arab peoples and to use them as a new means of pressure upon the British constable on his difficult beat.

I have yet to learn any reason which should lure us into such a trap. Certain I am that if the Jewish and Arab States, both members of the League of Nations, and over neither of which we are to have any control, are set up on either side of the small British zone, our responsibilities would become impossible to discharge. It would be the only logical conclusion of such a policy that the Holy Places should themselves be put under international control. I find it difficult, as at present informed, to resist the conclusion that the Commission's scheme would lead inevitably to the complete evacuation of Palestine by Great Britain. Here again is a set of grave strategic problems coming into view, none of which appear to have been sufficiently envisaged at the present time.

For all these reasons the House of Commons was surely wise in declining to commit itself finally to the principle of Partition. The Government, treating the House with becoming consideration, did not seek to force this premature decision upon them. It undertook to make further inquiries and then, if the plan is found workable, to lay it in a completed form before Parliament for decision. May we not hope that in this interval the Jews and Arabs will try to come together and make a further effort to restore the peace and revive the prosperity of their joint estate?[1]

---

[1]Within less than a year His Majesty's Government abandoned the scheme of Partition, to which they had prematurely committed themselves. So far they have not announced any other policy.

ANGLO-ITALIAN FRIENDSHIP—HOW?
AUGUST 6, 1937

The letters exchanged between Mr. Chamberlain and Signor Mussolini, although expressing only assurances and desire for friendship, have been rightly rated throughout Europe as of high importance. They must be judged in relation to Mr. Eden's increasingly plain warnings that the territorial integrity of Spain, her islands and colonies, is a matter of major British importance. The British have no wish to quarrel with Italy. On the contrary, the peace of the Mediterranean requires the continuance of the Anglo-Italian friendship and goodwill never broken until recent years. We cannot hold ourselves responsible for the unfortunate change. It was at the instance of Italy, against our advice, that Abyssinia was admitted to the League of Nations. The conquest of Abyssinia by Italy was plainly a breach of solemn undertakings. It could not fail to set in motion the procedure of the League of Nations which Britain was bound to support. Italians have often been scornful that a power which has made more oversea conquests than any other in the world, and which within the last forty years annexed the Boer republics and conquered the Sudan, should have appeared so strangely moved by the Abyssinian war.

But the main point upon which British public opinion has centred has been not so much the fact of conquest, as the open breach of covenants upon which so many hopes were based for maintaining European peace. It is natural that public opinion in a parliamentary and democratic country should be antagonistic to the totalitarian form of government and should be vigilant in marking aggressive action by Dictators. The League of Nations has hitherto refused to recognise the Italian conquest of Abyssinia, and so far, at any rate, the House of Commons has been very ready to resist such a step. The portentous groupings of France and Britain, with Russia in the background, on the one hand, and Germany and Italy on the other, have cast their shadow increasingly across the future of the whole world. It is the duty of all sensible men to try to prevent such a dire confrontation.

The question of recognition of the incorporation of Abyssinia in the Italian Empire must be viewed in relation to these Titanic issues. The question is whether the League has marked its protest against the Italian breach of the Covenant by the refusal to accept the grim undoubted fact. Is this protest to stand indefinitely? Is there to be a time-limit to reproaches however just? Or is the world to move forward with an increasing load of black-listed nations, and of grievances all duly entered in the ledgers at Geneva? If that were so, our security against a second Armageddon would certainly be seriously weakened.

The situation in the Mediterranean has become far more important than any difference between Great Britain and Italy about Abyssinia. If the Spanish Civil War should end in the, victory of General Franco, as on the whole seems more probable, relations between the new Spain and the Fascist and Nazi countries will inevitably be fraught with the utmost gravity. Large howitzers and many secondary guns have been mounted on both sides of the Straits of Gibraltar at Algeciras and Ceuta. The fire of these guns interlaces across the waterway. Although a fleet of armoured ships at night and amid smoke screens could run the gauntlet with comparative immunity, the potential obstruction of the highway of world commerce remains in a most serious form. It is one thing for a fortress to fire at a gun and quite another for a gun to fire at a harbour. The anchorage of Gibraltar might at any time be rendered unusable by the British fleet.

But it does not stand alone. Conditions in the Balearic Islands are in the last degree unsatisfactory. The proximity of Malta to the main Italian air force has already made that naval base unsuitable in time of war. The fortification by Italy of the barren rock of Pantellaria, between Malta and the African promontory, is aimed at Great Britain, and Great Britain alone. The very heavy fortifications, batteries and air stations at Rhodes and at Leros, both of which have been recently strengthened, affect the eastern Mediterranean. In the Red Sea another heavily fortified Italian base has been created at Massowah. Ambitious eyes are being cast at the eastern shore of the Red Sea. There is also the numerous Italian army in Libya, the coastal route 'for tourist purposes' to the Egyptian frontier, and the ceaseless propaganda of the Italian wireless throughout the Middle East. All this process, while it continues, carries danger with it with increasing momentum and in the most direct form.

The freedom of the Mediterranean is a prime British interest. We have valued friends and obligations there. There is the kingdom of Yugoslavia. There is the kingdom of Greece, so long united to us in sympathy and policy. There is the modernised Turkey, now most harmoniously related to Greece, under its champion and remarkable military commander of the Great War, Mustapha Kemal. There is Palestine, and all that that means. There is the kingdom of Egypt, newly established as a member of the League of Nations. We cannot allow ourselves, however peaceable our desires, to be cut off from these friendships and associations. They count as much to us as our free highway along the main arterial road to the East. We should make it clear, and make it clear in good time, that we could not agree to the doors of the Mediterranean being shut in our faces, and that we should have to range ourselves against any who tried to do it, or any who lent themselves to such an attempt. Sometimes, in these questions, it is better that plain language should be used. The new First Lord of the Admiralty[1] has made an appeal for a revival of the ancient Anglo-Italian friendship, but he does not explain on what basis this is to be re-established. It certainly cannot be re-established on the basis of an attempt to make the Mediterranean an Italian lake!

The assurances of European peace depend upon the preponderance of the British fleet and the strength of the French Army. They depend also upon factors which

---

[1]Mr. Duff Cooper.

cannot be measured: the value of sea power uniting across the oceans all the resources of the world and all well-disposed countries; the effective wealth which comes from credit and from gold; and thirdly, most potent of all, the force of democracy and free institutions, which not only unites the parliamentary nations, but undermines dictatorship in its own citadels. These forces should not be ignored in any discussion which may ensue.

A PLAIN WORD TO THE NAZIS
AUGUST 20, 1937

Nazi Germany is not only an anxiety but a world-puzzle. The step the Nazis have taken in expelling the Berlin correspondent of *The Times* leaves their friends and enemies equally bewildered. Those of us who labour to build up a strong international confederation against a potential aggressor have long been dissatisfied with the attitude of *The Times*. This great organ, with all its influence on governing circles at home and upon opinion abroad, has been consistently an apologist of Germany in most of her recent manifestations. *The Times* correspondent, Mr. Ebbutt, has never twisted the facts against Germany; he has reported them—that is all.

Of course, if any government in the twentieth century is engaged in persecuting people because of their race or of their religion, irrespective of their civic behaviour, and if these victims of ill-usage make feeble demonstrations of protest, the mere recording of these facts will be prejudicial to that government in the outer world. But to fasten on this particular correspondent, the doyen of all the foreign journalists in Berlin, and expel him—as he has been expelled this week—was not merely unfair but silly.

It would almost seem as if the present German Government were resolved to isolate themselves morally as well as economically from the other great nations in the West. They seem to care nothing for world public opinion. Nothing matters but food and weapons—weapons first. All the more will it be necessary that the nations adhering to the Covenant of the League should be increasingly conscious of their identity of peaceful aims, and increasingly well armed.

But this incident itself arose from a more serious cause. There are a large number of Germans resident in foreign countries. Many of them are refugees from the present regime, but of course the bulk represents Germans who have either accepted it, or are its active partisans. This last class are everywhere to be found—in Poland, Czechoslovakia, Austria, Yugoslavia, Italy, Switzerland, France, Belgium, Holland and Scandinavia, and last but not least, in England. It is with Great Britain that we are especially concerned. But what applies to us applies to other countries. Foreigners have hitherto come to our island as individuals. They have dwelt among us under the freedom and protection of our laws. We have welcomed them and wish them well. But the last two or three years have witnessed a development which would cause disquietude to any Government.

Everyone is of course familiar with the methods of Communist propaganda. Poisonous doctrines are spread, germ-cells are created in many walks of life and in many parts of the country. Communists in every country are linked to the Comintern in Moscow, and thence controlled by discipline and by funds. In Britain our broad political institutions, the robust attitude of our Trade Unions, and the long enfranchisement of the working classes, have made Communist machinations comparatively harmless. But if this were not so, the police have ample power and good arrangements to cope with Communist sedition. Parliament would certainly sustain any British Government in taking most drastic action, whether by imprisonment or expulsion, against organised disturbers of the peace.

But now we find that in this as in other aspects the German Nazi regime, and to a lesser extent the Italian Fascists, follow the Moscow model. There are perhaps twenty thousand Germans living in our peaceful country at present. There is a regular national political party organisation in which it is thought to bind them together. A Nazi minister and department have been actually set up in Berlin within the present year to promote and concert the action of Nazi Germans living abroad. These aliens have to report at frequent intervals to regular centres, where they receive instructions as to what they should observe, what language they should hold in moving about among our population, and what they should do in case of an emergency. Apart from objectionable surveillance of the unfortunate German refugees, there seems to be developing a definite threat to the State. In countries like Czechoslovakia and Austria these Nazi organisations play a dangerous part in stirring up pan-German agitation. That is a matter which may concern the independent existence of those States.

Our case is not so serious. But it is an affront to national sovereignty that a foreign power should in a time of peace organise its subjects within the bosom of a friendly State. It is a menace of the same character as is presented by the foreign-paid Communist conspiracy. I have for some months past drawn the attention of the House of Commons to this hitherto unprecedented process. When Parliament meets in the autumn, it will concern itself seriously with the question of foreign organisations in Great Britain, and ministers will be asked to show that they have effectual control. It should not be difficult to deal with the problem. If, for instance, a foreigner can find time to attend at frequent intervals a meeting of his Communist or Nazi association, he might be asked to attend equally often at the police station to have his permit inspected, and there he might be invited to give special proofs of his good behaviour if he desired to profit further by British hospitality. As for ringleaders actively engaged in building up an alien power within the State, they should be asked to go home without delay.

We have little to fear from a policy of reprisals upon British residents in Germany. Many more Germans get a good living in England than there are British subjects in Germany. We should certainly not suffer in comparison by any process of reciprocal repatriation, however far it was carried. I write plainly upon this matter because it is to be hoped that the German Government, with whom we are so anxious for good relations, will, in a tactful and helpful manner, meet our reasonable desires, if they know them in good time.

THE WOUNDED DRAGON
SEPTEMBER 3, 1937

Not only the British Empire and the United States, but the greater part of Europe, have a lively interest in what is happening to China. China, as the years pass, is being eaten by Japan like an artichoke, leaf by leaf. One province after another is being subjugated, and still we are told it is the Chinese who gave the provocation.

The government of Japan has become a military despotism. It is not a despotism of war lords or military chiefs. The driving power comes from secret societies in the army which in the name of an exalted patriotism murder statesmen, generals or admirals, thought to be weaklings in effecting Japanese Imperial expansion. Only the half-mystic authority of the Mikado commands a measure of respect and procures a measure of restraint.

During the present century the Japanese Navy has established a ratio of three to five against either the British or the American Navy. The enormous ocean spaces which separate Japan from all other naval powers make the Japanese Navy supreme in its own waters and upon the Asiatic shores of the Pacific. No single power, except after long preparation, could impose its will upon Japan in the Yellow Sea. If the United States and Great Britain acted together jointly for several years, and if they were supported by Soviet Russia, representations could no doubt be made to which Japan would have to defer. But the United States is naturally absorbed in her internal economic problems, and Britain, with Mussolini on her flank in the Mediterranean, will not for some years be able to do more than hold Singapore and thus preserve her contacts with Australasia. Singapore, it may be repeated, is as far from Japan as Portsmouth is from New York. It is evident, therefore, that Japan would suffer, in attacking Singapore, the same difficulties as either Great Britain or the United States in an offensive against Japan. It is necessary that these facts should be understood because they govern—or ought to govern—policy in the Far East.

We may deplore the fate of China. There will be deep indignation and sorrow in British and American breasts at this renewed aggression upon a peaceful, if disorderly, mass of industrious folk, upon whose already hard existence heavier burdens must now be laid. Everyone is revolted by the horrible tragedy of the clumsy Chinese airmen who dropped their gigantic bombs, meant for the Japanese flagship, upon the British hotel and doomed to death or mutilation many hundreds of their helpless fellow-countrymen. The spectacle of the wounded frantic Chinese dragon lashing out in the most senseless directions, injuring itself, striking even at the friendly American ship, is pitiful in the last degree.

But there is another side. There are nearly four hundred million Chinese. Their manhood is of exceptional physical strength and toughness. They can march great distances and carry great weights. They have an ancient civilisation which has developed a high intelligence and in many cases an admirable fidelity. But they have always rated the profession of a soldier as among the most degraded which the human being can adopt, and in consequence their soldiers, and particularly their generals, up to the present have fully conformed to their countrymen's estimate. If the Chinese now suffer the cruel malice and oppression of their enemies, it is the fault of the base and perverted conception of pacifism their rulers have ingrained for two or three thousand years in their people. It is certain that if the Chinese are not capable of defending China, no one else in the present state of the world is going to do it for them.

It may be that under the impact of Japan, China will gradually develop a military spirit. There have already been signs of this. In any case the conquest of even a portion of China will involve Japan in great exertions and take a long time. We European and American spectators must confine ourselves to the protection of our own interests, commercial, cultural and moral. We have created great establishments and businesses in China which have done nothing but good to the Chinese. The noble port and city of Shanghai has been reared upon its mud flats mainly by British enterprise and thought. European and American missionaries have carried their message fearlessly into the recesses of China. Many other countries have valuable and peaceful traffic with the Chinese. Germany in particular has in the last few years developed an important trade. Railway and mining concessions have been called into being and used for the benefit of all parties. Is all this to be encroached upon and gradually wiped out? It certainly will be while Europe remains torn by its internal divisions and while the United States holds aloof from all external affairs.

These facts also should be realised. If Europe wishes to talk to the East, she will have to clean up her home lines first. The outrage upon the British Ambassador arising out of the ruthless bombing of non-combatants in areas behind the fighting zones, has rightly been made the subject of a strong British Note. It is unlikely that such a Note would have been sent without a previous British decision upon the action to be taken if honourable amends are denied. There can, of course, be no question of the use of force to obtain satisfaction for what was certainly no accident. The matter lies rather in the field of good manners and correct international usage in which Japan has hitherto prided herself upon being punctilious. There is therefore no danger at this moment of any other war in the Far East except the undeclared war proceeding between Japan and China. Indeed, although it may seem strange to say it, the fact that Japan has chosen this autumn to make a further inroad upon China confirms the prevailing impression that the peace of Europe will not be broken in the present year. Germany, for instance, would be unlikely to make any move which would lead to a collision with Soviet Russia, while Japan is not free to devote undivided attention to Russia in the Far East.

What a comment it is upon present conditions of world civilisation that Czechoslovakia may breathe more freely because Chinese non-combatants are being slaughtered in the slums of Shanghai! Painful as it is to witness what is happening in the Far East, earnest as must be the desire of decent men and women in every land to bring it to a conclusion, it would be a wrong deduction to assume that the peace among the great powers of the world has been rendered more insecure and uncertain by this new conflagration. On the contrary, so far as it counts at all, it is a greater assurance that a further interval will be accorded to the peace-seeking nations in Europe.

Let them use this interval to strengthen their defences, to unite themselves into effective and faithful associations for the promotion and defence of the reign of law among themselves, and thereafter to extend its merciful scope to these distracted but, fortunately for us, far distant regions.

FRIENDSHIP WITH GERMANY
SEPTEMBER 17, 1937

I find myself pilloried by Dr. Goebbels's Press as an enemy of Germany. That description is quite untrue. Before the war I proposed to Von Tirpitz a naval holiday. If this had been accepted, it would enormously have eased the European tension, and possibly have averted the catastrophe. At the moment of the Armistice, as is well known, I proposed filling a dozen great liners with food, and rushing them into Hamburg as a gesture of humanity. As Secretary of State for War in 1919, I pressed upon the Supreme Council the need of lifting the blockade, and laid before them the reports from our generals on the Rhine which eventually procured that step. I took a great deal of personal responsibility in sending home, months before they would otherwise have been liberated, about one hundred thousand German prisoners, who were caged up in the Pas de Calais. I was vehemently opposed to the French invasion of the Ruhr. In order to prevent a repetition of it, I exerted myself in Mr. Baldwin's Cabinet to have the Treaty of Locarno made to cut both ways, so that Germany as well as France had British protection against aggression. Therefore no one has a right to describe me as the enemy of Germany except in wartime.

But my duty lies to my own country. As an independent Conservative member I felt bound to give the alarm when, five years ago, the vast secret process of German rearmament, contrary to Treaty, began to be apparent. I also felt bound to point out to the Government in 1934 that Germany had already created a powerful military air force which would soon be stronger than the British Air Force. My only regret is that I was not believed. I can quite understand that this action of mine would not be popular in Germany. Indeed, it was not popular anywhere. I was told I was making ill will between the two countries. I am sure that if Herr Hitler had been in my position, and had believed what I believed, he would have acted in the same way. In times like these the safety of one's own country must count for more than saying smooth things about other countries. At any rate, I did not feel at all penitent when, six months later, I heard Mr. Baldwin admit that the Government had been wrong in their figures and information. And ever since ministers have been bewailing 'the years that the locusts have eaten.'

Similarly, for the last few months, in Parliament and in these letters which are so widely published throughout Europe, I drew attention to a serious danger to Anglo-German relations which arises out of the organisation of German residents in Britain into a closely knit, strictly disciplined body. I wonder what Dr. Goebbels would think if we had fifteen or twenty thousand Englishmen in Berlin, all strong anti-Nazis, who, while they kept within the law, were none the less all bound together, attending meetings at frequent intervals, and putting pressure on any British refugees, if such there were, to toe the line of some British party or other. Moreover, this process of Nazi organisation abroad is undoubtedly becoming an obstacle in the way of British and German cordiality. Sir Walter Citrine, at the Trade Union Congress, has protested in the name of British Labour against the persecution of German refugees in England by other German visitors to our shores.

We have always been an asylum for refugees. It was only the other day that I was reading how in 1709 we gave refuge and shelter to a very large number of Germans from the Palatinate, which had been overrun by Marshal Villars with fire and sword. We could never allow foreign visitors to pursue their national feuds in the bosom of our country still less to be organised in such a way as to affect our military security. The Germans would not tolerate it for a moment in their country, nor should they take it amiss that we do not like it in ours. I see Herr Bohle has expressed a wish to talk this over with me. I should be delighted to do so in the most friendly manner, and do anything in the power of a private member to remove this new embarrassment to Anglo-German goodwill.[1]

I have had from time to time conversations with eminent German supporters of the present regime. When they say, as they so often do, 'Will not England grasp the extended friendly hand of Germany?' nearly everyone in England will reply, 'Certainly, yes.' We cannot pretend to like your new institutions, and we have long freed ourselves from racial and religious intolerance. We cannot say that we admire your treatment of the Jews or of the Protestants and Catholics of Germany. We even think our methods of dealing with Communism are better than yours. But after all, these matters, so long as they are confined inside Germany, are not our business. 'It is our duty and our sincere desire to live in a good and neighbourly fashion with so great a nation united to us by many ties of history and of race. Indeed, we will grasp the outstretched German hand.'

'But,' we must ask, 'what happens next? Are we expected to do anything special to prove our friendship, and if so, what?' We cannot be expected to help Germany financially while she is spending nearly a thousand millions sterling a year upon her tremendous rearmament. That would be unfair to our own people. We cannot hand over colonies irrespective of the wishes of their inhabitants and of a great many other considerations. We should be very wrong if we were to give Germany a guarantee that so long as she left Britain and France alone in the West, she could do what she liked to the peoples of the centre and south-east of Europe. To give such an assurance at other people's expense would not only be callous and cynical, but it might actually lead to a war the end of which no man can foresee.

To hold these opinions is not to be hostile to the German Government, and still less to the Germans as a nation. To feel deep concern about the armed power of Germany is in no way derogatory to Germany. On the contrary, it is a tribute to the wonderful and terrible strength which Germany exerted in the Great War, when almost single-handed she fought nearly all the world and nearly beat them. Naturally, when a people who have shown such magnificent military qualities are arming night and day, its neighbours, who

---

[1] He visited me a few weeks later.

bear the scars of previous conflicts, must be anxious and ought to be vigilant. One may dislike Hitler's system and yet admire his patriotic achievement. If our country were defeated I hope we should find a champion as indomitable to restore our courage and lead us back to our place among the nations.

I have on more than one occasion made my appeal in public that the Fuehrer of Germany should now become the Hitler of peace. When a man is fighting in a desperate conflict he may have to grind his teeth and flash his eyes. Anger and hatred nerve the arm of strife. But success should bring a mellow, genial air and, by altering the mood to suit the new circumstances, preserve and consolidate in tolerance and goodwill what has been gained by conflict.

In September 1937, Mr. Eden, the Foreign Secretary, indignant at the sinking of British ships in the Mediterranean by submarines of no proved origin, called a conference of Mediterranean powers to suppress this piracy. The conference met at Nyon in Switzerland; and as soon as it was seen that concerted steps would be taken to destroy the pirates, all outrages on shipping ceased. It was with great satisfaction that the assembled Powers received the co-operation of Signor Mussolini in such resolute action. This ensured success.

THE DICTATORS HAVE SMILED
OCTOBER 1, 1937

In spite of all the horrors that are happening in China, the world has got better in the last month. The meeting of the two great Dictators in Rome has passed off very pleasantly. They have feasted their eyes upon cannon and soldiers. They have exulted in the contemplation of their own power. They have substantially put up the market in bunting. They have vowed themselves anew to the sacred cause of Anti-Bolshevism, and we all hope they have both enjoyed themselves thoroughly. Upon the whole, they have smiled rather than scowled upon mankind. One even detects a certain willingness to offer explanations outside their own countries, and to place themselves in a polite relation to the Parliamentary democracies of the West. Certainly the upshot of the Hitler-Mussolini meeting has been a momentary easement in the anxieties of the 'Live-and-let-live' countries.

Then from the Mediterranean comes good news. Where are the pirate submarines? A month ago they were sinking merchant ships from one end of the inland sea to the other, and leaving the crews to shift for themselves, or drown. But now we do not see them any more. Eighty British and French destroyers, with cruisers and aircraft in attendance, scour the blue waters for a pirate periscope in vain. Was it all a nightmare? Were all these piracies, these ships foundering, these sailors choking in the deep waters—was this all a mere figment of the imagination, or, like the sea serpent, a hectic contraption of the world-press in 'the silly season'?

The pirate submarines have vanished as mysteriously as they appeared. It was particularly satisfactory that Italy should join the Mediterranean patrol on terms of perfect equality with Great Britain and France. This made assurance doubly sure. It would have been a great shame if Italy had been deprived of her rightful share of honour in bringing the Mediterranean submarine piracy to an end. Now that the three great Mediterranean Powers are united in repressing this hateful form of sea-murder, they must keep together. The patrol which has been established is doing admirable work. It must not be discontinued in a hurry. One never knows when piracy will raise its head again.

For Great Britain, the association with France in the Mediterranean is more than a matter of convenience. It is of real consequence. If Franco's cannon could disturb the anchorage at Gibraltar, if Malta harbour is rather too near to the mainland of Europe, the facilities of Toulon and Bizerta become invaluable to the British fleet in any war against piracy. It is therefore of the highest importance that what has been started should go forward, and that Britain, France and Italy should be closely associated in the solution of any difficulties which may arise out of the Spanish Civil War. Such co-operation will be cordially welcomed by the other Mediterranean powers. Turkey and Greece, for instance, whose old quarrels are healed, have a joint interest in the repression of piracy. So have Yugoslavia and Egypt. Let us all keep together, and now we have got the pirates down, let us make sure we keep them down. Out of this anti-pirate patrol may develop an accord between Mediterranean powers which will secure ships of all nations the right to traverse these classic waters on their lawful occasions without the danger of being destroyed by sea-assassins.

In Spain also the war comes to an equipoise which should encourage Spaniards to come together for the rebuilding of their country. The Spanish Nationalists have proved their right to be respected. So have the stout-hearted defenders of Madrid. The frenzied ideologies of Nazi-Fascism on the one hand, and of Anarchy or Communism on the other, are fading. The problem becomes one in which brave soldiers who have fought each other hard, and are now organised in disciplined forces, may well find that they have much in common, including among other things their own tortured country. When human society is ruined in any country by villainous politicians and fanatics, it can only be rebuilt by its fighting men, who even on opposite sides develop a confraternity of their own. Let the Spanish soldiers come together on the basis of throwing out the foreign interlopers, and upon the slogan of 'Spain for the Spaniards.' This is a theme which is waxing and not waning.

But after assembling these hopeful points, I must say how sorry I am that the two Dictators did not do the really big thing. They had a chance of helping the world which may never come to them again. Only fancy what a leap forward into the sunshine would have been taken by all mankind if Hitler and Mussolini, after surveying the whole scene, had declared jointly that this horrible butchery which is going on in China had got to stop; that the wholesale massacre of helpless coolies and poor toiling fishermen by air-bombing and submarines was an offence against the light of day which Europe would no longer tolerate. Hitler has already two years ago declared against the deliberate air-bombing of non-combatants. Both he and Mussolini have protested against the excesses of the secret societies that have gripped the civilisation of Japan. If these two potentates of the hour had invited the Western democracies to join with them in bringing to an end these Asiatic atrocities, what a reception their declaration would have had!

There is nothing like the sympathy of a common cause to make the settlement of other differences easy. The Western democracies, now armed and arming heavily, have much to give to these harassed Dictators, if they would only prove that they mean to be the friends and not the bane of our common humanity. If the true concert of Europe were re-established, our collective remonstrances would not go unheeded in the Far East. And there is always the United States, which has great interests and no small duties in China, and is not so timid as it sometimes makes itself out to be. Certainly a common policy by the great European nations in the Far East at this juncture would not only call a halt to the measureless crimes of the Yellow Seas, but would also give to Europe what it needs above all things, and now above all moments—the spirit of unity and mutual help.

WAR IS NOT IMMINENT
OCTOBER 15, 1937

It is the fear of ordinary men and women in many countries that their homes, their pleasures, their prudential thrift, their conceptions of right and wrong, their whole way of life and means of living, will be broken up at no distant date by war. We have already seen how this fear can be reflected in the stock markets. It may well become a factor in proving itself true. It is therefore an object of high importance to allay Fear. Yet no one wishes to be taken unawares. Between dwelling in a Fool's Paradise or in a Fool's Inferno there ought to be some middle space, be it only a Purgatory for Fools. An American writer on nervous diseases has drawn a clear and just distinction between what he calls 'Fearthought' and 'Forethought.' Fearthought is futile worrying over what cannot be averted or will probably never happen. Forethought is taking the best means at one's command to ward off perils or surmount them if they come. What we need now is vigilance and preparation without panic, and cool heads without cold hearts or cold feet.

Three or four years ago I was myself a loud alarmist. I tried to bring home to all the dangers that were coming upon the world, and to arouse Parliament, and the Government who were misleading Parliament, to the need of rearming. In those days the danger was distant and the time ample. Now the dangers are more clearly defined, and at the same time great exertions are being made to meet them. This, therefore, is not the time to exaggerate dangers. On the contrary, they must be faced with courage. In spite of the risks which wait on prophecy I declare my belief that a major war is not imminent, and I still believe there is a good chance of no major war taking place again in our time. More than that, I believe that Great Britain, especially if countenanced by the United States, can play what may be a decisive part in laying the War Ghost. Had she armed in time, it would not now haunt the capitals of Europe.

Let us, then, survey the scene as it unfolds so sullenly before us in Asia and in Europe. Unless the United States, as the result of a Nine Power Conference, is prepared to lead a general intervention and boycott of Japan, the invasion and subjugation of great areas in China, and the gradual freezing-out of European and American interests there, will proceed unchecked on the spot, but also without involving others. The fire will burn in China, but it will not spread elsewhere. If, on the other hand, the United States were prepared to act in earnest, they would find themselves so strongly supported by Great Britain and other powers, that Japanese aggression might be arrested. Nothing is more certain than that Japan could not indefinitely resist the economic pressure of the English-speaking world. Therefore, in the Far East the issue turns upon the decision of the United States. If they will not act, no one can act, and events must take their course. If they will act, then though there are risks, there are also high hopes of a favourable settlement.

Let us then turn to the near and immediate situation in the Mediterranean. We may take it for granted that Signor Mussolini does not wish to become embroiled in war with Great Britain, still less with Great Britain and France. What he wishes to do is to increase his hold upon the Mediterranean steadily in time of peace, by fortifying and preparing naval and air bases at various points in Italian territory, especially the island of Pantellaria; by establishing a large army, highly mechanised, in Libya, and also by constructing strong naval and air bases, if possible, on both sides of the Red Sea. He is working away at all this with great vigour, and much has already been accomplished.

The situation in the Balearic Islands is an extension of this general Italian policy, which has arisen out of the Spanish conflict. It is believed that Italian forces are gathered in Majorca, which is held for Franco, and that an attack by Franco's troops with Italian assistance might be made upon Minorca, with its famous war-harbour of Port Mahon, for losing which Admiral Byng was shot 150 years ago. It may be taken as certain that Italian control under any form of the Balearic Islands would involve the national safety of the French Republic. It would close the Mediterranean to the passage of the French African forces, which play a substantial and essential part in the defence of the French Northern Frontier. There is no doubt that the Balearic position is being watched by those responsible for the defence of France as a matter of major consequence.

It is extremely important that Signor Mussolini should not be under any illusions about this. He is engaged in what is called 'power diplomacy,' and so far he is getting step by step almost everything that he wishes by it. Wherever he finds himself opposed by the settled will of Great Britain and France, as at Nyon, he withdraws diplomatically and tries some new point of advance. But the danger lies in the fact that he may well believe that under any direct threat of war the British Government would recoil, as they did in the Abyssinian dispute. He has hitherto been extraordinarily successful in the vast scheme of expansion and Mediterranean control, upon which he is leading Italy. If at any time in these anxious months France or Great Britain were separated from one another, even in appearance, he might be led into some act of imprudence, from which withdrawal would be impossible. It is therefore absolutely vital to our safety and to the peace of the world that the British and French Governments should act in the closest possible accord in the Mediterranean, and also that they should leave Signor Mussolini in no doubt as to the points to which in the last resort they would feel bound to adhere.

Nothing would bring war nearer than an impression that the two Parliamentary nations would let themselves be pushed from point to point, would watch helplessly the deterioration of their interests in the Mediterranean, and would in no circumstances defend themselves unitedly by force. If perfectly plain, precise and categorical notifications are made by Britain and France together about encroachments which they could not endure, it is almost certain that their wishes would be respected. It cannot be taken for certain that as time passes the general balance of European armaments will become more favourable to the Parliamentary nations. Well was it written, 'Agree with thine adversary quickly whilst thou art in the way with him.'

YUGOSLAVIA AND EUROPE
OCTOBER 29, 1937

The new unity established among the Opposition parties in Yugoslavia deserve attention. Yugoslavia is one of the key States of Europe, and its action may be a potent factor in maintaining peace among the Great Powers. There was throughout the war a strong sympathy in Great Britain for Serbia in its heroic resistance and fearful ordeal. It was with lively pleasure that the victorious Allies contemplated the inauguration of the new State. For many years we had heard how keenly the Southern Slavs wished to be united. This cherished object was finally achieved, and the kingdom of the Serbs, Croats and Slovenes came into being. It comprises upwards of fourteen million souls dwelling in some of the most romantic and beautiful country in Europe, whose soldiers are admired for their physique and stamina and justly renowned for their indomitable tenacity. It was understood that the Southern Slavs had at last got what they wanted, and that they would live happily together ever afterwards.

Perplexity and disappointment arose among the liberating powers when it was seen that the new State was distressed by faction and feud. Secret societies were active; blood was shed in the Parliament House; finally a well-loved King was assassinated. Friction between the Croats and Serbs became apparent to Europe. Passionate religious differences have attended the attempt to confer what may be called concurrent recognition upon the Catholic minority. Nevertheless, I believe that at the root the differences which disturb Yugoslavia are neither deep nor incurable. We are told that a question of fundamental principle is involved. The ruling forces in Serbia have adopted the ideal of welding the three elements among the people into one integral Southern Slav nation. For this purpose they are willing to renounce their own Serbian characteristics and traditions, and they demand equivalent sacrifices from the other two partners. They proclaim that Yugoslavia consists of three tribes merged into a new national entity. On the other hand, the Opposition forces declare that the Serbs, Croats and Slovenes are three separate nations joined in a common government.

Considering that all accept one Crown, one Parliament, one Army and one Customs Union, it seems difficult for British observers to understand what all this rage is about. No one in England has ever wished to prevent the fullest expression of Scottish or Welsh traditions and customs. Indeed, their manifestation is regarded with pleasure and pride by the English people. We have reaped great advantages from this tolerant mood. It seems essential that a new country with such high hopes before it and serious dangers on either side should not hamper itself in its most important years by a quarrel which is largely academic in character. Ill-feeling and internal stresses have led the Regent, Prince Paul, and the Government to maintain measures of restraint which are very far from their desires, and have emphasised the divisions which already exist. Attempts are being made to represent the differences between the parties as similar to those existing between a Nazi dictatorship and a democratic Parliamentary regime.

There is no doubt that there are elements of Nazism on the one side and elements of Communism on the other. But it is absurd to represent the conflict in this form. In fact, there never was a country in which there were such favourable prospects of making a central block with a modern liberal outlook equally opposed to either of the totalitarian extremes. The mass of agreement enormously outweighs the differences, and the need of national survival and prosperity should foster a broad-based settlement. These are not the times when young nations can afford to have needless friction. It is known that Prince Paul, the liberal-minded Regent, has no desire but to do his duty till the new King comes of age, and that he has a deep comprehension of British democratic ideals. There are, therefore, good hopes of a genuine unification for all practical purposes in Yugoslavia.

This would have a bearing on the peace of Europe. It would be a disaster, far-reaching in its consequences, if Yugoslavia were quite needlessly ranged among the dictatorial or totalitarian states. Great internal stresses would immediately arise. The Little Entente would be completely ruptured. The fate of Czechoslovakia might be sealed. Bohemia and Moravia would soon be incorporated in Nazidom, and these convulsions might well produce a world war with its incalculable possibilities. The position of Yugoslavia as a poor relation to Rome and Berlin would be pitiful in the last degree. In fact, from the moment when the armed Western democracies, Britain and France, lost their interest in the fortunes of South-Eastern Europe, Yugoslavia would be left to bargain for her existence with the two dictators, one of whom, the Italian, views the Dalmatian coast and its harbours with avid eyes. Far safer and wiser would it be for this new kingdom of the Southern Slavs to throw in her lot boldly upon the side of Peace, Freedom and Parliamentary democracy. In this way alone would she realise that internal strength and unity which is vital to her in these critical decades of her life.

The Western democracies have no interest but to see Yugoslavia strong, prosperous and independent. They desire nothing from her, and have no axe to grind at her expense. Her young valiant people, marching forward on the road of life, must proclaim high ideals for the rights of the individual, the conscious share of all citizens in the government of their country, the respect for law, the freedom of speech and writing, and free Parliamentary debate. Thus in this attractive part of Europe a stronghold of liberal civilisation and tolerance would arise, all the more admirable because defended by brave armies.

Yugoslavia stands at the parting of the ways. By inclining towards a system of free government she may not only avert domestic discord, but play a prominent and possibly a decisive part in driving away the war-clouds which darken and disturb European life. The Southern Slavs would be neither happy nor glorious if they found themselves in a Central and Southern Europe dominated by the military apparatus and reactionary doctrines of Nazism, Fascism or Bolshevism. There is an ardent desire in Great Britain to see the country of the Serbs, Croats and Slovenes a happy land where freedom reigns, and where justice has not been driven from the Judgment Seat.

ARMISTICE—OR PEACE?
NOVEMBER 11, 1937

A wild surge of joy swept across the greater part of the world nineteen years ago to-day. A feeling of intense relief from intolerable effort descended upon us in healing floods. Victory was won, and beyond Victory—Peace and Plenty. By measureless sacrifices and toils mankind was absolved, and all men at the front—grim, harassed; and women at home, hard-driven, gnawed with anxiety, had the sensation that the doors of a glorious and sunlit age were opening to them. The word 'Armistice', which few people had had occasion to use, suddenly came on every lip to mean the salvation of the world. Armistice Day! Armistice Night!—when haggard, wardrawn London crowds expressed their joy in such a frenzy that the marks abide to this hour upon the granite plinths of Trafalgar Square. It was over then—the long and frightful ordeal—honourably over, triumphantly over, over for ever, and now there would be Peace.

But Armistice does not mean Peace. The dictionary calls it 'a cessation from arms; a truce'—nay, 'a short truce'. The Peace had still to be made, and Peace was never made, except on paper. The 'short truce' has lasted for nineteen years. We have dwelt under the Armistice most of that time. Peace, the reconciliation of Christendom, and the revival of civilisation are as far off as ever. In the first phase, when the war of the Giants was over, the war of the Pygmies began. All sorts of races who counted for nothing, or stood aside from, or were protected in, the dire struggle of the world, hurried up with their pretensions while the great combatants lay gasping. Then came a period which it was easy to predict, when the victors forgot, and the vanquished remembered.

In Britain, after a brief interval of absurd demands, it became a positive virtue to cast away what had been gained by infinite labours. The tides of reaction and remorse blotted out all practical thought. The nation which had sacrificed hundreds of thousands of men to gain obscure villages in the mud of Flanders, recoiled aghast from those small, well-considered perseverances which would have made victory safe. We entered upon that strange period in our history which may be called 'The Aftermath'. This phrase marks the state of national prostration, the loss of theme, which will long excite the curiosity of historians. The disease of Defeat was Bolshevism. But Bolshevism, in Foch's remarkable words, 'never crossed the frontiers of Victory'. The disease of Victory was different. It was an incapacity to make Peace.

Our ancestors after the Napoleonic wars at least sought for finality. They left Bonaparte to die in St. Helena. They organised Europe into the Holy Alliance—or Unholy Alliance as others called it—and they had peace for more than thirty years. In fact, never was there a period after the battle of Waterloo when France, so long the dominating power, could be a menace to Europe. I was about to write that we had never had a Peace, only an Armistice renewed from time to time at heavier interest, like a usurer's short-dated bill.

But is not this putting it too high? Have we even got an Armistice now? Can anyone call the present condition of Europe—or of Asia, for the matter of that—'a cessation from arms'? We have never had Peace. We have not even got Armistice. What we now have is War, without the engagement of the great armies and fleets. The truce, long or short, has been over for some years. What is happening now is War without the cannons of the great nations being fired; War without millions of people being killed or wounded. War, as it were, on the map and on paper, but none the less, War. We dwell in a state of affairs where, broadly speaking, the old groupings face one another as they did on the eleventh hour of the eleventh day of the eleventh month in 1918.

Italy has changed sides as she did in 1915; but then the Austro-Hungarian Empire is split into fragments divided up on both sides. Japan has changed sides. But, on the other hand, the Russian power in Siberia is incomparably greater than in 1914. Besides this, Turkey, no longer the enemy of Russia or of Greece, is, under the leadership of Mustapha Kemal—the only Dictator with the aureole of martial achievement—reconciled with what used to be called 'the Allied and Associated Powers'.[1] Finally, the United States allows no day to pass without declaring that she will not come in to the next war unless she decides to do so.

Nearly twenty years have passed. The trenches have been levelled. The plough drives its furrows to and fro across the Western Front. But the balanced array of the great powers and their adherents remains on each side, in presence of each other, and under arms. 'Under arms,' did I say? Never were they armed like this. Night and day the forges roar, the hammers descend, the hellish implements of slaughter pour out to multitudes of training troops. Statecraft is bankrupt. The unity of Christendom is a mockery. Nay, even the idea of Christianity is repudiated by a new paganism. No longer can the leading nations of the European family appeal to one another upon the New Testament. Grim war-gods from remote ages have stalked upon the scene. International good faith; the public law of Europe; the greatest good of the greatest number; the ideal of a fertile, tolerant, progressive, demilitarised, infinitely varied society, is shattered. Dictators ride to and fro upon tigers from which they dare not dismount. And the tigers are getting hungry.

Yet what is it that three hundred million Europeans want? They want Peace and comfort. They want a larger share of life. They want to cast upon the ground some of the needless burdens which they bear. They would like to dwell together in comradeship, rendering each other service for mutual and common profit. Why cannot they achieve their heart's desire? Is it not worth their while to make the great effort, the supreme effort on the grandest scale to prevent Armistice lapsing into actual War, and to make Armistice ripen into real Peace?

These are the thoughts for Armistice Day.

---

[1]The Anglo-Turkish Alliance was announced in May 1939.

SPAIN'S ROAD TO PEACE
NOVEMBER 26, 1937

A deep and indeed a solemn hush overspreads the Iberian Peninsula. For weeks hardly a salvo of cannon has disturbed the hundreds of miles of front upon which the armies of Nationalist and Republican Spain are thinly spread. Yet for many weeks past General Franco has been free to move a hundred thousand of his best troops, his Italian batteries, and his German aviation from the Biscayan coast to any point on the Government front which he may select for a new major offensive. That very large movements have been in progress is certain, and it is remarkable that the point of attack should apparently have remained a secret from the outer world. Whether the blow will be delivered under the cruel conditions of winter among the Spanish mountains or whether it will be delayed till the spring is also uncertain.

War is full of surprises; but it is now generally recognised that Nationalist Spain has proved itself definitely and decisively the stronger side. The Nationalists hold two-thirds of the country and its population. Unbroken peace and active industry reign behind their lines. Their *peseta* commands double the price of the Government paper money, although the latter is based upon the whole gold reserve of Spain. Alone of the armies the Nationalists have both the strategic initiative and the capacity to deliver attacks. Alone they possess a naval power. For a long time past there has been no justification in precedent or policy for withholding from Nationalist Spain appropriate belligerent rights.

The British Socialist Party insist that Franco is only a rebel at the head of a gang of mutinous officers, supported by foreign faction-fighters from Germany and Italy; and that opposed to him is a constitutional Parliamentary Government of the Spanish Republic, ardently championed by the mass of the Spanish nation, apart from the priests, nobles and capitalists. This affectation, which never remotely corresponded to the truth, has now become patently nonsensical. It has become foolish in the last degree for neutral Powers like Britain and France to deny that measure of recognition to the *de facto* Government of the greater part of Spain which is necessary to safeguard their commercial and political interests. The appointment of British agents to Nationalist Spain is only to be criticised on the score that it was too long delayed. It is to be hoped that this process will be continued and extended, and that France will copy it, until the two great armed liberal Parliamentary Powers have established equally convenient and honourable relations with both Spanish belligerents.

In the interests of humanity it has for a long time been a mistake of the parties of the Left, both in Britain and in France, to brand large organised bodies of resolute armed men as 'rebels' and 'outlaws' whom the *de jure* government may justly execute when captured. This attitude has only intensified the ferocity of the conflict. When men are denied all status, it is natural that in desperation they should prove their credentials by terror and show that force at least is on their side. If Britain wishes to mitigate the horrors of the Spanish Civil War, it is indispensable that she should have formal friendly diplomatic relations with both sides, and should encourage by every means the regularisation of the conditions of war between the two combatants. In this way only can the preparatory stage be reached out of which a new life for Spaniards of all classes and political records may emerge.

Meanwhile, during the past year, a marked advance towards an ordered system of government and war has simultaneously produced itself in the character of the Spanish Republican Government. The shameful wholesale atrocities which the extremists committed in the days when the Communists and Anarchists ruled the tragic scene, have been repressed, and the Anarchists have been quelled by fire and steel. Communists, Anarchists, and ordinary folk who support the Government have alike been woven into a disciplined army. That army lacks military efficiency, and there is no Government fleet, because of the wholesale murder or execution of almost all the professional officers in Government hands during the early months of the struggle. It may now be realised that this butchery was perhaps shortsighted.

But an army which has a coherent entity, a strict organisation and a hierarchy of command has been formed. It is just as wrong to call the Valencian and Catalonian Governments a mob of savage Bolshevists as to dub the Nationalist movement a mere body of rebels, traitors and reactionaries. When in any country the whole structure of civilised and social life is destroyed by atavistic hatreds, the State can only be reconstituted upon a military framework. War, the hardest of all teachers, is the only one to whom attention is paid. From a welter of hideous events the structure of an organised society gradually rises again. In its new army, which has not yet been seriously tested, the Spanish Republic has an instrument not only of military but of political significance.

Moreover, the complexion of the Government is profoundly changed. President Azaña still remains at the summit; Liberals, and even Conservative Parliamentarians, have found it possible to return to Republican Spain. The meeting of the Cortes this year was attended by a hundred and eighty members. Señor Indalecio Prieto is throughout Spain a man of mark. Thus during the cruel struggle both sides have progressed steadily towards a coherent expression of the Spanish mind. Is not this the time when every effort should be made by all true friends of Spain to bring about a pacification?

What could be more helpful to this than the restoration of a constitutional monarchy as a guarantee that all Spaniards who have not committed crimes of moral turpitude will find their places in the New Spain? This week in Austria, when the Monarchists were celebrating the natal day of the Habsburg heir to the throne, they were assaulted by a combination of Nazis and Communists. Does not such an episode strike a note which should be audible to all that great majority of Europeans who wish to see totalitarian tyrannies pass from the life of Europe, and to that end would rejoice to see Spain resume a united and independent place among its leading nations?

It must be remembered that at the beginning of the Spanish Civil War the French Government proposed, and the British Government accepted, the policy of Non-intervention. This was agreed to by Germany, Italy and Russia. It meant that no one should help either side. The Spanish Government were denied the right to purchase arms with their own gold. Belligerency was denied to both. This was a great advantage at the outset to General Franco. But such a policy required to be honourably observed by all parties. It was reduced to mockery by Italy, Germany and Russia. I still think that both sides should have been accorded belligerent rights at an early stage, and that the Spanish Government should have been allowed to purchase whatever they could pay for and import. They having been penalised at the outset, and the whole 'Non-intervention' becoming a fraud, would have been still more hardly treated if belligerent rights had been accorded to General Franco at a stage when this would have favoured him.

WHAT WE ASK OF THE UNITED STATES
DECEMBER 10, 1937

There never was a time in all our history when the good relations between the British Empire and the United States stood so high. There is throughout the great Republic active widespread comprehension of the dangers and difficulties to which the liberal Parliamentary countries are exposed from the rise, character, and ambitions of the aggressive dictators. This has evoked lively sympathy both with Great Powers like France and Britain and helpless countries like China and Abyssinia which have been attacked, or other small European States which are menaced. There is even more strongly marked hostility to the totalitarian Dictators.

The American public as a whole, in spite of its large Italian and German infusions, reads with gusto the scathing attacks upon Nazism and Fascism, or above all upon the Japanese aggression, with which they are copiously supplied by the American Press. Public expression has been given to these feelings by the President in powerful speeches and by United States ambassadors both in Paris and London. The United States and British Admiralties, instead of bickering about guns and cruisers, watch with mutual satisfaction the enormous expansion of each other's fleets. An Anglo-American trade agreement[1] or an harmonious settlement of the Debt question would be a manifestation of goodwill now existing between these vast communities, which in all essentials feel the same way. There can be no doubt that United States sentiment is far more favourable to Great Britain than it was in 1914.

But this must not mislead the Parliamentary nations into supposing that the United States is coming over again to fight their battles. On the contrary, the first resolve of the great majority of American citizens is to avoid European, or even Far Eastern, entanglements, and at all costs to keep out of war. These are natural views for a gigantic self-contained country with three thousand miles of ocean on one side of it and seven thousand on the other. Wars have a way of drawing nations into their vortex in spite of all that they can do; but it would be a profound mistake for Britain or France, or any of the minor States gathered together in the League of Nations, to count for their safety upon any force save that of their own right arm.

There are, however, ways in which the United States, without exposing herself to the risk or toil of war, can give effect to the moral feelings of her people and Government, and powerful aid to causes which she deems righteous. The interpretation placed upon United States neutrality in time of war would be of immense consequence to Great

---

[1] This has since been made. February 1939.

Britain and France. The principle embodied in recent American proposals of 'cash and carry' is highly favourable to any Power possessing the command of the sea. But even in time of peace the economic and financial policy of the United States may exercise an appreciable check upon the war preparations of potential aggressors.

We have seen this week the fury with which Signor Mussolini's mouthpiece has denounced the proposals of the *New York Times* for a talk about concerting all economic and financial policy against law-breaking nations. This outburst only shows how much this form of deterrent is dreaded. The Italian Dictator is more sensitive to such processes than his Nazi confrère, and far more dependent upon external supplies than his Japanese associate. Yet the Italian remedy is very simple. They have only to act in a loyal and friendly manner to other countries, to keep the Treaties and Covenants into which they have entered, and to desist from their attitude of challenge, in order to regain the goodwill of the democratic world. Many people on both sides of the Atlantic have watched with pleasure the rise and reorganisation of Italy, and still feel warmly towards that industrious and agreeable nation. Certainly no effort would be lacking to restore the old relationships.

But there is one way above all others in which the United States can aid the European democracies. Let her regain and maintain her normal prosperity. A prosperous United States exerts, directly and indirectly, an immense beneficent force upon world affairs. A United States thrown into financial and economic collapse spreads evil far and wide, and weakens France and England just at the time when they have most need to be strong. The quarrel in which President Roosevelt has become involved with Wealth and Business may produce results profoundly harmful to ideals which to him and his people are dear. It is surely far better to allow the productive force of Capital and Credit to create wealth and abundance, and then by corrective taxation on profits meet the needs of the weak and poor.

Instead, the Washington administration has waged so ruthless a war on private enterprise that the United States, with none of the perils and burdens of Europe upon it, is actually at the present moment leading the world back into the trough of depression. This warfare has taken three main forms: first the attack upon the capital reserves of great corporations, which has woefully crippled their power to make future plans and give future work; secondly, the remorseless pressure of uncertainty and ill will which has been maintained against the immense sphere of public utility undertakings; thirdly, the irksomely hampering restrictions imposed upon market and Stock Exchange transactions. The effect has been to range the Executive of the United States against all the great wealth-producing agencies of the capitalist system. On both sides blood is up, and between them in their fury they can undoubtedly tear the financial and economic strength of the American people to pieces.

In quiet times there is much to be said for some of these issues being patiently fought out. But even the most enthusiastic New Dealer might ask himself whether, with Europe and indeed the whole world in its present condition, this is a good time for the United States to indulge in this devastating internecine war. Those who are keeping the flag of Peace and Free Government flying in the Old World have almost a right to ask that their comrades in the New World should, during these years of exceptional and not diminishing danger, set an example of strength and stability. The well-being of the United States may spell not only the well-being but the safety of all sorts and conditions of men.

During the whole of the year of grace 1937 the more highly educated portions of the human race have been arming upon a scale never before imagined. All the preparations of the years before the outbreak of the Great War were upon a petty scale compared to this. Not only has the expense in service and in money been vastly greater, and the weapons all far more deadly, but arrangements are made in all so-called civilised countries to bring the whole population into the national war effort and to expose both sexes, all classes, aged and young, weak, sick and wounded impartially, to the flail and torment of destruction.

At the same time, the mass of every nation in the world is earnestly desirous of peace, and asks very little but to live in it, and enjoy the ever-ripening fruit of their labours which science can bring. Those that dwell under totalitarian dictatorships are gripped by an all-pervading apparatus of propaganda and compulsion which welds them into a State machine primarily adapted to war. The liberal and Parliamentary countries have had in their turn to arm upon an enormous scale in self-defence, and seek in a tentative and as yet imperfect manner to join themselves together for mutual protection and insurance. The cost of warlike preparation has thrown the finances of the dictatorship governments into a condition which is leaving ordinary bankruptcy far behind, and which compels them to enforce privations and discipline upon their peoples which hitherto have been tolerated only in times of war. The modern world is taking the aspect of a series of feudal fortresses victualled for a siege. Such have been the dominant tendencies of the year 1937, and such is the strange panorama which unfolds before our eyes at this Christmastide.

The events of the year have corresponded to the forces which have been at work. The Civil War in Spain has been fought feebly but cruelly and incessantly throughout the year. The strength of the Spanish Nationalist and monarchical forces has increasingly gained upon the Republican and Left-wing elements. This Spanish quarrel has been taken up by the Dictatorships of both extremes who have sought to transform it into an ideological contest between Nazism and Communism. While promising solemnly and repeatedly not to intervene, the German and Italian Dictators have thrown their weight in on one side, while the Soviet Czar has done his utmost to help the other. France has been neutral and Great Britain strictly neutral. The British Government and Foreign Secretary deserve applause for the patience and good faith with which they have acted, and it may well be that when this bitter struggle ends, Great Britain will not be found to be the most unpopular or uninfluential Power in Spain.

The secret military societies which control the Government of Japan having virtually suppressed its Parliament, and murdered politicians who were thought to be lukewarm in their patriotism, have led their people into an invasion of China marked by ruthlessness and frightfulness on the latest models. The Japanese are now deeply involved in China, and no one can tell how far this adventure may carry them. The Chinese have defended their country as well as they could, and a new spirit of unity and patriotism is alive in the hearts of the Chinese race, the most numerous in all the world. The Japanese onslaught upon China has been marked by a succession of outrages against neutral powers, particularly Great Britain and the United States, followed in all cases by apologies. So far these apologies have had to be accepted, but it may be that further injuries are in store and that little else than the destruction of British, United States and European interests in the Far East may be in contemplation.

Signor Mussolini's conquest of Abyssinia has weighed heavily upon the Italian people. The whole of that wild mountainous region is seething with sporadic rebellion, and the maintenance of an Italian army of several hundred thousand men amid a hostile population has become a serious drain upon the Italian resources of all kinds. The Italian dictator, having also sent a considerable army to Spain and another even larger to Libya, has certainly spread his resources widely. At the same time he is fortifying his ports in the Mediterranean and the Red Sea with feverish zeal. The cost of these excursions and exertions, together with the immense host of uniformed functionaries and military establishments associated with Dictatorships, have thrown a burden upon the Italian peasants, artisans, and mercantile classes which they bear with astonishing docility and increasing strain.

The embarrassments or the ambitions of the Dictator Powers have led Germany, Italy, and Japan to form a triangle of authoritarian and militaristic governments nominally to resist Communism, of which they profess to stand in great dread. Such a combination is fraught with danger not only to the soil of Russia but to the prosperity and freedom of Parliamentary democracies alike in the Old World and the New. It is fortunate therefore in these circumstances, and quite natural, that the British Empire and the French Republic should draw ever closer together. The British Navy even at present is far stronger relatively to European fleets than in 1914. The programmes now in rapid construction will emphasise this reassuring fact. The French Army has not yet been surpassed in the numbers of formed divisions by the Germans, and its formations are of full maturity. The combination of the British fleet and the French army in resistance to any violent or unprovoked aggression should give confidence to the secondary or small Powers of Europe to hold firmly to the Covenant of the League of Nations, and to make the greatest contribution they can to their own safety. Under the usual appearance of party and Parliamentary bickerings there is a greater measure of unity upon essentials in the French and British nations than has ever been known in time of peace. Finally, the goodwill extended towards the free Governments of Europe by the United States has become more apparent as the months have passed.

There is therefore no need for us to feel unequal to the stresses of 1938, and we must all try to use that year so as to bring about a healthier atmosphere and a more easy and sane situation. Let me, then, close with a thought which may appeal to all.

On Christmas Day, 1914, the German soldiers on the Western Front ceased firing. They placed small Christmas trees on their trenches and declared that on this day there should be peace and goodwill among suffering men. Both sides came out of their trenches and met in the blasted No-Man's Land. They clasped each other's hands, they exchanged gifts and kind words. Together they buried the dead hitherto inaccessible and deprived of the rites which raise man above the brute. Let no man worthy of human stature banish this inspiration from his mind.

BRITAIN REARMS
JANUARY 7, 1938

In 1938, the civilised nations of the world will receive consideration principally on account of the armaments they possess, and are able to pay for. The contentment of their peoples, the freedom of their institutions, the impartiality of their courts, their ancient traditions, their standard of working-class comfort, their philosophy, poetry and art, will not count very much for fame in this degraded age. Arms and the men to use them will be the criterion by which hungry aggressive States will measure their steps and the small countries their behaviour.

We must be glad in these circumstances that the British Navy is strong. Even during the years of disarmament, at least £50,000,000 sterling was spent every year upon keeping in order the plant and organisation already established on the largest scale. A proportion of the battleships and cruisers have been completely rebuilt in the guise of refitting. Since the Italian alarm in 1935 the Admiralty have had whatever money they cared to ask in order to fit all the vessels of the fleet with every kind of modern appliance and equipment. In particular, protection by guns and armour against air attack has been revolutionised. Lord Fisher used to say, 'The British Navy always travels first-class.' I can hardly believe that so capable a body as the Naval Lords have not made good use of their opportunities.

We are now spending at the rate of about four times as much on the fleet as, for instance, Italy; and no doubt the new estimates will show a very large upward surge. An immense programme of new construction in vessels of every kind is now clanging its way through the dockyards and private firms. Five battleships are being built. Obviously another squadron of the largest type must be begun in the programme of 1938. All other branches of the fleet are being developed in due proportion, and the man-power of the long-service professional Navy rises as fast as possible, subject only to training efficiency. The methods of dealing with the submarine menace are incomparably superior to any discovered in the Great War. There is the growing conviction that the air menace against properly armed and protected ships of war will not be of a decisive character.

If this be so, the ultimate command of the seas will rest with whichever Power can at any moment draw out the strongest line of battle in blue water. At the present time no other Power in Europe, except the British, can attempt to form a line of battle, nor, indeed, all the Powers of Europe together. By treaty the United States is entitled to build to full parity with Great Britain. As far as we can see, President Roosevelt has every intention of acting up to the spirit of that agreement. Therefore we may be easy on that score. A feeble, ill-armed United States Navy would at the present time be an additional danger to the world. A strong and efficient United States fleet inspires no one with fear but evil-doers.

The French Navy is also an important element in the problem of world security. In all the circumstances it may be safely said that the control of the oceans and great waters rests with the Parliamentary nations, and that this control will sustain their commerce and their credit. It is surely well that this should be so, for none of these Powers have any designs against the independence, welfare or prosperity of other countries. They may have their own opinions about the way these countries are governed, but they seek nothing from them, neither their ox nor their ass nor anything that is theirs.

Great Britain has never had a large army in time of peace. She has a small professional force which is little more than an Imperial police reserve. Indeed, it is a prodigy to see the vast tracts of the world, and multitudes of people who dwell in composure, and for the most part in goodwill under the British Flag, protected by smaller military forces than even a third-class European State could mobilise. Nevertheless, it is necessary that the modest military establishment we maintain should be kept at its full strength, and should be equipped with the latest appliances and fullest supplies. Recruiting has greatly improved, and the rejuvenation of the High Command, for which the new Secretary for War, Mr. Hore-Belisha, has been praised, should initiate a period of overhaul and replenishment throughout our small army.

The British Army must not, however, be considered otherwise than in relation to the French Army, which during the year 1938 will certainly not be surpassed in the number of formed divisions by any European country except Russia, and will be superior in the maturity and cohesion of its cadres to any country. These conditions, however, are not unchanging. Although in a few years time the British Navy will increase its preponderance in Europe, the man-power of Germany will gradually become organised upon a far larger scale and in a higher degree of perfection.

If we only had to consider the fleets and armies of Europe in the immediate future, there would be no excuse for the Central and Southern European States to subject themselves to the rigours of dictatorship, and make their obeisance to the Nazi power. It is in the new element of the air that the weakness of the free peoples resides. General Weygand, who certainly would not speak without authority, defined some time ago the proportions of the European air forces as follows: Germany 3000, Italy 1200, Great Britain 1500, and France 1000. If these figures are approximately a true guide, it is very discreditable to France and Great Britain that with all their wealth and resources they have not been able to make in freedom a proper use of this delicate and superfine arm. When the House of Commons meets, it will be the duty of Parliament to seek reassurances from the British Government, not only upon the effort which is being made, but upon the results which have been achieved. We were solemnly promised by Mr. Baldwin that our metropolitan air strength should not be inferior to that of any power within striking distance. If this undertaking has not been made good, a most grievous responsibility rests upon those public men who so long delayed the process of expansion.

Money for defence is certainly pouring out in all directions in Britain. The Co-ordination Minister assures us that the expenditure will far exceed the estimate of fifteen hundred millions sterling forecasted less than a year ago. Happily, British credit is so good that no difficulty in financing these enormous charges need be expected. The friends of political and democratic freedom in Europe need not therefore look upon the sombre year now opening with undue despondency and alarm.

WHAT JAPAN THINKS OF US
JANUARY 21, 1938

The changes in the French Government, the health of the franc, the visits and conferences of the Little Entente Powers and others in Central Europe—and the wandering planet which might perhaps have ended all our troubles—have dominated the newspapers this week. But I still feel that the attitude of Japan to the rest of the world deserves our continued attention. Several unpleasant things have happened. British policemen in the International Settlement of Shanghai have been punched and man-handled by Japanese soldiers in a manner which shows a deep-seated hatred towards white people. Japanese apologies for sinking the American gunboat *Panay* and killing considerable numbers of American citizens and others who enjoyed their protection, have not carried conviction either to the Government or to the people of the United States. A Japanese Admiral, by name Suetsugu, of whom the world had not previously heard, has declared himself in favour of driving the white race out of the Far East, and immediately after this declaration this Admiral has acquired a controlling position in making Japanese plans.

These plans are directed to a four years' war upon China and meeting any foreign complications that may arise therefrom. Since the Japanese armies broke into the Shanghai district, numerous opportunities have been afforded to the representatives of the white races of learning the sort of mood they are in, and the kind of respect they are likely to show to British, United States and European rights in China. It has been obvious that the small respect of Japanese soldiers and sailors for the Chinese is nothing compared to the contempt with which they regard the non-yellow races, and in particular, unhappily, the British and Americans. All this is too bad, because it was the British and Americans who cordially fostered and aided for many years the modernisation of Japan. No nations in the civilised world have watched with so much practical sympathy the great advances which Japan has made in the last fifty years. Certainly no other governments have done so much to befriend Japan or have yielded themselves more readily to the hope that Western science and knowledge would be in this case a unifying force between Japan and her world companions.

We must recognise, however reluctantly, that the Mikado's Government has only an imperfect authority over the naval and military warriors of Japan, and still less over their aviators. The secret societies in the Japanese army and navy have very largely taken charge of the policy of their country. They have murdered so many politicians who were thought to be weaklings or backsliders that they have terrified the rest. It is painful to say it, but there are moments when we must feel ourselves in the presence of an army and navy which are running amok.

It must be stated quite plainly that the United States, Great Britain and the European countries have no designs upon the safety or prosperity of Japan. They have been good purchasers of Japanese merchandise. They have willingly extended the hand of courtesy to Japanese Ambassadors and Envoys. They have no aims in China except to see the Chinese people happy and free and to render them the normal services of commerce and enterprise. However, at the end of it all there is Admiral Suetsugu with his plan for driving all white people out of the East, and the bloody decks of the *Panay* with United States sailors trying to save helpless refugees from aeroplane bombs and subsequent machine-gun fire. One must recognise this as a very serious disappointment for the great democracies of the Western world. Evidently we should not lose heart. On the contrary, we should persevere, but we may have to persevere along a somewhat different path.

At this point one begins to look at the strength of the Japanese Navy in relation to the other great Naval Powers of the world. The Washington Conference of 1920 agreed to a ratio of five British and five American to three Japanese naval units, and to certain limits of tonnage and cannon. But that Treaty has now expired, and it is said that Japan has already embarked upon the construction of several battleships which exceed in tonnage and size of cannon those that are being built in Britain and America. The United States Navy Board will of course be compelled to review its programmes and types very searchingly. President Roosevelt's declarations seem to show that the Government of the United States would not be willing to see their naval power seriously rivalled in the Pacific Ocean at the present time. They have an ample superiority, but this might pass in a few years unless timely measures are taken.

It seems probable that a large programme of naval expansion will be undertaken in the United States, and that the American Navy will keep good pace with the British Navy in accordance with the principles of parity which govern our relations. Neither Government need be afraid of what is called starting a naval race with Japan. It is quite certain that Japan cannot possibly compete with the productive energies of either branch of the English-speaking peoples.

The immediate problem is of a different character. Its solution depends entirely upon the view—moral, political, economic—which the people of the United States take of their responsibilities in the Pacific. It is certain that no American Government is going to 'pull the chestnuts out of the fire' for the sake of British or European interest in China. It is not certain that they may not feel an interest and duty of their own. The absorption and organisation of a great part of China by Japan into a vast Asiatic naval and military power, with hundreds of millions of subjects under its sway, and animated by the principles which Admiral Suetsugu has so frankly expressed, might not upon a long view be in accordance with the safety and freedom of the people of the United States. The issue is one entirely for the decision of the American Government and people, and none of us in Europe should presume to intervene in that tremendous cogitation. No one in Great Britain would venture to ask or urge any particular course upon the Washington Government.

The British Government is, however, entitled to say that if the United States for their own purposes chose to take a lead in preserving peace and civilisation in and around the China Seas, they would be supported by Great Britain and the British Empire to the full limit of their strength. There were Anglo-American misunderstandings in 1931, but there should be no misunderstandings now. If President Roosevelt's Government feel it their duty for purely American or world purposes, to make their weight tell in the cause of peace and order in the Far East, the British Empire will associate itself with them heart and hand.

THE DUSK OF THE LEAGUE
FEBRUARY 4, 1938

The attempt to produce a crisis at Geneva fatal to the League of Nations, upon which so many weak, foolish or baleful wishes were set, has failed. The declarations made by Great Britain, France and Russia of fidelity to the principles of the Covenant have tided the League over a dangerous conjuncture. It would, indeed, have been a sorry spectacle if at a time like this the notables of so many countries gathered at Geneva had embarked upon an endless theoretical discussion about the exact interpretation of Article XVI, or, even worse, upon the task of redrafting it. Such as it is, the Covenant of the League represents the noblest and most coherent endeavour of the peoples of the world to escape from the horrors of war by confronting aggression collectively with serious deterrents. Whether this hope will fail or not no one can tell. But it would be better to allow it to fade and fall as it is, than to fabricate a patchwork of shams. The League at the present time is not strong enough to undergo a surgical operation. It would die under the knife. Even the chloroform might prove fatal. There is nothing for it but to let the healing forces of natural vitality work, and await the result.

The secondary and smaller States of Europe are terrified by the decision and ruthlessness of the Dictator Powers, and their apparent readiness to use military force to achieve their ends. They have no confidence that Britain or France has the will or the power to protect them. Russia to them is a mystery which when unfolded may count either way. Many of the minor Powers have failed to make any contribution to the strength of the League corresponding either to their resources or their dangers. Belgium, which owes its existence to the former Allies, and with its magnificent colonial estate defended only by public law, is eager to emphasise its neutrality. Holland, with enormous tropical possessions at the mercy of predatory aggression, has taken the lead in urging the Scandinavian powers to recognise the Italian conquest of Abyssinia. Mr. de Valera, oblivious to the claims of conquered peoples, has also given his croak in this sense. No sooner had he clambered from the arena into the Imperial box, than he hastened to turn his thumb down upon the first prostrate gladiator he saw.

In Yugoslavia and Rumania the Governments, by an extreme use of the executive power, have forced their peoples towards the policy of Nazism. There is a general inclination among the governments of the smaller Powers to leave Czechoslovakia and Austria to their fate. This mighty Europe, which could so easily if it willed secure freedom and avert war, seems inclined at the moment—and it is a very dangerous moment—to yield itself to the apparition of Nazi-Fascist prestige. Whether these appearances are merely superficial can be known only when some overt aggression takes place.

Nearly all European States are anxious for a quiet life. It may not be heroic, but it is only natural that many of them should wish to keep out of any trouble that is coming, although this may involve them in much greater troubles later on. But how they would act in the presence of some terrible and wrongful act cannot be judged by the cautious disclaimers in which they now indulge. The pity is that this attitude of caution may bring about the very evils it is designed to avoid. Whereas united declarations at Geneva might keep Europe on an even keel, the apparent gaining of adherents by the totalitarian States may precipitate unpleasant developments.

Nevertheless, the best has been done in the circumstances at Geneva. The strong unity between Great Britain and France has again been emphasised. The two Western Parliamentary States have made it clear that they do not take sides or seek to enlist others in the present quarrel of rival ideologies. There is the Nazi-Fascist ideology, and the Communist ideology. Britain and France are equally opposed to both. But that does not mean that the League of Nations should not have a strong conception of its own. The Parliamentary States think that small peoples acting within their rights should not be trampled down by stronger ones. They think that civilisation implies in any society the freedom to criticise the Government of the day; free speech; free Press; free thought; free religious observance; no racial persecution; fair treatment of minorities; courts of law and justice which have an authority independent of the executive and untainted by party bias. These are the ideals which centre around the League of Nations. These are the hopes of the world. These are the means by which an abundant prosperity would come to this generation. Are they to be dubbed a mere 'ideology'? On the contrary they represent that sober, decent, righteous middle path which not only the majority of nations but the vast majority in every nation would desire to follow. They are well worth defending over all Europe as long as it is possible to defend them.

What is the alternative to the League of Nations and the maintenance of its authority, weakened as it now is? The alternative is sombre. It is for Britain and France, rich, powerful, heavily armed, to stand aside and allow Central and Eastern Europe to clatter into anarchy, or congeal into a Nazi domination. If that is what the smaller countries of Europe want, the Western democracies cannot stop them having it. Already voices are raised, not only in Britain but in France, saying, 'let them stew in their own juice.' This process would not be pleasant to any of the States now existing in Middle Europe. It would be accompanied by intense internal stresses such as destroyed the empire of the great Napoleon. It would be melancholy for the world. It seems very likely that the Western democracies would remain erect at the end of it. But what a cataract of misfortune would be opened upon these shortsighted governments and unfortunate peoples, who through mere incapacity to combine upon a broad international platform had left themselves the prey to measureless tribulation!

On February 16 the Austrian Prime Minister, Dr. Schuschnigg, having been summoned to Munich, was compelled by Herr Hitler under dire threats to admit Nazi agents as Ministers in his Government. This was described in the German press as a 'new joint contribution to the peace of Central Europe.' The sequel followed promptly.

IT'S NOT ALL OVER YET
FEBRUARY 17, 1938

This eventful fortnight contains good news as well as bad. The lamentable fate of Austria requires discussion separately when we can measure more truly what has actually happened. It is clear, however, that this prejudices the interests of the Italian Dictator as much as it wounds the sympathies of the Western Powers. We must see what are the guarantees which Herr Hitler has given of Austrian independence and in what way they will be carried out. It is not at all certain yet what the reactions in Austria will be, and whether the violent scenes at Berchtesgaden will produce all the recruits for the Nazi cause in Austria which were expected from them. If there is any general rally by the Austrian people, deeply religious as they are, to the cause of national independence, it may be that some breathing space will be secured. Peoples do not like being bullied into any ideology. In Rumania, the Jewbaiter, Goga, has been pitched out of his brief authority, and the munition contracts of the Rumanian army are once again restored to France. It is evident that the forces at work in Rumania cannot easily be made to join the pro-Nazi axis.

'The masses,' said Napoleon in one of his most pessimistic pronouncements, 'care little for liberty, but much for equality.' But more than a hundred years have passed since then, and the world has moved on. To-day individual freedom, especially when combined with a higher standard of living, makes a potent appeal to the men and women of every country under every system. Why should not an ordinary toiler have the chance to keep a home together and rear a family, without being vilely trodden in upon by well-paid uniformed officials and professional party agents? Why should the police harry ordinary households in so many lands more than they do in England? Why should the ordinary wage-earner not be allowed to express his opinion about the government of his country, and say whether he thinks it is being wisely or honestly conducted? Why should men's opinions be condemned as crimes, and buzzing functionaries conduct an inquisition into the political or party views of law-abiding folk? Why should religion be the subject of oppression? Why should racial persecution endure? Was it not Frederick the Great who said, 'In Prussia every man must get to Heaven in his own way'? Can anyone help being born with red hair or a hook nose?

After centuries of widening education and of liberal culture these primary conceptions are deeply implanted in all communities, civilised and militarised alike. Thus it is not at all surprising that the Goga stunt in Rumania has had to be summarily curtailed. It is to be hoped that Prince Paul of Yugoslavia and his Prime Minister, M. Stoyadinovitch, who are confronted with a far more formidable political and Parliamentary movement than has manifested itself in Rumania, will not be unresponsive to these invincible and unquenchable promptings, which spring alike from the true needs of the working people and from the day-spring genius of mankind.

In the Far East, the Japanese have declined to reassure the Naval Powers about the size of the battleships they are building. This can only mean that they are building ships of larger tonnage and cannon than those which the American-Franco-British self-denying ordinance permits to themselves. This is all to the good in the long run. Great Britain and the United States have too long hampered each other in their naval construction by their praiseworthy wish to keep naval armaments on a low level. Henceforward they will feel absolutely free to utilise their immense economic and financial superiority to design and construct whatever vessels and navies are necessary for their respective national safeties. There is happily no question of a naval race. In a few years the Japanese navy will have fallen back into a relative position far inferior to the ratio of five-five-three.

It is a tribute to the great place held by the German people among the nations, that the dismissals of generals and other ebullitions which have occurred in that country should have given rise to such wild and widespread rumours. Everyone is looking towards Germany with attention. Anyone can see that the world needs not merely the concurrence but the active aid of the German people, in order to bestow a better life upon the wage-earning masses in every land. It is an odd commentary upon latter-day politics that the class prejudices of Prussian generals should win a measure of sympathy in the Parliamentary States. They are, it seems, the element of toleration and prudence. It is a relief and a reassurance to find that in a totalitarian State some differences of opinion may become manifest without the recurrence of another June 30. Most people in England would rejoice sincerely to welcome a tolerant, peace-seeking Germany into the very van of world leadership. It would be our duty to aid and salute this process by every means in our power.

No one can measure, still less predict, the course of events in Germany. The German army may continue to preserve under its iron discipline the breath of tolerance and freedom: in which case there will be a considerable gain in international security. On the other hand, the Nazi party, aided by the Secret Police, may succeed in creating a party-army dominated by Nazi principles in this world, and by the Nazi religion as their guide to the next. In this case also we should all breathe easier, because no army can be formed on party lines without very serious diminution of its military efficiency. Once the process of heresy-hunting pervades an army, true comradeship dies. Officers are promoted not for professional knowledge but for being glib in the party patter. Pretence infects every rank and every unit. A bad officer gets on by mouthing orthodox political doctrines. Resolute men needed to stand the strain of battle are no good at this game. We hear a lot from time to time of French degeneracy, but the French Army, from Commander-in-Chief to private soldier, from Monarchist to Communist, is a harmonious engine for the defence of France against aggression. Their experienced Chiefs could certainly watch the Nazification of the German army with a considerable degree of composure.

Last, but not least, we must turn our eyes to Italy, or rather to the extraordinary man who at the present moment embodies and expresses all that Italy means. The English newspapers have been indulging this week in many rumours about a deal with Mussolini.

Certainly all parties in the House of Commons would like to see the old relations in the Mediterranean restored with Italy, but it is comforting to read Mr. Eden's declarations at Birmingham that 'In any agreements we make to-day there must be no sacrifice of principles and no shirking of responsibilities merely to obtain quick results.' And 'It is not by seeking to buy temporary goodwill that peace is made, but on a basis of frank reciprocity with mutual respect.' These words may be taken to represent not only the views of the Foreign Secretary, but those of Mr. Neville Chamberlain and consequently of His Majesty's Government and the British Parliament.

On February 18 Mr. Eden resigned the office of Secretary of State for Foreign Affairs. It was apparent then, and is obvious now, that the Prime Minister, in his hopes of appeasing the Dictators, had decided to assume control of Foreign Affairs.

CARRY ON!
MARCH 4, 1938

The sudden and lamentable events which have taken place in England during the last fortnight must not be exaggerated. They have greatly weakened the Conservative Party in the constituencies. The Liberal, Labour and non-party voters whom Mr. Baldwin had painstakingly gathered, have been summarily dismissed and will not be easy to recall. In Mr. Eden the National Government have lost their only popular figure. A fortnight ago they could have appealed to the electors with confidence. No friend would recommend them to do so now. The growing association on parallel lines between Great Britain and the United States has received a very severe setback. British foreign policy has become for the moment even more than usually incomprehensible to her friends and well-wishers on the Continent and all over the world. No explanation has been offered why, at this moment of all others, we should have gone to the rescue of the one Dictator whose misdeeds were already beginning to find him out. He was very near to collapse. By so doing we have set him up again on a pinnacle, and generally have exalted the dominance and prestige of Dictatorships in all countries.

It would, however, be a mistake to read into the motions of the British Government more than they intended themselves. It is certain that they do not mean to disinterest themselves in European affairs. Mr. Chamberlain has been eager to assert that our relations with France, which include a military arrangement, are unchanged. There is no intention to abandon the League of Nations. The process of rearmament will be pressed forward if possible at increased speed. In the upshot Great Britain, though herself substantially weakened and her enemies encouraged, is in the main standing where she stood. We have now to await the results of the conversations which Lord Perth will hold in Rome with Count Ciano, or perhaps with Signor Mussolini in person. The triumph of the Italian Dictator is remarkable. With one bound he has been carried from a position of desperate embarrassment to be courted at once by the British and German Governments. Chamberlain and Hitler alike seek his friendship. The British are negotiating with him. Hitler is about to visit Rome himself. There has never been in history any example of such magnificent bluffing.

But this is not the end. The underlying realities and verities of Europe will increasingly assert themselves. In a short time we shall know whether Mr. Chamberlain's hope of detaching Mussolini from Hitler will be realised. If it is not realised, nothing else that Mussolini could give us is of the slightest value. The withdrawal of 10,000 or 20,000 Italian troops from Spain, if balanced against a similar withdrawal of volunteers from the Republican forces, would be a great advantage to General Franco. The British recognition of the Italian 'Empire' of Ethiopia, though mortifying to great numbers of good people in

England, does not solve Mussolini's problem in the slightest degree. The withdrawal of some troops from Libya, and the stopping of the abuse poured out from the Bari radio, will only benefit Britain till the weather changes.

What Mussolini wants is money. It will not be at all easy to procure this for him. It is very unlikely that the Government will face the prolonged ordeal of carrying a Loan Bill through the House of Commons. Therefore it seems that the Prime Minister has somewhat precipitately embarked upon most unpromising negotiations. If Mussolini is willing to separate from Hitler, to take his stand with France and Britain, and help sustain the independence of Austria, there will be an undoubted gain. But what chance is there of this? We shall not have to wait long before we know.

Meanwhile the constancy and stolidity of the democratic forces in Europe excites admiration. The high spirit of the French nation was evident in the great debate in the Chamber. It is extremely improbable that M. Delbos would have spoken so confidently if he had not received very considerable reassurances from the British Government. The new British Foreign Secretary, Lord Halifax, must not be dismissed as a pious devotee of 'peace at any price.' Hitherto he has wielded undue influence in the Cabinet as a vague, sincere advocate of making friends with everybody. Now in the collar of a great Department he will be brought face to face with grim duties arising from the movement of events, and I for one shall not assume he will be found unworthy of them.

Elsewhere this crowded fortnight has revealed in several quarters the innate strength of the cause of freedom in Europe. The brutal bullying of Herr Schuschnigg at Berchtesgaden, where the most horrible threats were uttered, is in its secondary stage producing a very strong national rally throughout Austria. The union of the Socialists with the Catholics gives a broad foundation to the Vienna Government which they have never had before. They have now probably two-thirds of the people of Austria behind them in defence of their independence. They could now probably face a plebiscite conducted under fair conditions without fear. But no one can tell what the reactions in Nazi Germany will be, or what new shattering blows impend upon a small unhappy State.

Czechoslovakia has also made it clear that she will fight for her independence. People underrate the strength of this virile community. They could no doubt be trampled down by Prussian boots, but the process would not be easy. Their new fortifications are formidable. Their army of 24 divisions is loyal, efficient and well supplied. The capacity of Czechoslovakia to consume steel, which is some index of war-power, is equal to that of Italy. Czechoslovakia is also protected by her alliances with Russia and with France. It was surely a great hour for the French Republic when a few days ago by an overwhelming majority the Chamber proclaimed its resolve to stand by its alliance with Czechoslovakia. Since Germany by all accounts is not yet in a position to undertake a major war in which she would be the aggressor, such a solemn declaration may do much to preserve the peace of Europe for some time. These are solid facts, and if their force is not weakened by shortsighted British action, a further breathing space may be secured while the tardy but ponderous rearmament of Britain develops.

Note

On March 13 Herr Hitler having launched his armies upon Austria while Europe gaped, declared the Federal State of Austria dissolved and annexed to the German Reich. France and Russia renewed their pledges to aid Czechoslovakia in the event of German aggression. Field-Marshal Goering assured the Czechoslovak Government, 'on the honour of a soldier,' of Germany's determination to respect the territorial integrity of Czechoslovakia. Lord Halifax announced that Great Britain took formal note of this assurance.

THE AUSTRIAN EYE-OPENER
MARCH 18, 1938

The Nazi seizure and subjugation of Austria has produced an effect in Britain deeper and stronger than anything that has occurred since the Great War. The scales of illusion have fallen from many eyes, especially in high quarters. There is a new spirit stirring throughout the nation. It is not a mood of nervous or superficial excitement, but a widespread conviction, sober and solid; first, that the expansion of British defences must be pressed forward with a new and intense energy; and secondly that our country must bear her part with the French Republic in a joint effort to avert a European war. It is now generally realised that this can only be done by strength and not by weakness, by firmness and not by deference. Time and precious advantages have been lost by a misreading in influential circles of the German mind.

But if concerted diplomatic action is now taken upon the basis of active rearmament, it ought to be possible to accumulate a mass of deterrents against further acts of aggression. These deterrents must then be assembled upon the basis of the Covenant of the League of Nations and must be in strict harmony with the principles and ideals of the League. It must be made plain that any combination of Powers, who may find themselves prepared to act as special mandatories of the League, will carry their action as far as may be necessary to deter or, failing that, to resist, further instances of unprovoked aggression. In such a policy Mr. Chamberlain and his Government would have behind them the united support of all parties in Great Britain, and by proceeding on the basis of the Covenant they might confidently expect the broad concurrence of the Dominions, over whose individual decisions the Mother Country has, of course, no control. The urgency of the undertaking arises from the fact that the hope of producing peace by concerted action is greater in 1938 than it would be in 1939, and far greater than in 1940. To continue delaying from month to month while the degeneration of European morale proceeds apace, would seem to make war certain at a later date.[1]

Many high authorities believe that the German army is not yet in a condition to undertake a major aggressive land war. Neither her stores of raw material nor the state of her officer-cadres are sufficiently complete to encourage during the present year a hasty challenge to a group of well-armed States, with Great Britain and France at the core. No one, of course, can predict with certainty, but in any case the facts must be faced

---

[1] This policy of a Peace block of nations pledged and organised to resist further acts of Nazi aggression was adopted by Mr. Chamberlain a year later in March 1939, after the occupation of Prague by the Nazis, the dispersal of the Czechoslovak armies, and the capture of their munition arsenals.

with resolution, as they offer the best hopes of peace; and, failing peace, of national self-preservation.

The first step is to find out which of the Powers of the second rank in Europe would be willing to join with Great Britain and France for special action, not excluding armed resistance, under the Covenant of the League. If none of these States, however menaced, is found willing to join with the two Western democracies, then Nazi domination over the greater part of Europe is inevitable at no distant date. Alone, Great Britain and France cannot save Europe and avert war. If the larger hope fails through the weakness of the States of second rank, a mutually defensive role will alone be open to France and Britain. With their backs to the ocean and the command of the seas, they will be the heavily armed spectators of the horrible events and indefinite tyranny which will involve all countries from the Baltic to the Black Sea, and after that Holland and Belgium and the Scandinavian countries. It is not necessary to think of this sombre alternative until the hope of coming to lasting terms with Germany upon the basis of superior strength has been finally abandoned. Why should this hope not be converted into reality? It is the duty of any free country that wishes for peace and the reign of law to strive its utmost to rescue mankind from the steadily approaching catastrophe.

British and French thoughts are focussed now particularly upon Czechoslovakia. The French Republic have proclaimed their intention to make good their Treaty obligations to Czechoslovakia in the event of her becoming the victim of an unprovoked act of aggression. A further declaration of the intentions of the British Government in such an event must soon be made. Everything must be done to make it easy for Nazi Germany to live in a neighbourly fashion with Czechoslovakia. Dr. Benes and his Government owe it to themselves to convince the world that the German minority in their country is accorded every form of good treatment and equal citizenship, not incompatible with the safety and integrity of the State. The proper place for such an issue to be thrashed out is clearly Geneva. The fact that such a process was taking place at Geneva would be beneficial in itself, especially if it were simultaneous with the gathering of the Powers ready to undertake special service in resisting aggression. It must also be made clear that there is no desire to encircle Germany, but only to encircle an aggressor. If Germany does not become again the aggressor she would herself be entitled to the fullest measure of assistance from the allied Powers in case she were herself the object of attack. There is therefore nothing invidious or provocative in the procedure.

But the seizure of Austria cannot be allowed to lie as it does. I pointed out on Monday in the House of Commons that the Nazi mastery of Vienna dominates all the roads, railways and rivers upon which the States of the Little Entente depend for their military cohesion, and all the countries of Central and South-Eastern Europe depend for their economic life. Vienna, the ancient capital of a once mighty empire, is the ganglion nerve-centre of the trade and communications of all countries of the Danube basin, and others besides. It would be possible for the Berlin Government, by an abuse of tolls and tariffs on the Danube and on the Austrian railways, to paralyse the trade of Czechoslovakia and Yugoslavia and to sever these countries irretrievably from one another, even without firing a shot. Czechoslovakia could, therefore, be strangled into unwilling submission.

This should be the subject of early discussion before any question of accepting the fate of Austria can arise. Here again Geneva seems to be the centre, apart from other channels, through which Great Britain and France should apply their influence.

Two essential requirements stand out. First, effective guarantees for the protection of minorities, and, secondly, a reasonable freedom of trans-Austrian communications for commercial purposes. Both these questions are of vital import to the States of the Little Entente, and of scarcely less consequence to Hungary, Bulgaria, Greece and Turkey. The salvation of these countries and their future is at stake, and upon these issues they can found a means of immediate common action. If the policy which I have outlined should be adopted and should prosper, the 'Austrian eye-opener' may yet be made the means of saving Europe and the world from miseries beyond the dreams of Hell.

RED SUNSET IN SPAIN
APRIL 5, 1938

Another act of the Spanish tragedy is drawing to its close. The advance of General Franco's three corps attacking on a broad front, and the increasing demoralisation of the Republican forces, must, in the absence of some miraculous recovery, be decisive. Under the smashing weight of German and Italian artillery and aviation, all resistance is breaking down, and the Governments of Barcelona and Madrid will soon be cut off from supplies from France or from the sea. Considering their shortage of munitions of every kind, and their immense difficulty in feeding the population, the Republican leaders would be wise to make the best terms they can while time remains, and while they still have some remaining capacity for resistance. They should invoke without delay the mediation of Great Britain or France, or both, and thus avert useless slaughter on the battlefield, and procure a mitigation of the severities which it is to be feared will follow the subjugation of one half of Spain by the other.

No help can be expected from any quarter. The Anti-Nazi forces throughout Europe are so cowed and disorganised that they can only bow their heads in sombre acquiescence. One may measure the ascendancy acquired by the Dictator Powers by the two Italian communiqués which appeared simultaneously. The first warned France in strident terms of the risks she would run in intervening in Spain, and lectured her upon her responsibility to avoid a European war. The second was a statement of nearly 2,000 casualties in the Italian divisions which are taking part in General Franco's present offensive; and everyone knows besides that it is German artillery and aviation which has decided this phase of the struggle. Thus Dictator Powers may do anything; the others nothing. At this moment the Dictators are giving the law to Europe, and their decrees are being dutifully accepted by the Parliamentary democracies.

As between Spanish Nationalists and Republicans, British sympathies are divided. Strong elements in the Conservative Party regard the cause of Franco as their own. All the Parties of the 'Left' feel outraged by its triumph. But only a small minority would have urged that Britain should actively intervene, and in fact the division is so deep and balanced that no coherent action was at any time possible. We can only claim that we have passed through these hideous episodes with clean hands; have aided both sides by works of mercy; and have faithfully fulfilled our declarations both in the letter and the spirit. It is the violent intrusion of the German and Italian Governments, in utter scorn of every vestige of international faith and honour, which leaves a lasting sense of being wronged and cheated.

But let us look ahead across the closing agonies and horrors to the scene which awaits General Franco, and indeed all Europe, on the morrow of his victory. By foreign aid, and mainly by foreign aid, he will be the victor. His vanquished fellow-countrymen will lie prostrate beneath his feet. Between the two Spains there flows a river of blood both deep and wide. Its rills and rivulets run through every province, almost through every village in the stony devastated peninsula. Most of it is not clean blood shed in fair fight. Murders and executions by the tens of thousands have left their curse and vendetta behind. A long period of iron repression and aching poverty is all that lies before the Spanish people in their desolate homes. Only a very great statesman, uplifted above the passions of the hour and armed with august and independent authority, could rebuild under these conditions. Does General Franco possess these advantages?

It may be true that the blackest atrocities, such as the bombing of Guernica and Barcelona, with their wholesale indiscriminate butchery of women and children, were the work of his allies. The Germans in particular have been anxious to experiment with air power and find out with professional curiosity which kind of bombs are technically the best adapted to the destruction of great cities or the torture of civilian populations. Such allies are not easily controllable. Still, upon Franco's shoulders rests the formal responsibility. But has he independent authority? It is no doubt true that a complete victory by the Spanish Government would have been followed by a second savage internal struggle between the moderate elements in their ranks and the Communists and Anarchists, and thereafter further strife between the Communists and Anarchists themselves. But Franco, too, lives upon forces profoundly divided. Self-preservation has united them. Victory will expose their suspended animosities. Between the Phalangists and the Requetes and other representatives of Old Spain burns a fierce rivalry and a complete diversity of outlook. This is the schism which will dominate the new phase. Here again the struggle for power among the victors might safely be left to work itself out if it were confined only to Spaniards.

But what part are the foreign intruders going to play? Granted sufficient time, one might trust to a general rally by Spaniards of all sections—conquerors and beaten alike—against them. A passion of xenophobia might unite all parties and both sides upon the cry of 'Spain for the Spaniards.' But this would take time to develop, and many things will happen meanwhile. Will the Italians go? Certainly they are already unpopular with those they are helping. Signor Mussolini is prodigal of his assurances to the British Government that he will withdraw his forces, and that Italy has no designs upon the territorial, economic or political life of Spain. It may be that the Anglo-Italian negotiations may bear this fruit.

But what of the Germans? They have not fought in the field, but their highly competent technical assistance has permeated every part of the Nationalist system and administration. They possess a very powerful and efficient air force in Spain. Their airfields lie within easy striking distance of the munition establishments of Southern France. At any moment they can treat the great city of Toulouse as they have treated Barcelona. They will be directed from Berlin in accordance with the general plan of Nazi expansion, and, of course, in relation to any approaching war. It would be natural for them to seek to impose upon General Franco and the forces of which he disposes the Nazi system and characteristics, and in this the Phalangists will be their instruments.

Even if Franco desired a more merciful and more gentle course and a system Spanish in its character, these formidable efficient interlopers stimulating and guiding the Phalangist movement may well be too strong for him. A thoroughly Nazified Spain, retaining its German nucleus, would be a cause of profound anxiety both to France and Britain. At any rate, it appears to be a matter upon which they should exert themselves, if indeed the faculty of action still resides among them.

THE NEW FRENCH GOVERNMENT
APRIL 14, 1938

If France broke, everything would break, and the Nazi domination of Europe, and potentially of a large part of the world, would seem to be inevitable. It is therefore with keen and somewhat strained attention that all countries—especially friendly countries, great and small—have watched the prolonged deadlock in French Parliamentary affairs. One stop-gap Government has succeeded another. The many interesting personalities involved, the intricate warfare of the various groups and parties, the vivid, indeed hectic, collective life of the Chamber, provide all the elements of a most thrilling political game—if only this were the time to play one. The Deputies and the Chamber have, as anyone can see, a very jolly time. They are perpetually making and unmaking Governments. Thirty or forty distinguished and astonishingly able men take it in turns to be Prime Minister, Foreign Secretary, Finance Minister, etc. They have a much more amusing time than their opposite numbers in Great Britain or the United States.

In both these English-speaking democracies when a man's in, he's in; and when he's out, he's out for a good long time. But the accomplished players at the French musical chairs monopolise with their own fads and prejudices, their own airs and graces, their own personal egotisms or partyisms, an altogether undue part of the life of France, and thus of the life of the free democracies. What splendid attitudes they are able to take—and how often! How they strut and pose! Here is a good man capable of giving the necessary directions, but if he moves one inch this way he loses the Left, or one inch that way he loses the Right. Shuffle the cards again; shake the kaleidoscope; bring forth another highly competent personage and let him have a chance! Ministers of State pass through their departments like week-end guests at Le Touquet. The experienced hard-bitten Chef de Cabinet has hardly time to make their acquaintance, offer the usual compliments and good wishes to a new Minister taking office, before the highly competent visitor has departed and another equally able successor is knocking at the door.

In England we only have a Cabinet crisis once in a blue moon, and when it happens it is both serious and exciting. Its consequences last for years. But in Paris Cabinet-making is a perpetual sport. The question which has now arisen is whether this kind of sport is one which the French people 'risen against tyrants' can afford to enjoy so frequently. After all one can have too much of a good thing. A joke is a joke; but it palls with repetition. I have for a generation taken the view that British fortunes are linked in many vital matters with those of France. For the first time since the war I have seen a real advance in British public opinion and in the declarations of his Majesty's Government towards a close, rigorous defensive alliance with the French Republic. No Englishman would presume to have a preference about the particular Ministers or the party groupings upon which any French Government depends. But Mr. Chamberlain said the other day that we would fight in defence of France and Belgium. Therefore we naturally feel that we should like to know who are the men with whom we are to deal and whether they are likely to stay for any length of time in their present jobs. It seems to me that this is a reasonable request.

I wonder whether the French people realise how bitter and persistent is the pro-German propaganda in this island? The strongest point, repeatedly made, is that France is on the verge of collapse. She is portrayed as about to go down the same bloody sewer as Spain has done. All the 'Heil Hitler' brigade in London society exploit and gloat over what they are pleased to call 'the Parliamentary impotence of the French democracy.' Thus the amusing game in which French politicians rejoice is turned in deadly fashion to their detriment—and to our common danger. There surely ought to be an effort to put this right.

It is upon this footing that we come to the events of the hour. They are important. A very capable and sincere man has been chosen in M. Daladier. He has for nearly two years been identified with the French army and the defence of France. He cannot command the pledged allegiance of either the Right or the Left; but he has formed a small Inner Cabinet which has been welcomed by the almost unanimous vote of the buzzing Chamber; and he asks for power to give them a brief holiday while he and this small group govern the country. The French finances are in great disorder. There is a nasty row about money. The urban working-class, in acute and natural distress about the massacre of the Spanish Republic through Nazi and Fascist intervention, and otherwise angered by the rise in prices, has yielded itself to an epidemic of strikes. On Tuesday 150,000 men were said to have ceased work. Some sulked in their homes; others occupied the factories. The production of munitions, especially aeroplane engines, the most tardy and necessary of all, was for the moment arrested.

The well-meant 40-hours week has produced an inefficiency and slowing-down in painful contrast with the vast iron-driven German munitions supply. Competition in such circumstances would be too unequal. The awful sentence may be pronounced: 'Thou art weighed in the balance and found wanting.' Unless Nazi rule is to spread throughout Europe, these superficial yet vicious and morbid disharmonies must be brought to a speedy end. The agreement now reached is doubly welcome. Those who know France well, or have long worked with French statesmen and generals, realise the immense latent strength of France. They see what is not apparent to the casual observer. They see the French army always on the watch. Part of it mans the ramparts round the country. The rest constitutes the most perfectly trained and faithful mobile force in Europe. The French army means to France what the Monarchy means to Britain. It is above all parties. It serves all parties. It is cherished by all parties. Never interfering in politics, though by no means unobservant of them, the officers and men of the French army discharge their professional duties and keep their vigil upon the frontiers of the land. Behind them lies the solid peasantry of millions of families rooted in the soil they own. Behind them stands this agitated intellectualism which presents so perfectly and expresses so volubly the vital ideas. There is also the inspiration in the soul of a people who feel themselves in a marked degree, and at this particular moment with intensity, the trustees of freedom throughout Europe.

We in Britain wish all success to the Daladier Government, and we hope it will last long enough to afford a solid foundation upon which the necessary arrangements for mutual security can be made. M. Daladier has had disappointments in the formation of his Ministry. He has had to express upon a narrow front needs that deserve a much broader basis. But he has one important political force in reserve. M. Blum will not fail the cause of European freedom. His influence with the Socialist party is commanding. He will certainly give loyal aid.

BRITAIN'S DEFICIENCIES IN AIRCRAFT MANUFACTURE
APRIL 28, 1938

In the last month a very definite change has passed over British public opinion about the progress of rearmament, and particularly rearmament in the air. Until a few weeks ago, except in specially informed circles, there was an easy-going feeling that the whole process of equipping the Air Force and the Army was hurrying forward, no doubt at great expense, but also at great speed. The Government, it was felt, might have started late, but they were doing their best—no one could do better—and the power and flexibility of British industry would soon produce incomparable results. Those who had given warnings two, three and four years ago were held to be stultified because no great war had broken out in Europe, and nothing tangible had happened to the British Empire. Even those who should have known better yielded themselves to the comfortable belief that all troubles would 'blow over' abroad, and that we should very soon be in a strong position at home.

This reposeful and complacent mood has somehow or other received a sudden internal jolt. It is not easy to fix or describe precisely what has caused that jolt. There are, of course, rumours of disputes among Ministers upon the facts of Air Force expansion. All this is pure surmise, for the secrets of the Government are admirably kept at the present time. Nevertheless, the demeanour of many persons who would have an opportunity of knowing the facts has become markedly less assured. The Air Force now comprises a very large, influential and widely distributed section of the population, and the bold pretence that all is well, and that everything is proceeding 'according to plan,' is found to lack confirmation at numberless individual points. Then there are the aircraft manufacturers, a powerful and prosperous body, who cannot help being irritated by inefficiency in the Contract and Design departments of the Air Ministry. They complain that no broad layout of the British aircraft industry was made at the beginning of the expansion; that orders were given, and are given, piecemeal, in little packets; that they have never been able to prepare their works for mass production; that designs are repeatedly altered, to the delay of production, and that very often there is a gaping void between the execution of one contract and the assignment of another.

All these rivulets of opinion have flowed towards Parliament. The House of Commons, hitherto so very ready to be satisfied wherever Government action is concerned, or unwilling to credit any statement not made from the Treasury Bench, was already becoming somewhat disquieted by the ceaseless accumulation of facts and evidence even before a new light was thrown upon the scene. This new light was the decision of the Government to make, in principle, important purchases of aircraft in the United States and to set up large new aircraft factories in Canada. Such a resolve on the part of the Government is wholly admirable, and must be vigorously supported by all who wish to see the gathering dangers warded off. It of course infuriates many of the aircraft firms, and there is a natural prejudice against money going out of the country for machines which we ought to have been building quite easily in almost unlimited numbers at home.

Resentment is increased when from many quarters there are assertions that the existing capacity is not being used to the full or to the best advantage. We are told of important aircraft firms only working to two-thirds of their possible output, and of skilled workers being paid off in appreciable numbers at many places. Why, then, it is asked, should we send so many millions across the ocean when good management and strong hands could swiftly produce all that is wanted at home? There can be no doubt of the ability of British industry to produce a vast output of war aeroplanes. At the end of the Great War the Ministry of Munitions were delivering machines at the rate of 2,000 a month, or 24,000 a year. The plans for the—happily unfought—campaign of 1919 contemplated an output of nearly double this colossal total. Given an office table, an empty field, and a sufficiency of money and labour, it ought to be possible to produce a steady flow of aircraft from the eighteenth month. It is now the thirty-third month since the Baldwin Government decided to triple the Royal Air Force. Why, then, is there not this copious flow? This remains a mystery to those who had wartime experience. It is true that we are not now working under war conditions, but war conditions cut both ways. All production by the Ministry of Munitions in 1917 and 1918 was grievously, but rightly, hampered by the repeated drafts of men for the Front and the ceaseless process of dilution.

The Government, though not choosing to equip them with emergency powers, have let the Air Ministry enjoy for nearly three years unlimited money and—provided due priorities are given—a superabundant man-power. Yet at the end of the third year of expansion, already tardily begun, we are not overtaking the German monthly outputs. Indeed, if we may credit the allegations which are made more loudly every day, we are at the moment falling back not only relatively but even actually. These charges must be examined by Parliament at an early date, and it is greatly to be hoped that members will not lack the public spirit necessary to strengthen the hands of the Government in any measures, however drastic, which may be required. Certainly no party or personal considerations ought to stand in the way of what is so necessary for our own safety and for the peace of Europe.

Nothing, however, that can be done at this stage in Great Britain can obviate the need of placing the largest possible orders in the United States and Canada. Nearly two years ago I personally urged the Government by every means at my disposal to adopt this policy. It would indeed only have been prudent, when the expansion first began, to place the largest possible orders across the Atlantic. We have never been likely to get into trouble by having an extra thousand or two of up-to-date aeroplanes at our disposal. Starting as late as we did, we should at once have opened our own industry to the fullest compass and at the same time used our wealth to buy to the utmost extent abroad. As the man whose mother-in-law had died in Brazil replied, when asked how the remains should be disposed of, 'Embalm, cremate and bury. Take no risks!'

Colonel Moore-Brabazon, the Member of Parliament who enjoys the distinction of possessing the first pilot's certificate in Great Britain, has laid before us all the arguments for the creation of great factories in Canada. Here everything, including boundless plains, is available for fast independent production of the latest types of war aircraft and also for armament training. Far beyond the reach of hostile attack gigantic factories can be established from which an almost limitless supply of heavy bombers of the maximum range can be created. With the command of the seas which Great Britain will certainly hold, these could be shipped in vessels, perhaps specially constructed to carry them in fighting trim, to the air bases in the British Isles. Indeed, the range which it is now possible to give to the heavy bomber might well enable such machines upon a favouring wind at certain periods of the year to fly direct to their operating stations in Britain, or perhaps Ireland. We must regard such a policy as one of the ultimate safeguards of the British Empire. It should have been done long ago, but even now plans upon the largest scale should be put into instant operation.

The friendly co-operation of the United States, both in the making of aircraft and in the necessary association of Canadian industry, should be invoked. It will be forthcoming in generous measure in time of peace so long as the policy of Great Britain and her associates is clearly seen to be in harmony with the broad principles of Parliamentary democracy, the reign of law, and resistance to tyranny and aggression. The effect of this policy upon the free countries of Europe has already been bracing in a high degree. Everywhere it is seen that the reserves of wealth, and the possession of sea power enjoyed by the English-speaking peoples and those associated with their ideals, bring a new, a potent, indeed an omnipotent, factor into the dread scales upon which the future of historic civilisation depends.

BRITAIN AND ITALY
MAY 12, 1938

The painful emotions excited by Mr. Eden's resignation and its circumstances, must not be allowed to obscure the general issues involved in an agreement between Great Britain and Italy. The former Foreign Secretary himself was perfectly ready to negotiate with Italy. He was, in fact, conducting conversations with the Italians when he was superseded. Moreover, he had made the 'gentleman's agreement' of January 1937. This agreement, of which I was an advocate, was founded upon a mutual guarantee for the freedom of communications through the Mediterranean for both Powers. It was in this connection that Signor Mussolini drew his agreeable distinction of 'Vita' and 'Via'—*to Italy her life, to Britain her road.*

The freedom of the Suez Canal for all nations in peace and war has always been a matter of universal acceptance. The question of Italian troops in Libya, or of British battleships in the Mediterranean is not susceptible to real agreement, because nothing can prevent Italian troops returning to Libya,[1] or the British fleet in any strength required re-entering the Mediterranean in a quarrel. The question of the fortification of the Mediterranean by Italy, presumably against Great Britain, was more serious, and has not proved itself capable of any satisfactory settlement. But the 'gentleman's agreement' *was intended to place these issues upon an easy and amicable footing.* It was hoped that an 'atmosphere' of goodwill would be created, which might lead to a closer association of the two nations so long united by ties and traditions of friendship.

The reason why this result was not achieved was certainly not the fault of Great Britain or of its Foreign Secretary. It was solely due to the violent manner in which Signor Mussolini 'non-intervened' in Spain. When whole army corps of foreign regular troops participated, contrary to solemn promises, in a civil war, and when submarines sank large numbers of vessels under the British flag, leaving the crews to their fate, a certain amount of unpleasantness—to put it mildly—was bound to arise, and the friendly atmosphere which it was hoped would be evoked was inevitably vitiated. Nevertheless, Great Britain and Italy have so many common interests that even these acts of ill-usage and bad faith were not held by the Foreign Office or by Mr. Eden to be a bar to a renewed effort to come to terms. Many people think that a better agreement could have been obtained by a stiffer attitude on the part of Great Britain. But upon the desirability, and even the need of coming to an agreement, there is a preponderant consensus of opinion.

Mr. Chamberlain's agreement itself, it must be admitted, represents the unstinted triumph of the Italian Dictator. Although at the head of a country incomparably weaker

---

[1] They have now returned in larger numbers.

than Britain and the British Empire, he has gained from us every point in dispute. He has fortified the Mediterranean against us. We have cordially accepted this position, and have even promised not to fortify Cyprus, Haifa, or other precious strategic points without what is called 'notification.' This means that we shall not be allowed to do it unless we are prepared to face a complete breakdown of the present understanding. Secondly, he continues to beat down the remains of the Spanish Republic by Italian divisions, fighting in Spain. We have dropped our opposition to such proceedings. His army will remain in Spain until General Franco's victory is complete. When 'all is over bar the shooting' he will withdraw his troops. We shall then clasp his hand and recognise that he has conquered Abyssinia.

We are told we are only recognising the accomplished fact. But this is a very doubtful matter. No one can tell what the situation in Abyssinia will be by the time the Spanish Civil War is over. We are, however, to recognise this conquest, and to draw the French into recognising it as well. When we look back upon the action this country has taken about Abyssinia in leading the League of Nations into a combination, which might have cost Signor Mussolini not only his office but his life, we must think of his own memories as well as our own. Italy successfully withstood 'fifty-two nations led by one,' and this is the one which now sets its seal upon his triumph, if triumph indeed it be.

However, that situation is not the one which confronts us to-day. New events of capital importance have profoundly altered the balance and relationships of the European Powers. Every country has been affected by the Nazi seizure of Austria, and the incorporation of Vienna and all that Vienna means, within the sovereignty of the German Reich. Everyone must take count of this deep and violent change. The effect produced upon the Italian people by the seizure of Austria has been intense. Their pride has been lowered and their apprehensions raised. The Italian Ambassador in Vienna, who a few months ago was almost Viceroy of Austria, who held much the same position in the capital as the British High Commissioner in Cairo, is now replaced by a Consul-General. The Italians find themselves in the presence of the most formidable military power in Europe along a frontier which, though mountainous, extends for nearly two hundred miles. Mountains are treacherous barriers, and military history affords numberless examples of how easily they can be pierced.

But there is a second new fact. We cannot consider the policy of the Government towards Italy without at the same time giving full weight to its policy towards France, which commands almost universal assent. The Prime Minister has made the plainest declarations ever uttered of our defensive alliance with France. He has proclaimed our resolve to fight in defence of France and Belgium if they are the victims of unprovoked aggression. I have, therefore, urged that these declarations and commitments should be implemented and made as safe and effectual as possible by precise, formal technical arrangements for the combination of British and French forces, sea, air and land, should the worst come to the worst. This has now been settled.[2] Such staff arrangements in no way carry the Government or Parliament beyond the position declared by the

---

[2] Very little serious progress was made until after the seizure of Prague in 1939.

Prime Minister. Not to make them would only have been to accept an increase of our risks without any corresponding insurance. Before the Great War we had no political commitments to France, but very detailed hypothetical military arrangements. To have the most blunt commitments, but no technical arrangements, would be to make sure of the disadvantages of both worlds. We should have the certainty of being in, and the minumum chances of coming through.

The Government have, from their independent study of our affairs, very largely adopted this view. Not only are we given the most positive assurances that nothing in the Anglo-Italian agreement will allow a wedge to be driven between us and the French Republic, but our association has become even more close. Mr. Chamberlain's policy towards Italy and France must be judged as a whole. France and Britain, more closely associated than ever, are both entering into arrangements with Italy, designed if possible, and if they are kept, to make the Mediterranean an area excluded from a possible war. This leads directly to the question of the Danube basin, to the States of the 'Little Entente' and the Balkan League. Undoubtedly all these countries have heard with relief that all the Mediterranean Powers are trying to keep war out of the Mediterranean, and all of them feel a strong sense of easement and an added freedom of action as the result of the hope—and growing belief—that common interests will increasingly unite Italy with France and Britain.

No one can pretend that what is called the 'Berlin-Rome axis' has been broken, but at least we may feel that no sparks from Vesuvius or Etna will light up the forests of the North. It would be foolish to undervalue this hope at the present time. If Europe is to be stabilised and the destruction of civilisation averted, it is imperative that as many Powers as possible, all heavily armed, should be linked together in a non-war area and system. From such an association, a more practical form of collective security may develop.

JAPAN ENTANGLED*
MAY 26, 1938

Officially there is no war. The celestial regions are lapped in peace. For the last ten months, however, this peace has taken the form of the movement of very large armies, and of slaughter and devastation on a gigantic scale. But the Japanese friendship for China is, we are assured, unbroken. They tell us they long to enjoy again happy and fruitful relations with the Chinese. On no account would they willingly do them any injury, or allow ill will to grow up between ancient races who have so much in common. Nothing would induce them to annex an inch of Chinese territory. They are resolved to maintain the integrity and independence of China. All they want is to have a Chinese Government which will live with them on neighbourly terms, and not leave undone the things they like or do anything they do not like. Merely that! Such is the grimace which the Imperial Japanese Government presents to the world.

But then there has been an 'incident.' Trouble has arisen between the peace-loving Japanese and the Chinese bandits—they are Bolsheviks, of course—who seemed determined to obstruct all the Japanese plans to develop and civilise China. In order to help the Chinese set up a government which will restrain these bandits and Bolsheviks from causing 'incidents,' over 600,000 Japanese troops have felt themselves compelled to go a long way into China and do a lot of things to the Chinese. But all for their ultimate good! However, the Chinese bandits (and Bolsheviks) have turned out to be more numerous than was foreseen. Thus, the 'incident' has been protracted, and extra protection has to be offered by Japan to China against their evil behaviour.

The first great offensive of the Japanese invading armies was launched against Shanghai and Nanking. It was an unpleasant surprise that the Chinese resisted so long and that, after resisting, they escaped to fight again another day.

They are very good at this. The second main Japanese offensive has now been delivered. The struggle has proceeded 300 miles north of Shanghai on the line of the East and West railway of China around the important railway junction of Suchow (sometimes spelt Hsuchow). Along this line the Chinese had constructed a carefully prepared system of defence. It is extremely important for the Japanese to take Suchow. All that mattered to the Chinese, on the other hand, was to escape from the net, and go on fighting somewhere, somehow, in their vast country. It seems they are succeeding in this. It may be that they will learn to combine their ardent patriotism with a persistent use of guerrilla warfare, and will not attach too much importance to fixed positions or large-scale encounters; for the Chinese maxim should be to fight everywhere and be

---

*See map of China facing p. 225.

fought nowhere. It looks as if they were finding this out. If so, the position of Japan will become increasingly more embarrassed.

If a million Japanese soldiers were sent into China and you were to go and look for them six months later it would not be so easy to find them. As the lines of communication lengthen, the difficulties of an invader multiply. Every day all these Japanese soldiers have to be paid upon a scale far more expensive than when they live at home. Then there are the munitions of war, which are very costly, and pour out daily in a copious flow. It is difficult for a foreign observer to see how Japan can conquer China unless the Chinese give in. In Japan everyone counted upon their giving in. The fact that they have not done so is described in Tokyo as 'the worst disaster in our history.' Many authorities think that the Chinese have only to endure to put a strain almost blasting in its intensity upon the life-strength of Japan.

For this 'incident' in China does not stand alone. There is always the Russian Anxiety. Russian armies, aggregating nearly a million, well-equipped and largely self-contained, with their arsenals and munition plants on the spot, lie far to the north along the Siberian frontier or, more precisely, the Siberian front; for it is a front of silent war. Against this heavy impending weight Japan must set nearly half a million of her finest troops. Whether these would be sufficient to stem a sudden Russian advance no one can tell. It is, at any rate, a daring adventure for Japan to try to ward off the Russian masses with her right hand while strangling this voluminous China with the other. On the one side, a great bear growling low; on the other, an enormous jelly-fish stinging poisonously. Altogether, a nasty job for an over-strained, none-too-contented nation to tackle. Japan is sprawled in China; Russia is crouched ready to spring in the North. 'Incidentally,' to follow the Japanese mode, the Russian air force can inflict frightful damage upon Tokyo and other Japanese cities any fine night.

Here we must recognise the services which Soviet Russia is rendering in the Far East to civilisation and also to British and United States interests. Russia is holding the best army of Japan gripped upon her front. At the same time, by a wonderful motor-road from Russian Turkestan to the Chinese Western Province of Kansu, and thence on into the heart of China, a constant stream of lorries carry Russian munitions to the Chinese forces. Half a million coolies toil continuously upon this road, and some at least of the weapons of modern war are placed in the hands of those who are defending their native soil. It is certainly neither in the interests of the British Empire nor of world peace that this traffic should stop. The Western democracies should recognise the part Soviet Russia, albeit for her own purposes, is playing in the Far East.

The fighting has rolled away from Shanghai, and the immediate danger to British life and property has become less intense. The Government at Tokyo has grown more polite; and although the rough and hostile attitude of the Japanese soldiers towards British subjects and other Europeans in Shanghai has not changed, there is not the same danger of a major clash. Major-General Telfer-Smollett, whose steely composure through a score of dangerous collisions has gained the respect and, indeed, admiration of all Europeans in the Far East, must be conscious of a temporary relief. They feel more comfortable, too, for the moment in Hong Kong. It is greatly to be hoped that our Foreign Office and

Conservative members of Parliament will not overlook the source, however unpopular it may be, from which this easement comes.

On the top of their immense commitments in China the Japanese military and naval secret societies, who have displaced the Elder Statesmen, have also managed to start a naval race in battleships, etc., with Great Britain and the United States, either of which can easily outdo them. It was not a clever move for them to start their ancient and honoured country upon so vain a rivalry.

But after all the grand and cardinal event in the Far East is the revival of China. Japan has done for the Chinese people what they could, perhaps, never have done for themselves. It has unified them once more. General Chiang Kai-shek is a national hero amongst the most numerous race of mankind. He may well become a world hero, as a patriot and a leader who, amid a thousand difficulties and wants, does not despair of saving China from a base and merciless exploitation. It may thus be that from the opposite side of the earth will come that exemplary discomfiture of a brutal aggression which will cheer the democracies of the Western world and teach them to stand up for themselves while time remains.

On the 30th of May Sir Thomas Inskip, Minister for Coordination of Defence, made a speech in the House of Commons in which he indicated that the Government had plans ready which would provide for universal national service in time of war.

NATIONAL SERVICE
JUNE 9, 1938

The announcement which Sir Thomas Inskip made last week about national service in time of war ought not to have been thrown out casually to an empty House in an unimportant Debate. Such a declaration ought to have come from the Prime Minister with all formality, in words carefully chosen, and upon a great occasion. It might then have exercised a beneficial effect upon the European situation.

There is no doubt that the record of the British Empire in the Great War acts as a shield to us all in these anxious years. Whatever may be thought of the present state of our defences, it is realised on the Continent that if Great Britain should be forced to enter a war, she will fight it with her whole strength, keeping nothing back from the common cause. Foreigners remember that although we had only a small army in 1914, we had 5,000,000 soldiers overseas in 1918. They remember also that the longer the struggle lasted, and the more grievous its character became, the greater was the effort made by the British Empire, and that the will-power of our race to win was found to be inexhaustible. Thus the noble deeds and sacrifices of the generation that is gone constitute a real security alike to European peace and our present safety. When on various anniversaries we lay our wreaths at the foot of the Cenotaph or other monuments, we may cherish the thought that the heroic dead still, in a most practical sense, protect the living as they go about their daily business.

Great Britain will certainly not enter any war unless she is forced to do so for what the mass of the people judge to be her own life and honour. She will do everything in her power to prevent war, and if, in spite of all, the worst comes to the worst, we shall fight with the assent of the whole nation, for our own survival as a State and Empire, and only in strict accordance with the spirit of the Covenant of the League of Nations. We cannot contemplate being engaged in any war except one approved by the heart and conscience of the British race all over the world. If the awful event should ever occur, we may be sure there will be no half-measures. It will be victory or destruction. Once entered, we shall have no choice but that. Therefore the idea that Britain will fight only with her professional army and the patriotic Territorials who train themselves in time of peace would have evoked from the great Duke of Marlborough his famous comment, 'Silly! Silly!'

Moreover, upon the next occasion the bombing of British cities and townships will be a frequent occurrence. Our manhood will experience an irresistible incentive to fight from the fact that they will see around them women and children killed by this cowardly method. No man worthy of the name but will demand to take part in the struggle. Even in the last war, every time a few bombs were dropped in London, or some bombardment of our maritime towns took place, there was an intense reaction throughout all classes to serve. How much more potent will be these terrible stimuli in the future?

Our Government, who are upon all hands admitted to be profoundly pacific, are bound none the less to look ahead and face with steady eye the situation which would arise if all our efforts failed. In 1914, the well-to-do and so-called ruling classes were at first more convinced of the duty to fight than the wage-earning masses. It required the German atrocities in Belgium to rouse the whole people. Now it is somewhat different. The wage-earning classes are resolved not to submit to Nazism or Fascism, and there is more doubt and division in the other ranks of society. But if a Government trusted for its peace record felt bound to give the signal, which they would only do if all saw it was inevitable, the response would be practically universal, and it would run like an electric current from one end of the Empire to the other.

In the first few months of the last war more than 1,000,000 men, most of whom had never dreamed of being soldiers, came forward as volunteers. Ultimately nearly 2,000,000 actually demanded of their own free will to be sent overseas to the bloody trenches in France and Flanders. In far-off New Zealand nearly one-tenth of the entire population of the country traversed voluntarily more than half the globe in order to fight and die in a cause upon which they had never been consulted beforehand. Nothing like the voluntary effort of the British Empire was seen in any other country or has ever been paralleled in history.

Then ensued the tragical and agonising experience of vast numbers of ardent fighting men with no weapons. We witnessed the sorry spectacle of hundreds of thousands of our manhood training in the camps and marching along the roads of our island, often without even rifles in their hands, while all the cannon and shell which we made had to be sent at once to our comparatively small army at the front, which nevertheless amounted to 15 divisions by Christmas. But another evil made itself manifest. The flower of the nation volunteered. Whole regiments were formed out of men whose education and ability fitted them to be capable officers. All that was most brilliant, gifted and glorious in our country hurried to the field, and the wounded returned time and again in virtue of their original voluntary engagement. Thus a great injustice was inflicted upon the best, and moreover a ruinous, unthrifty use was made of our strength.

Eventually, when about two million homes had their fighting man at the Front, sometimes already wounded once or twice, while other sturdy millions went about their ordinary work at higher pay, there was so fierce a roar for universal compulsory service that no Government, even when backed by Lord Kitchener, could stand against it. His Majesty's present Ministers are bound not to overlook these facts imprinted indelibly in the minds of all who passed through that ordeal. It is therefore their duty to prepare a scientific, fair and equal plan which, if the nation and Parliament decide to go to war, will enable our full strength to be realised, not only at the earliest moment but throughout the struggle and in the best way. Nothing should be said to weaken the force of the statement made by the Defence Minister, because the prospect of an immense British Army cast into the scales is one of the greatest deterrents to an aggressor, and one of the surest bulwarks of peace.

The establishment of a National Register, enabling a survey to be made of all our resources in man power, has become all the more urgent after what has been said in Parliament. The whole process of voluntary recruitment for the Air Raid Precautions services is inevitably prejudiced when many a would-be volunteer has to ask himself whether it is any use preparing himself in peace-time for one task and being set to do another in war; and when men of military age who volunteer may be aspersed by the suggestion that they are installing themselves in safe jobs betimes. Having gone so far, the Government cannot stop short of a complete scheme for national service, which would come into operation on the outbreak of war if Parliament approved. Such measures would naturally have to be accompanied by legislation 'to take the profit out of war,' upon the study of which great progress has been made in the United States of America. The idea of large numbers of men being made liable to be sent abroad on military service is not compatible with others remaining at home to pile up inflated wartime profits, under conditions when free competition is largely suspended.

The principle that no man, whatever his calling, shall become richer out of war should be proclaimed, and a special financial bill should be drafted for this purpose and submitted to Parliament, if an emergency should arise, simultaneously with the national service proposals. Such a measure of social justice would be the most effective answer to those shrill voices which, in the name of the 'conscription of wealth' seek to take advantage of war to establish Communism by a short cut.

SHADOWS OVER CZECHOSLOVAKIA
JUNE 23, 1938

Although the Spanish Civil War and its surrounding complications have lately held the first place in the public mind, Czechoslovakia remains beyond all question the immediate danger-point of Europe. There is no doubt that Henlein, Hodza and President Benes are working for a settlement, and that a good settlement is possible between them on the basis of Home Rule for the Sudeten German regions within the Czechoslovakian State. Why, then, should not this be achieved? The Czechoslovakian Government owe it to France and Great Britain that nothing which reason and justice can claim should be withheld. The Sudetens have never sought annexation by Germany, except as a last and desperate resort and threat. The enthusiasm even of their leaders for incorporation in the steel framework of Prussian Nazidom has been markedly chilled by the disillusionment of the Austrian local Nazis.

It seems daily more attractive to Sudeten leaders to play a distinguished part as equal partners in a small State like Czechoslovakia than to be swallowed whole by Berlin and reduced to shapeless pulp by the close-grinding mandibles of the Gestapo. Above all, there must weigh upon both sides and all parties in Czechoslovakia the deadly thought that if in their quarrels they strike forth the flames of general war, the one consequence which can be most surely foreseen is that their land and homes, their families and possessions will be shattered and consumed in utter devastation.

Without the championship of armed Germany, Sudeten wrongs might never have been redressed. From the moment they are redressed, further interference by Germany will bring not more blessings, but only misery and ruin. Thus all paths in Czechoslovakia lead to Prague and to agreement. Such a settlement, if accepted by Germany, would be a notable contribution to peace, and might well be the herald of better days for all Europe. No one knows, however, what are the resolves and plans of the group of high personages who wield and direct the might of Germany. The persistent campaign of the German controlled Press against the Czechs is not a favourable sign. One must admire the discipline and astonishing self-restraint which has characterised the Czech authorities, military and police, and still more the Czech population, during these weeks of electioneering excitement and keenly felt danger. When one large section of the population seems to be inviting a foreign army to invade and conquer the homeland, when flags, songs, badges, white stockings, offer numberless causes of provocation, and when any hothead on either side can start a riot, it is indeed wonderful that this agitated month should have passed without any widespread outbreak of passion or violence. Evidently these people are serious-minded. Evidently they have need to be. This again is a reassuring factor.

But, of course, if it were the deliberate purpose of the German Government to bring great issues to a head, there would be no difficulty in creating incidents, capable of being represented as mortal affronts. If existing Sudeten leaders were thought too accommodating, there are many means by which they could be corrected or displaced. All depends upon the brooding figure at Berchtesgaden and the clash of his fierce lieutenants in Berlin. It is to this process of reflection that efforts for peace should be directed.

The Czechoslovakian Government have decided to keep strong forces on guard along their frontiers. Their object is no doubt to make the invasion of their country an operation which will require very large troop movements in Germany. The larger the scale of the movements the harder it is to conceal them. Thus there should be time to mobilise the whole national defence. This constitutes a very substantial deterrent upon a sudden onslaught. Pro-German propaganda in Great Britain is eager to suggest that the overrunning of Czechoslovakia, if not as easy as that of Austria, would at most be a matter of a few days. We are told how swiftly armoured divisions will rush in from every side breaking down all opposition with irresistible fury. But this is not the picture which presents itself to the experienced student of modern war. A well-conceived system of forts and concrete pill-boxes, a judicious improvement of natural obstacles, the thorough mining of roads and bridges, should, if backed by a stubborn army, bring any rapid thrust to a standstill. It would then be necessary for the invader to move up the masses of men, and assemble and supply the immense artillery, necessary for the reduction of fortified positions.

Thus, whatever else may happen, an easy walk-over transforms itself into a grave and costly operation of war. Before embarking on such a plan, an aggressive Government would have to contemplate general mobilisation, the employment of a large portion of its whole army, and at least three or four hundred thousand casualties. Even taken by itself, such an enterprise would be heart-shaking to any modern Power, especially to one just recovering from a defeat in which nearly the whole world gradually came against her. But would the issue stand by itself? Would Czechoslovakia be left to struggle week after week against an avalanche of fire and steel? There is the explicit French declaration to the contrary. There is the Russian engagement, which should not be lightly discounted. There is the statement which the Prime Minister made in the House of Commons about Czechoslovakia. No poorer service can be done to peace than to belittle these massive deterrents. We have only to recall the swift rise of temperature which occurred in British public opinion during the annexation of Austria, bloodless as it was, to imagine the effects of a fearful conflict raging day by day between the invading armies of a great Power and the heroic defenders of a small civilised State. Until, in 1914, the German armies actually broke into Belgium, not one out of twenty in the British nation but would have voted against Continental war. Forty-eight hours later it was a hundred to one the other way.

Parliament and the public have approved the circumspect and restrained position which Mr. Chamberlain and his Majesty's Government have adopted, but no one who remembers the past can doubt that circumstances and national feeling may upon occasion pass beyond the control even of the most sincerely peace-loving British Administration. It may be that some of these reflections played their part in the very definite easement of the Czechoslovakian problem which occurred a month ago. It is certain that the great mass of the German people of all classes, while deeply grateful to their Fuehrer for leading them back from the trough of defeat to the uplands of power, would regard the renewal of the late world war—for this is what it may well prove— with the utmost grief and alarm. It is well known that the German military leaders are foremost in counselling caution and delay. The honourable rehabilitation of General Von Fritsch is a proof that the influence of the German army with the Fuehrer has not been overborne by the machinations of extremists in the Nazi party and its instrument the political police.

These summer months may well be anxious; but no one has a right to despair of a good solution. A settlement and reconciliation in Czechoslovakia would be no humiliation to Herr Hitler. On the contrary, he could rightly claim that his exertions had won for the Sudeten Germans honourable status and a rightful place in the land of their birth; and that the process by which these reforms had been achieved had strengthened rather than shaken the foundations of European peace.

THE RAPE OF AUSTRIA
JULY 6, 1938

Two months ago I reminded the House of Commons that after a boa-constrictor had devoured a goat or a deer it usually slept the sleep of repletion for several months. It may, however, happen that this agreeable process is disturbed by indigestion. If the prey has not been sufficiently crushed or covered with slime beforehand, especially if it has been swallowed horns and all, very violent spasms, accompanied by writhings and contortions, retchings and gaspings, are suffered by the great snake. These purely general zoological observations, of which further details can be found in Buffon's Natural History, suggest a parallel—no doubt very remote—to what has happened since Austria was incorporated in the German Reich.

Although many of the most experienced foreign correspondents have been turned out, a continuous stream of trustworthy information continues to reach London from all parts of that unhappy country. There is, in fact, no part of Europe more naturally obnoxious to the German Nazi regime than the ancient capital of the Holy Roman Empire, round which the old-gold lustre of a thousand years' pre-eminence still lingers. Indeed, throughout the whole of the truncated Austrian State there exist all the forces and factors against which the cult of Nazism wages its unrelenting war. There are Jews in very large numbers; there are Catholics by the million; there are Monarchists faithful to a Habsburg restoration, and the numerous remains of what was once the high society of the Austro-Hungarian Empire. Lastly, there are strong Socialist and Left-wing elements in every working-class district. All these constituents of Austrian life excite, for one reason or another, the hatred and antagonism of the German Nazi party.

It is easy to ruin and persecute the Jews; to steal their private property; to drive them out of every profession and employment; to fling a Rothschild into a prison or a sponging-house; to compel Jewish ladies to scrub the pavements; and to maroon clusters of helpless refugees on islands in the Danube; and these sports continue to give satisfaction. But 300,000 Jews in Vienna present a problem of large dimensions and intractable quality to a policy of extirpation. Already it is admitted the process will take some years. Meanwhile, a very serious loss to the already straitened economic life of Vienna is incurred when a busy, ingenious, industrious community, making themselves useful in a thousand ways, is reduced to a mass of helpless, miserable folk, who nevertheless cannot quite be allowed to starve wholesale. The tale of their tribulation spreads widely through the world, and it is astonishing that the German rulers are not more concerned at the tides of abhorrence and anger which are rising ceaselessly against them throughout the heavily-arming United States.

The Austrian Catholics have for the time being made through their Cardinal a separate truce for themselves, and so far there has been no attempt to visit upon the Austrian Catholic clergy and schools the severities which prevail in Bavaria. The 'Heil Hitler' declaration of the Austrian Cardinal Innitzer is exploited in Bavarian railway stations in reproach of the more robust attitude of Cardinal Faulhaber of Munich. In short, the Austrian Catholics are deemed in Berlin too tough to be tackled at present. The oppression of the Monarchists, the gentlefolk, the supporters of the Schuschnigg regime, is implacable. It is strange that the gaining of so great a prize as Austria, so swiftly and so cheaply, should not have induced more magnanimity in the triumphant captors. Almost any other set of men would have been inclined, in an hour of unexpected triumph, to let bygones be bygones and start fair. But it is part of the policy of German Nazism to treat with exemplary rigour all persons of German race and speech who have not identified themselves with Nazi interests and ambitions. By this means it is hoped to unify through fear the Germanic populations in other countries and so prepare the ground for further adventures. It must be remembered, however, that the Austrian nobility and landowners have many affiliations with the same classes in Germany which shelter behind and within the dignified structure of the German Army.

But the strongest and the only overt resistance to the Nazification of Austria has, oddly enough, come from the very class of Austrian Nazis who were the prime cause and pretext of the invasion. The Austrian-Nazi legionaries, 30,000 strong, returned from their exile in Munich and other Bavarian cities in the highest hopes of becoming the masters of the land they had betrayed. They were welcomed by their associates who had been undermining the Austrian Republic from the inside. Both bands naturally regarded themselves as the heroes of the day, and both were infuriated when they found themselves excluded from nearly all positions of power, profit and control. At every point they were confronted by officials of the German Nazi party, who deprived them of all the longed-for sweets of office. They saw themselves the catspaws who had pulled the chestnuts out of the fire for stronger hands to seize. They broke out in loud complaint, and even renewed the sabotage with which they had embarrassed the former Schuschnigg Government. In the Post Office, on the railways, and in many factories, incidents occurred manifesting the disappointment of a faction robbed in the moment of triumph of what they thought was their own.

Here, however, the German administration was on strong ground. The Austrian Nazis are a peculiarly virulent type. They carried pillage, corruption and brutality beyond the wide limits of political discretion. They were animated by an intense desire for revenge upon their Austrian fellow-countrymen who had opposed their views. It was necessary for the German authorities to displace and control them, and Herr Buerckel, the virtual Governor of the Province, is no doubt right in declaring the bulk of them unfit for positions of trust. They remain a snarling but somewhat intimidated and thoroughly disillusioned tribe in the midst of a gloomy scene.

It remains to consider the effect of the annexation upon the unorganised mass of the Austrian wage-earners and peasants. There is no doubt that the standard of living in Austria was unduly low. Years of deflation necessary for a strictly regulated finance and the service of foreign loans had depressed the conditions of the workers in town and country. It cannot be said that they would be injured in an economic sense by being brought to the level, harsh though it be, of the German population. On the contrary, although they do not relish being exhorted to lay aside their 'easy-going ways' and put more thrust and energy into their daily toil, there might even be an appreciable improvement in basic factors.

Meanwhile, their masters proceed with high-handed authority to mete out rewards and tasks at their good pleasure. Two opposite kinds of immigration into Germany are in progress. Numerous trains carry enormous droves of Austrian wage-earners to labour under stern rule in the Old Reich. At a time when all Germans are under industrial or military conscription, the life of these deportees must tend in many ways to resemble the older forms of servitude. Far from home, under hard taskmasters, they labour to build up that martial strength, the final purposes of which Europe has yet to learn. Side by side with these unfortunates run the excursion trains of those who are chosen by favour for the 'Strength through Joy' organisation. These elect are permitted to gape in awe-struck admiration at the spectacle of Nazi power. Thus, by every device from the stick to the carrot, the emaciated Austrian donkey is made to pull the Nazi barrow up an ever-steepening hill.

THOUGHTS ON THE ROYAL VISIT
JULY 26, 1938

The famous Royal visit to Paris is over, and surely it must be very rare for official ceremonies to give so much real pleasure and joy to all who share in them. The King, with his fresh youthful personality and frank manly regard; the Queen with her magnetic charm and 'world's sweetheart' smile, captivated Paris, and through Paris, France. The Royal couple, married for love, ascending the Throne with diffidence when called by duty, presented in their visit to the French Republic that spectacle of happy family life so dear to the French heart, so precious to the life of France. The singular quality of the welcome and the hospitality they received lifted the whole episode out of the sphere of parades and protocols, of formal pageantry and etiquette. We saw again in France that 'unbought grace of life, the cheap defence of nations' which Burke had deemed the treasure of a vanished age. New bridges spanned the gulfs which have opened in the centuries, and the history of France and its traditions marched forward in unbroken procession into the modern world.

Although the flash of arms and the roar of warlike engines played their part, these were not the dominant or characteristic features. Other great countries can rival—though not yet surpass—the sombre magnificence of such displays. But the entertainment offered to the British Sovereigns had a charm and elegance, a quality of gentle peace and culture, of art and poetry, of music and dance, which only French genius can command. The scenes at Bagatelle, at the Opéra, in the chapel of Versailles, at the Bosquet d'Apollon, might well have been devised to show how much there is in human life above and beyond the blare of trumpets or the webs of diplomacy. It was as if a clear voice were calling upon the peoples of Europe to turn their thoughts from harsh ambition, iron regimentation, bitter creeds and hatreds, to all the joy and fun and splendour to be gained without pain or crime. Poor indeed must be the heart which could not delight in this day-dream amid the mellow sunshine of freedom and of France. How fair the world could be, how bountiful the gifts of Nature, how bright the inheritance of man, if only the great States and Governments of Europe would take unitedly a few resolute and simple steps together!

The days are gone by when Sovereigns, rulers and Ministers could by themselves decree the friendships of nations. All such celebrations, however imposing, however well staged, are vain unless they have with them the people's hearts. It is in cottage homes and workmen's dwellings that treaties of union and comradeship must nowadays be unrolled. Expert draughtsmen may prepare them, the Heads of States may write their names upon them, but, to be valid, such instruments must be witnessed and countersigned by hands rough with toil in forge and field. It is this sense of solemn social contract, upborne by the will of scores of millions, acclaimed by every class and creed, and by every political philosophy in a free and tolerant civilisation, that invests the association of the British and French peoples with its world significance, and also in no small degree with its formidable strength. There glinted no kindlier welcome to the Sovereigns of the venerable British Monarchy than in the eyes of the poorest citizens of the French Republic. The multitudes who thronged the streets of Paris laid aside, be it only for a spell, the divisions of faction and of doctrine which loom so large to ignorant, uncomprehending, foreign minds; and we saw again the vision of the 'union sacrée' which binds all Frenchmen together in a bond stronger than terror or death.

I walked about among the troops. Every race prides itself upon its military manhood, but there is something in the French soldier which is unique. He is the product of a hundred years of political and religious liberty, and of his ownership of the soil he tills. These potent forces have liberated his intelligence and moulded his character. A strong personality is evident in his face—the lineaments are grim and hard, the jaw closes like a steel trap. Yet withal there is an indefinable expression of gaiety and humour. Freedom and the Land, these have been his teachers, and it has taken them a century to produce this type.

This is, of course, a period of serious preoccupation for the French and British democracies. They have nothing to gain by war and almost everything to lose. The idea of war for ambition, for aggrandisement, is odious to them. Nor would they in their present mood refuse to cede to right and justice what they will deny to violence. It is wonderful to observe the calm of a people where the nation is the army, where the people own the Government, who have been pledged openly by their leaders to enter upon the most terrible of ordeals if certain events, over which they can have no control, should take place in countries far removed from their own frontiers, and with whose peoples they have no contact but that of a common cause. There is no high explosive so powerful as the soul of a free people.

The visit of King George VI and Queen Elizabeth, with the overwhelming assent of the Parliaments and peoples of the British Empire, must be regarded as a new and additional security against the sudden onset of catastrophe. It has strengthened and emphasised the deep accord which unites the Governments and masses of France and Britain. It has enabled France to see herself once again in her true greatness. It has enabled the Ministers of both countries to make sure that the unity between the Western democracies will not be used to obstruct the necessary settlement which must be reached between the various races in Czechoslovakia. The Czech Government owe it to the Western Powers that every concession compatible with the sovereignty and integrity of their State shall be made, and made promptly. Just as we demand that Germany shall not stir up strife beyond her borders, so we must make sure that the clear definitions of our attitude which have become visible shall be no encouragement to obduracy on the part of a small State whose existence depends upon the conscience and the exertions of others.

Having myself heard at first hand the case for both sides in Czechoslovakia, I am sure that all the essential elements of a good and lasting settlement are present, unless it is wrecked by obstinacy on the one hand, or mischievous fomentations upon the other.

Goodwill and fair dealing, reciprocal concessions and forbearance, should achieve a result by which no great Power will be rebuffed or endangered. The scene is not, however, free from disquieting signs. Those who are best informed are not those who are the least anxious. It may be taken as certain that a military onslaught by Germany upon Czechoslovakia would lead, by stages which cannot be foretold, to the outbreak of a general war ultimately involving the greater part of the world, and leading certainly to the ruin for many years of its wealth and civilisation. The assurances lately received from Herr Hitler must be welcomed in a sincere spirit, and must be matched by renewed efforts on the part of the British and French Governments to secure a just and fair solution. As long as troops do not march, or cannon fire, patience and perseverance on all sides will surely in the end be crowned with success. But, meanwhile, there can be no greater security for peace than the broad solidarity of ideals and common safety which the Royal visit to Paris has proclaimed to exist between the parliamentary democracies of Western Europe.

THE UNITED STATES AND EUROPE
AUGUST 4, 1938

How heavily do the destinies of this generation hang upon the Government and people of the United States! From many lands in Europe and in Asia eyes are turned towards this large, strong English-speaking community, which lies doubly shielded by its oceans, and yet is responsive to the surge of world causes. Will the United States throw their weight into the scales of peace and law and freedom while time remains, or will they remain spectators until the disaster has occurred; and then, with infinite cost and labour, build up what need not have been cast down? This is the riddle of a Sphinx who under the mask of loquacity, affability, sentimentality, hard business, machine-made politics, wrong-feeling, right-feeling, vigour and weakness, efficiency and muddle, still preserves the power to pronounce a solemn and formidable word.

In what position, physical, moral or psychological, do the United States stand to-day? The fierce struggle which is proceeding between the anti-capitalist or anti-rich-men forces of that vast country on the one side, and the anxieties of its practical economic well-being on the other, has reached a kind of equipoise. It is good politics to hunt the millionaires, to break up the monopolies, to tax and discipline the vested interests. But these have great powers of resistance. They fight, they will keep on fighting; and until the quarrel is settled, prosperity stands a-tiptoe outside the door. Yet there never was a time when it was more important to the whole world for the United States to be prosperous as well as militarily strong. The European democracies have a real advantage over the Dictator States in wealth, credit and sea-borne trade; but their strength and energy at any given moment are intimately related to the prosperity or adversity of the United States.

When things are going well in America, the more solid pedestrian forces in the free countries of Europe are conscious of a new draught of strength. When things go ill, they are weakened through a hundred channels in those very elements of strength which ought to reward law-respecting, peace-interested, civilised States. Economic and financial disorder in the United States not only depresses all sister countries, but weakens them in those very forces which might either mitigate the hatreds of races or provide the means to resist tyranny. The first service which the United States can render to world causes is to be prosperous and well-armed.

The arming part is being achieved on a very large scale. Enormous supplies have been voted by Congress for the expansion of the armed forces, particularly the Navy, to levels far above what any immediate direct danger would seem to require. No American party resists the President's desire to make the United States one of the most heavily armed, scientifically prepared countries in the world. Pacifism and the cult of defencelessness have been discarded by all parties. There never was in peace a time when the American armaments by land, air and sea, reached so imposing a height, or were sustained by so much national conviction.

But the economic and financial strength which would impart itself so readily to like-minded countries across the oceans is still far from its natural level. The warfare between big business and the Administration continues at a grievous pitch. These great forces do not seem to realise how much they are dependent upon one another. The President continues blithely now to disturb, now to console, business and high finance. He blows hot, he blows cold, and confidence does not return. Immense use is made of the national borrowing power for relieving unemployment which would largely cure itself, if even for a single year the normal conditions of confidence were restored. Party politics invade every aspect of economic life. When one measures the prodigious sums which are being expended on various forms of relief, pump-priming and New Deal ideology, it is possible to visualise the innumerable official and semi-official classes or hierarchies inevitably called into being in the process, who will henceforward cherish a vested interest of their own.

The attempt to organise and administer a nation-wide scheme of unemployment relief without the essential mechanism of Labour Exchanges must have produced fraud, waste and imposture. The noble effort which the President has made towards a higher form of social justice requires to be corrected and consolidated by well-admimstered services running under strict conditions during several years of quiet perseverance. If, instead, there is to be another surge of electioneering at the expense of the national assets, then the stabilising part which the United States might play in the world will be crippled. The authority and prestige which spring from the great armament of a free people will be undermined by financial and political disorder. But we must hope that other counsels will prevail.

As a contribution to trade revival, and as an expression of the goodwill prevailing in the English-speaking world, the British-American Trade Agreement is of real importance. There is every prospect of a good arrangement being reached in the near future. The debt question, on the other hand, has encountered a new complication. The isolation forces in the United States are not favourable to a settlement which would free Great Britain from the ban imposed upon foreign loans to defaulting countries by the Johnson Act. These forces would naturally press for the most rigorous terms, and make it difficult for a reasonable compromise to be reached. The stirring of this question at this juncture, and when Congressional Elections are already looming, would not be helpful. Nevertheless there is an earnest desire in Great Britain for a fair and friendly agreement.

In the meanwhile, the movement of American opinion upon world affairs is remarkable. Side by side with the loudest reiterations of 'Never again will we be drawn in,' there is a ceaselessly growing interest in the great issues which are at stake both in Europe and the Far East. There never was a peace-time when the newspapers of the United States carried more foreign news to their readers, or when those readers showed themselves more anxious to be informed about affairs taking place thousands of miles away, or more inclined to develop strong intellectual and moral convictions about them.

There are literally scores of millions of men and women in the United States who feel as much opposed to the tyrannies of Totalitarian Governments, Communist or Nazi, as their grandfathers were to the continuance of slavery.

The feeling, not against Germany, but against the Nazi regime, is more pronounced and outspoken throughout the United States than in Great Britain. It is far more active and widespread than it was before 1914. This mood is not at all discouraged by the Administration. The speeches of important Ministers express, in ardent terms, all the feelings of British, French and Scandinavian liberal democracies. The American ex-Servicemen confront the Nazi movement with a stern, unrelenting hostility. German espionage in America rivets public attention. The New Yorkers have to be restrained from mobbing German ships. Hardly a week passes without some incident arising in politics or sport which affords the five-hundred-headed newspaper Press an opportunity of writing against Nazism the kind of things their readers want to read. Evidently, behind all this process, a sombre antagonism to tyranny and aggression in all their various forms is steadily growing. The attitude of American ambassadors and their staffs in many capitals is strongly bent towards the maintenance of the democratic deal, while at the same time in no way committing the United States to active intervention.

All these facts should be noted by those whom they concern. It would be foolish of the European democracies, in their military arrangements, to count on any direct aid from the United States. It would be still more foolish for war-making forces in the Dictator Governments of Europe to ignore or treat with contempt this slow but ceaseless marshalling of United States opinion around the standards of freedom and tolerance. The more weightily the personality of the United States is accounted in Europe in these years, perhaps even in these months, the better are our chances of escaping another lurch into the pit.

GERMAN MANŒUVRES
AUGUST 18, 1938

Opinion is divided upon the important question whether recent military developments in Germany are merely interesting exercises and tests of their new army machine, or whether they have some more serious purpose. When it is stated that Germany will have before the end of the month 1,500,000 soldiers under arms, that they have retained all serving conscripts with the colours for an indefinite period, that they have called up one, two, or perhaps three classes of reserves, it is pointed out that other countries have from time to time exercised portions of their reserves in peace manœuvres, and it is only natural that the German leaders should make a similar experiment, no doubt on a somewhat larger scale. When it is mentioned that all farm horses and all serviceable motor-lorries are being requisitioned for the artillery and transport from August 15, that all officials must be back at their posts from leave by the same date, and that no men under 65 may leave the country, it is explained that this is only an example of German thoroughness designed to lend an air of reality to the mimic warfare which will be proceeding in the various commands for an unspecified time to come.

When we learned that the regions in which the largest concentrations for manœuvre purposes were being made were on the Rhine front and the approaches to Czechoslovakia, it was suggested that it was no more than reasonable that the new German army should be acquainted with these areas of particular strategic interest. If the German public shows signs of nervousness and alarm, we must remember that under the Totalitarian System they are only told what is thought fit by their rulers, and are consequently an easy prey to rumour. If the Berlin Stock Exchange has experienced a severe fall, that is, no doubt, because the Jews are selling their securities out of spite. The sharp rise in the price of gold in the world market and the heaviness of Wall Street are simply another case of 'the jitters.'

Some months ago a decree of universal conscription for all purposes was made in Germany, and the Government assumed the power to take any men from any work and employ them as they please for as long as they like. This enormous measure attracted too little attention. When scores, and even hundreds, of thousands, of workmen were suddenly called from their civil occupations, and building schemes and public works were brought to a standstill, this was, of course, simply the fulfilment of the same decree. When these great masses of workmen and labourers were reported to have reinforced the large numbers already working upon the German fortifications opposite France, powerful British newspapers explained that this was purely defensive, and therefore, in essence, a pacific action wrung from the Nazi leaders of Germany by the fear lest they should be assaulted by the wicked Democracies on their western border.

A policy of feverish emergency-fortification on practically all frontiers against such a danger would naturally carry with it the need for extreme privacy, and hence the closing of wide zones of country to tourists, especially those who might hold military rank. Should anyone remark that a man wishing to commit a crime in his back garden might well begin by taking the precaution of locking his front gate, he would at once be answered that the well-known peaceful sentiments of the Nazi leaders, their respect for treaties and public law, their aversion from anything in the nature of violence or bloodshed, and their often-repeated desire to establish friendly relations with Great Britain, make any such comment entirely inappropriate. If any proof, we are told, were needed of the absence of all sinister motives on the part of the German Nazis, it would be found in the open manner in which all this immense peace-time mobilisation has been and is being conducted.

I have tried to set forth clearly the views of the optimists, and we must all fervently hope and pray that they are right. It is quite certain that if they are right, and if this vast and immensely costly embodiment of German armed strength should pass off in a perfectly peaceful, good-humoured manner, and if in a few months everything settles down again happily, there will be a universal sensation of relief and of renewed confidence. On the other hand, if the optimists were proved wrong, then it might be that the Governments and countries who had shared their views would find themselves at an enormous disadvantage in the opening stages of a world war. A great responsibility, therefore, rests on anyone who, through mental inertia, August holiday mood, or refusal to confront facts with a steady eye, misleads the mass of ordinary quiet and friendly people. It would be only common prudence for other countries besides Germany to have these same kind of manœuvres at the same time and to place their precautionary forces in such a position that, should the optimists be wrong, they would not be completely ruined. Indeed, any failure to take counter-measures in good time would only be an encouragement to evil ambitions, if, indeed, one can conceive such things being possible.

The British Government have sent Lord Runciman to Prague with a sincere desire to find the way to a fair and friendly settlement of the Sudeten-German problem. Those who know him are sure that he would feel in honour bound to state the truth and not to deny justice to either party. Assuming that his mission runs its normal course, we shall presently have a practical working compromise which will give the Sudeten-German a free and equal chance with other races inside a more broadly based Czechoslovak Republic. Such a plan might be the rallying ground of all the good forces which sustain the cause of world peace. There are many occasions when an outsider can help far better than those embroiled in controversy.

But, after all, the immediate fortunes of the world lie in the hands of Herr Hitler. He entertains Sir Ian Hamilton in his mountain retreat. Apparently there, according to the General's account, it is all birds' nests and goodwill. The idea, says the General, of war being planned in such surroundings is absurd. He may be right, and, if so, this period of increasing strain drawing to its climax will be succeeded by a far more solidly founded peace than we have at this moment.

There is only one further point which it is useful to make at the present time. No one can foresee the effects produced on himself and his fellows by the spectacle of bloody lethal violence. If a score of people are sitting round a conference table in strenuous argument, and one of them draws a pistol and shoots two or three of his opponents, the whole temper of the conference is altered, and it becomes very difficult to recall its members to the other points upon the agenda. Three days before Britain entered the Great War, four members out of five in the Cabinet and nine out of ten in the House of Commons would have been found inveterately opposed to our intervention upon the Continent. Four days later these proportions were reversed.

It was not argument or reflection that produced this change of view. People simply would not believe that Germany would really attack France and Belgium. But when the German vanguards broke into Luxemburg and began to hack their way through Belgium, when guns fired and men were slaughtered, everyone knew instinctively where they stood and what we ought to do. An episode like the trampling-down of Czechoslovakia by an overwhelming force would change the whole current of human ideas and would eventually draw upon the aggressor a wrath which would in the end involve all the greatest nations of the world.

IS AIR-POWER DECISIVE?
SEPTEMBER 1, 1938

The prime factor of uncertainty in the world to-day is the menace from the air. Nothing has bred fear and distrust among the nations or encouraged predatory ambitions so much as this new means of sudden assault, not only upon fighting men, but upon their women and children far behind the lines. It is, therefore, of capital importance to measure, if that be possible, the part which air-power would play in a modern war. At the same time the obscurities of the questions make all judgments little better than guesses. It may, however, be said with some assurance that the whole course of the war in Spain has seemed to show the limitations rather than the strength of the air weapon. The extravagant claims of a certain school of air experts have not been fulfilled.

Take, first, the case of warships. We were assured some time ago that navies were obsolete and that great battleships, costing seven or eight million pounds, would be easily destroyed by aeroplanes costing only a few thousands. I asked in the House of Commons eighteen months ago why it was that no Spanish warships on either side had been sunk by aircraft. The Spanish fleets are not well equipped with anti-aircraft artillery. Their vessels have no special armour against overhead attack. Yet we see them cruising about the coast, often in full view from the shore, apparently as free from danger as if aeroplanes had never been invented. Thus, two years have passed. All the time, each side in the Spanish war has possessed hundreds of aeroplanes of comparatively modern types, manned not only by a few ardent Spaniards, but in the main by pilots from Italy, Germany and Russia. Very often it would only take a quarter-of-an-hour's flying from the shore aerodrome to reach these ships. Not only have they not been destroyed, but apparently it is not thought worth while even to try. The sinking of the National cruiser Canarias would be a tremendous stroke for the Spanish Republicans. Why are they not able to do it? Similarly, the Republican destroyers would appear an easy target for the airmen of Italy and Germany, but nothing happens.

At the time of the Abyssinian tension in the Mediterranean we were warned by tales of how easy it would be for Mussolini's air force to blow the British fleet out of the water. Since then an enormous work of anti-aircraft defence, both active and passive, has been done upon the ships of the British Navy. It now looks as if the original danger was much exaggerated. Whatever it was three years ago, it is certainly much less to-day, when our ships have received such immense and formidable protection. I, therefore, continue to adhere to the opinion I have frequently expressed that aircraft will not be a mortal danger to properly-equipped modern war fleets, whether at sea or lying in harbour under the protection of their own very powerful anti-aircraft batteries reinforced by those on shore.

The attack on undefended merchant ships is more threatening, but even in this sphere, where the brave airmen run no risk and can come down as low as they like with impunity and even stop to machine-gun the escaping crews, it is said that in 500 attacks, only ten ships have been actually sunk. The arming of all merchant ships with anti-aircraft artillery and the institution of convoys under properly-equipped escorting vessels should reduce this new danger to manageable dimensions. It would seem to follow, therefore, that all the implications of sea power based upon the possession of a superior line of battleships still retain their validity. If this be true, and it is the view both of the British and American naval authorities, the command of the seas would appear to rest unchallenged with either of the navies of Britain or the United States. This, added to the undoubted obsolescence of the submarine as a decisive war weapon, should give a feeling of confidence and security, so far as the seas and oceans are concerned, to the Western democracies.

On land, the operations of the Spanish armies do not seem to have been decisively affected by the air weapon. The Republicans, being at a great inferiority in the air, have had to endure, often without any means of retaliation, very heavy and disproportionate air attack. This inequality has not quelled their spirit; on the contrary, all accounts declare that they are fighting more stubbornly than at the beginning of the war. But the most striking example of the limitations of the air arises from the operations across the Ebro. Here, for five weeks, 50,000 Republican troops have been fighting continuously on the south bank of that river, supplied from day to day by a number of bridges, all of which are plainly visible from the air and which are not defended by any very large number of anti-aircraft guns.

Why, we must ask, have these bridges not been destroyed by air bombing? Certainly, if this had been accomplished, the defeat and destruction of the Republican army would have followed immediately. There was, therefore, the highest incentive to General Franco and his German and Italian pilots to break down these bridges. He certainly possessed several hundred aircraft of modern types which could operate from aerodromes close at hand, returning, perhaps, every half hour to fetch a new consignment of bombs. In this case, they have tried, but we must still ask, why have they not succeeded? Inability to aim accurately and the unwillingness of alien pilots to come down low, even in the face of feeble fire, appear to be the only explanations.

We now come to the effects of air-bombing and machine-gunning on troops in trenches. The moral effect is, no doubt, very great, especially when the air attack is so one-sided. But everything goes to show that an air attack on trench lines and fortified points is far less effective than bombardment by artillery. Indeed, I have heard it said by soldiers of experience that the concentrated bombardment of two or three batteries of field-cannon would be far worse to bear than that of 100 aeroplanes. Certainly, in the advance against the Basque country it was not the aeroplanes but the powerful foreign batteries which cleared the way for General Franco's advance. It would seem, therefore, that so far as the fighting troops are concerned, aircraft are an additional complication rather than a decisive weapon. It is believed that these opinions are shared by the leading soldiers of France and of Germany. If they are right, the main basic conditions under which armies fight will, like those of navies, not be found to have undergone any revolutionary change. But, of course, the Spanish struggle may be peculiar and the conditions there no true guide.

There remains the air attack upon the civil population and upon the factories producing munitions and upon the economic springs of the country. It appears that in Spain very little accurate bombing has been achieved of particular small targets, especially when these had any kind of defence. As to the psychological effects upon the civil populations of Madrid, Barcelona and Valencia, these have been exactly the opposite of what the German and Italian air bombers expected. So far from producing panic and a wish to surrender, they have aroused a spirit of furious and unyielding resistance among all classes. They have united whole communities, otherwise deeply sundered, in a common hatred of such base and barbarous methods. I, therefore, remain convinced that where the strength of the air forces is equal, the side which consumes its energy upon slaughter of the civil population is likely to encounter surprising disappointments.

All these considerations might be vitiated by very much larger numbers of aircraft operating against much larger targets. I must, therefore, add, to avoid misunderstanding, that none of the conclusions which I have tried to draw from the Spanish civil war in the slightest degree diminishes the need for Great Britain, with her special dangers and vulnerabilities, to acquire at the earliest possible moment an air force at least equal to that of any Power within striking distance of her shores.

THE EUROPEAN CRISIS
SEPTEMBER 15, 1938

Fear, not unmanly fear, but none the less wearing, broods over Europe in these fateful days. The anxiety should not be so much about what Hitler has said, but about what he may do. His speech of menace must be judged in relation to what is actually in movement. It closes no door on evil. It marks time while preparations are being completed. The dominant facts are military.

Germany is very largely mobilised. The Fleet is mobilised; the Air Force is ready, and two-thirds of the army are on a war footing. The economic and industrial organisation of the country and its general life approximate to conditions of war. The chiefs of the Nazi regime have made these enormous demands upon their country, and nothing like it has happened before in time of peace. It seems impossible that these extreme conditions could remain in their present tension for very long. The armies must act, or they must disperse. Winter is approaching, and after the middle of October the weather may become severe. Therefore, it seems that the limit of time when these great forces are either launched in war, or sent to their homes, is very short. If they are dispersed without some clear triumph, the Nazi regime, already the object of much criticism in Germany, will have sustained a rebuff which may affect its future life.

Many credible witnesses declare that a programme is being executed step by step. Certainly the troop movements which carried great forces from Central Germany to the Rhine frontier, and have produced very heavy concentrations all round Czechoslovakia, and particularly in the newly-conquered Austrian Province, seem to be all part of a plan which will reach its climax before the end of the present month. The time that is passing has been well spent by the mobilised troops in welding the reservists into the formations, and shaking them together into fighting efficiency. We must suppose that everything is ready, or will be ready in the next ten days, for a converging attack upon Czechoslovakia with troops and weapons which the Nazi Party believe to be overwhelming. All that remains is for some bloody incident, or actual revolt, to be created at the moment prescribed by Hitler, and for the signal to advance to be given. It is not probable there would be any ultimatum. 'When I strike,' said Hitler a year ago in a little-remembered speech, 'I shall not waste time like Mussolini in discussion. I shall strike like lightning in the night.'

Inside the Czechoslovakian Republic there is an absolute determination to fight for life and freedom. All their frontiers, even that opposite Austria, are well fortified and guarded by a strong and devoted army. I am told that the Nazi conception of the onslaught upon this small neighbour is to pour in from all sides in great numbers, to plunge their German armoured divisions through some gap in the defences, and to blast

Prague and other ancient cities and towns with such a deluge of bombs from the air, that all resistance will collapse in a few days. If this be their dream, it is likely to have an unpleasant awakening. Air bombardment may efface the monuments of Prague, may inflict hideous slaughter upon the women and children, but it will not prevent the defending troops from reaching their stations, nor will it turn brave men out of carefully fortified positions. We see how stubbornly the Spanish Republicans are enduring an air bombardment to which they have no means of reply. But the Czechoslovakian army is one of the best equipped in the world. It has admirable tanks, anti-tank guns and anti-aircraft artillery. This resolute people have long prepared themselves for the ordeal. Systems of concrete pill-boxes and solid entrenchments, if defended, cannot be taken at a run.

It is always imprudent to attempt to forecast the unknown, but if the spirit of the Czechs has not been daunted by all the worry and pressure to which they have been subjected, three or four weeks and three or four hundred thousand casualties should be the least price in time and blood exacted from the invader. I do not believe that such a spectacle could be witnessed impassively by the civilised world. Very few people outside Germany are now misled by Nazi propaganda. No doubt the disorders which would precede the outrage have been prepared with the same meticulous care as the military movements. It may be that, as was plotted in the case of Austria, some attempt upon the life of one of the Sudeten German leaders will be staged. But from the moment that the first shot is fired and the German troops attempt to cross the Czechoslovakian frontier, the whole scene will be transformed, and a roar of fury will arise from the free peoples of the world, which will proclaim nothing less than a crusade against the aggressor. To the wage-earning masses of every land, the word 'Czechoslovakia,' lately so unfamiliar to their ears, spells nothing less than 'self-preservation.' Thus I believe that should these dark designs, now so remorselessly unfolding hour by hour, reach their appointed climax, Nazi Germany will find herself engaged in a world war, inexpiable in its character.

Some people still profess to believe that Herr Hitler and his confederates would never dream of using violence against the Czechs; that these vast preparations are only after all small local manœuvres entirely normal in their character, though perhaps a little extensive in their scale; and that soon the armies will disperse. If that be true, then we may all rejoice. But on the assumption that it is not true, and that the crime is planned and imminent, the question before us is whether we can stop it, and how? The British Government sustained by a united nation have made it clear that should a major war explode, they would be almost inevitably involved. But it is not enough to say that we shall probably be in the war if it happens. What above all is important is to prevent it happening. The ordinary smooth and balanced phrases of diplomacy, with all their refinements and reserves, are of little use in dealing with the fierce chiefs of German Nazidom. Only the most blunt, plain, even brutal language will make its effect. Moreover, whatever words are used must carry with them the conviction that they are spoken in deadly earnest. This is no time to bluff.

Everyone will sympathise with the high-minded statesmen who have laboured so patiently for peace. But one must ask whether they would add appreciably to our danger by declaring themselves unmistakably, while time remains. If, for instance, Great Britain, France and Russia were even now to present a joint or simultaneous note to Herr Hitler personally, setting forth that an attack on Czechoslovakia would immediately be followed by common action; and if at the same time President Roosevelt would proclaim that this note carried with it the moral sympathy of the United States, with all that would follow therefrom—there would be good hopes, if not indeed almost a certainty, of warding off the catastrophe which may so easily engulf our civilisation.

Why should we wait till the worst has happened before being ready to run risks? May not risks be run for peace, as great as those which, if the worst happens, will assuredly be run for victory? If this moment is lost through hesitancy, however well-meaning, and war should come, as come it may, perhaps quite soon, how vain will be reproaches and regrets, how vast the tragedy of mankind![1]

---

[1] Events took a different course. After visiting Herr Hitler at Berchtesgaden (September 15th), Mr. Chamberlain, in accord with Monsieur Daladier, adopted the policy of appeasement embodied in the agreement of Munich (September 28th). The Czechoslovak Government were induced to yield themselves without resistance to the German occupation of the regions claimed by Herr Hitler, and to deliver up the fortress-line upon which their power to defend themselves against further aggression depended.

FRANCE AFTER MUNICH
OCTOBER 4, 1938

British sympathy goes out in generous measure to France as she stands by this fateful milestone in her long history. It is a duty binding upon all public men, on both sides of the Channel, who write or speak about the tremendous events of the last fortnight, to make sure that no words of theirs weaken the ties which unite our two countries. That would be the last and crowning service that could be rendered to the triumphant Nazi power. If the French Republic and the British Empire were necessary to each other in days of war and in days of success, they are still more necessary in these times when conditions are so different. Above all, there must be no recrimination between the two countries whose future security and independence is more than ever bound up with their unity. In both countries there has been the same admirable composure in the whole mass of the people as long as the period of strain lasted, and the same frank, spontaneous, natural expression of relief and joy on learning that they were to be spared the terrible ordeal for which they had braced themselves.

Everyone admired the smooth efficiency with which the French military machine was brought into complete preparedness, and the loyalty and patriotism which animated the millions of men who left their homes and peaceful occupations and planted themselves upon the frontiers of their land to face the worst that fate might have in store. Equally reassuring was the sober confidence in which the Chiefs of the French Army found themselves able to confront their task, hampered though they were by the lamentable weakness in the air, which must on no account be overlooked. France has sustained several heavy shocks within living memory, and has emerged from them all the stronger. There is indeed a recuperative power in free democracy which enables it, for all its improvidences, to rise like Antæus after every contact with the earth. Nothing in history was more remarkable than the way in which France recovered her strength and confidence in the early years of this century, undaunted by the spectre of the heavy numerical preponderance of her warlike neighbour. It is in that spirit that the period which lies before us must now be traversed.

The changes which have taken place in Central Europe must certainly not be underestimated. The seizure of Austria, the ruin and neutralisation of Czechoslovakia, the collapse of the 'Little Entente', the defection of Poland, and, finally, the possible departure of Russia from the European system, lay open the path down the valley of the Danube to the Black Sea, without obstacle or hindrance, to exultant Nazidom. Unless this danger leads Poland, Rumania and Yugoslavia to realise how profoundly their position is affected, and draws from them new sources of strength and co-operation one with another, it might well be that this great operation of ambition, this dream of European overlordship, will be realised in fact if not in form without the firing of a single shot. The position of all States outside the German system, and particularly that of France and England, will have to be adjusted to these new dominating facts.

It would be affectation to deny that the whole basis of French foreign policy in Central and Eastern Europe has disappeared. On the other hand, no charge can be made against France of having broken her military engagement with Czechoslovakia. That promise did not become operative until the act of aggression was in fact perpetrated. It was the outbreak of an armed conflict which alone would have brought the French obligation into absolute being. 'Unbearable pressure' was brought by France and Great Britain upon the Czechoslovak Government, and beneath that pressure they bent and yielded.

It cannot be denied that a great nation, the ally of a small country, has a right to bring pressure to bear upon that country within certain limits, in order that very much larger interests should not be endangered. Nevertheless, if the Government of President Benes had refused to accept without due examination the terms thrust before them on September 20, and had in consequence been attacked by Nazi Germany and had valiantly resisted the cruel and bloody onslaught, it would have become imperative upon France to intervene, and upon Great Britain to go to the aid of France. Thus neither in form nor in reality can it be said that France has failed in her word. Still less, of course, can it be suggested that Great Britain, who had no special engagement with Czechoslovakia, and was bound only by the general obligations of the Covenant, is technically in default.

An injury has, however, been sustained by the prestige and authority of both the Western democracies which must woefully reduce their influence with small countries of all kinds. It will not be easy to regain the lost confidence. All those statesmen in the minor countries of Europe who have consistently endeavoured to incline their policy towards the Nazi channels, who have pointed out the weakness of the democracies and the impediments to action provided by their parliamentary systems, are now, of course, vindicated. All those who have hitherto laboured with France and Britain, remembering the achievements and results of the Great War, and who have represented elements opposed to the totalitarian system, are proportionately stultified and discouraged. This is true in Poland, in Rumania, in Yugoslavia and Bulgaria. Everywhere the temptation, and in some cases compulsion, to make the best terms possible with the one Power which is ready to use brutal violence without scruple, will be potent. One can only hope that the German proverb, 'The trees do not grow up to the sky' will operate, and that the reactions to the fate of Czechoslovakia may not be entirely one-sided.

Much will depend upon the attitude of the British and French Parliaments, and upon the new measures which they may consider necessary for meeting the grave deterioration in their positions. It is, no doubt, heartbreaking to look back over the last few years and see the enormous resources of military and political strength which have been squandered through lack of leadership and clarity of purpose. There has never been a moment up to the present when a firm stand by France and Britain together with the many countries who recently looked to them would not have called a halt to the

Nazi menace. At each stage, as each new breach of treaties was effected, timidity, lack of knowledge and foresight, have prevented the two peaceful Powers from marching in step. Thus we have the spectacle of a handful of men, who have a great nation in their grip, outfacing the enormously superior forces lately at the disposal of the Western democracies.

It is a crime to despair. We must learn to draw from misfortune the means of future strength. There must not be lacking in our leadership something of the spirit of that Austrian corporal who, when all had fallen into ruins about him, and when Germany seemed to have sunk for ever into chaos, did not hesitate to march forth against the vast array of victorious nations, and has already turned the tables so decisively upon them. It is the hour, not for despair, but for courage and rebuilding; and that is the spirit which should rule our minds.

On July 7, 1937, was published the report of the Royal Commission in favour of Partition. In August the report came before the Mandates Commission of the League of Nations which showed very little enthusiasm for the settlement proposed by the British Government.

By the beginning of 1938 the Arabs were in active rebellion, and there were hundreds of casualties. Meanwhile the Government sent out a technical commission to Palestine, under the chairmanship of Sir John Woodhead, which was supposedly to advise on how Partitions should be carried out. In the event, however, the Woodhead Commission advised against Partition. By midsummer, when the Colonial Secretary, Mr. Ormsby-Gore (now Lord Harlech) resigned, it was apparent that the British Government had decided to abandon Partition.

PALESTINE
OCTOBER 20, 1938

Amid world preoccupation the conditions in Palestine have passed into eclipse. The lull in Europe, while the victorious Nazis are gathering their spoil, forces us to turn our eyes to this distracted country, for which we are responsible.

It is indeed a shocking scene that meets the view. The whole of this small province is sinking into anarchy. Jew and Arab carry on hideous vendettas of murder and reprisal. Bombs are thrown among harmless villagers on market days. Women and children are massacred by Arab raiders in the night. The roads are being broken up. The railways have largely ceased to work. The pipe line, though heavily guarded, is repeatedly cut. A considerable proportion of the British regular army, together with large bodies of armed police, hold the main centres of Government, and sally forth upon foray and patrol. A rival administration has been set up by the Arab rebels, and rules over considerable areas. It is the Ireland of 1920 again, but in this case the rebels are powerfully aided by arms, explosives, money and propaganda from German and Italian sources.

The spectacle is vexatious and discreditable. Great Britain is called upon at immense expense and trouble, and some loss of life, to carry on a policy of severe repression, with all its painful features, not for her own sake, but because of the bitter racial feud which has now developed between the Arab and Jew. The dictators mock at the ill-success of our methods. They descant on the severities inseparable from the attempt to keep order, and point the moral of British inefficiency. For this last charge there is more than sufficient foundation. Up till 1934 Palestine was in every respect a credit to our administration. The country had gone ahead by leaps and bounds. There was peace and prosperity, roads and schools had been built; large power schemes set on foot. The area of cultivation was constantly extending. The process of bringing in the annual quota of Jews was being effected without serious friction. All this was being accomplished without the country being burdened by a heavy military establishment. In contrast with Syria, where the French kept an army of over 50,000 men, Palestine presented an orderly and hopeful aspect, with a force behind the rulers of only a few battalions and a few hundred police.

Hitler's persecution, and the piteous spectacle of the pillaged and hunted Jews, driven from the lands of their birth, led to an enormous expansion of the annual immigration quota. As many as 60,000 arrived in a single year, and although Jewish money and enterprise provided employment and settlement for all, the alarm of the Arabs was not unnatural. They saw themselves in near prospect of being outnumbered. A strain was put upon the absorptive capacity of Palestine which was more than it could bear.

Agitation began. In 1936 serious disorders broke out. The British Government found themselves unable to come to any clear decision. They allowed matters to drift. Differences among Ministers prevented a long overdue change in the High Commissionership. The line of least resistance seemed to be found in sending out a Royal Commission. Accordingly a body of estimable gentlemen, under the late Lord Peel, set forth to Palestine, toured the land, took a great body of evidence, heard and saw all sections and interests. They then returned home to write their report, which was deliberate and lengthy. When the report after further delay was published, it was found that the Commission recommended partition. The country was to be divided into three, a Jewish State, an Arab State, and a British zone between the two, with the British attempting to hold the balance fairly between the two races and keep them from each other's throats.

From the outset I denounced this policy as vicious and dangerous. It placed the British administration in an impossible position. It created two hostile States, both of which were to be members of the League of Nations, with full right to raise whatever armies they chose. Indeed, this scheme, although conceived by able men with the highest motives, was nothing more nor less than a recipe for war. Yet even this scheme, had it been put into force vigorously and promptly, would have been better than the hopeless indecision which followed. His Majesty's Government showed themselves unable to make up their minds. They adopted the report of the Royal Commission in principle, but evidently without conviction. After further delays during which the state of the country steadily deteriorated, a second Commission was sent out to report upon the methods by which the report of the first Commission should be brought into operation. Meanwhile everything grew worse; murders began and reprisals were taken, reinforcements were brought in driblets, strong measures were taken by halves, and so by an unbroken process of vacillation and weakness the country has degenerated into its present horrible plight; and a blood feud has grown between the Arab and Jew, of which the end cannot be foreseen.

Surely this is a case in which the British Government might make up their mind and bring to an end a policy of temporising and drifting. Everything that can be known about Palestine has long ago been in the possession of the Colonial Office. There never was any need for these Royal Commissions, except for the purpose of putting off the ugly day of choice. Parliament ought to be told in the next few weeks whether the Peel plan of partition is to be abandoned or not. If partition is rejected, ought we to throw up our task as insoluble and return the mandate to the League of Nations? This solution will certainly find its supporters in the British Press. We should have to admit that we had tried our best, and that we had found ourselves incapable of discharging our duty. The advocates of this course would no doubt contend that peace and the avoidance of worry and effort should have precedence over sentimental considerations like national pride and public obligation. But there are serious practical obstacles to such a policy.

There are, of course, three Powers which would be willing to undertake the task. Germany and Italy would eagerly come forward, if only for the strategic advantages which Palestine would offer to them. The third Power is Turkey, and we must to our sorrow admit that the present condition of Palestine no longer compares favourably with that prevailing before the war under Turkish rule. Nevertheless, the adoption of any of these alternatives would be painful and disgraceful in the last degree. Moreover, we may imagine that the controversy which would arise at Geneva would be protracted. The process of disentangling British interests, residents and troops from Palestine would be complicated and lengthy. Even at the quickest, a year would be required. Meanwhile we should have to keep order under circumstances of constantly increasing difficulty. The suggested transfer of mandate does not therefore offer that means of escape from unpleasant duty which renders it so attractive to its advocates. The more it is examined, the greater the repugnance it will excite.

What then remains? There remains only the policy of fidelity and perseverance. We must unflinchingly restore order, and suppress the campaign of murder and counter-murder between the two races. We must give protection to the large Jewish community already established in the country; but we should also give to the Arabs a solemn assurance, embodied if possible in an agreement to which Arab and Jew should be invited to subscribe, that the annual quota of Jewish immigration should not exceed a certain figure for a period of at least ten years.

No doubt such a course would arouse a furious outcry, and involve us in a long and thankless task; but should it seem the only way, we must face it with steadfastness and conviction if we are still to preserve our good name.

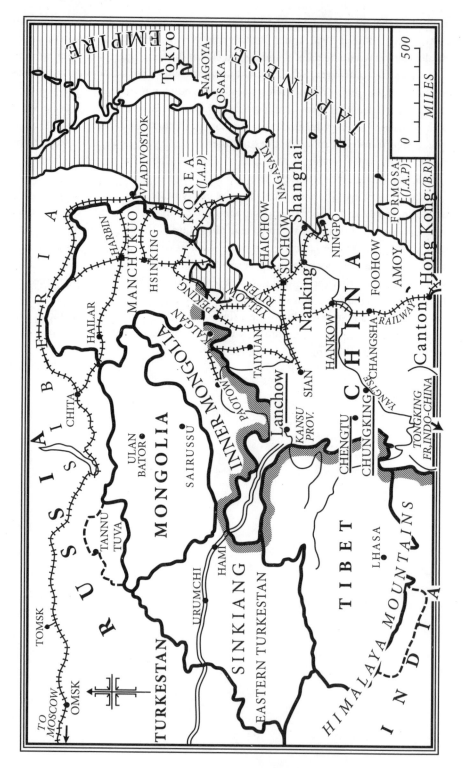

THE JAPANESE BURDEN
NOVEMBER 3, 1938

We turn upon the uneasy bed of European affairs and roll over to the other side. We are in the Celestial Regions. We are in China. Is it cooler there? Shall we rest more comfortably? How fares the cause of freedom, of right and law, against the forces of conquest and invasion in the Far East?

It is some months since I directed the attention of readers of these letters to the Japanese war upon China. Since then, two heavy blows have befallen the Chinese in a single week. After a year and a half of war, Hankow, the main military centre and arsenal of China, with its strong fortifications and stout defenders, and far to the southward, the great city of Canton, have both fallen into the hands of the invaders. What effect will this have upon the spirit of China, or upon the strength of Chinese resistance? Is the war in the Far East coming to a speedy end? Will China now collapse into servitude and exploitation, or can she continue the struggle? These are questions which are of direct importance to us; for the misfortunes of the Chinese react upon Europe, just as the rebuffs sustained by the French and British democracies carry their message of evil tidings to the East.

To seek to answer these questions, it is first of all necessary to look at the map. After eighteen months of fighting the Japanese armies have penetrated deeply into China. They have mastered railway and river communications which enable their military line to be drawn to-day on paper to enclose an area of roughly one-third of China. At many points their pickets stand along the Yellow River. Within this military front dwell over a hundred millions of Chinese. Are they all conquered? Have they submitted themselves to the Japanese yoke? Can we regard this military grip, imposed upon so great an expanse and such vast numbers, as representing a real transference of authority? The answer is surely to be found in the fact that there are probably not more than seven or eight hundred thousand Japanese troops in the whole of the invaded territory.

The Japanese still have to keep nearly half a million of their best-trained forces in the north against Russia. The three quarters of a million they are using in China have been able to advance along the railroads and rivers, but are quite unable to control the country. Behind the Japanese front nine-tenths of the area is still administered under the direction of the Chinese Central Government, and hundreds of towns and villages in regions as large as Yorkshire or Champagne, although lying in the so-called conquered zones, have never seen a Japanese soldier. Perhaps from time to time they see a hostile aeroplane fly across the sky; but for the rest they know of the invasion, and that they have been engulfed by it, only from the tales and rumours of the East, and from what they read in the few news-sheets that are printed.

Nevertheless, they are alive to their country's danger. They nurse and shelter the guerrilla forces which dominate the countryside. These forces are very considerable. The so-called 8th Route Army is the most formidable of them. This is the old Communist force which has had years of experience in fighting the Chinese Government, and now is whole-heartedly rallied to the national cause. These Communist guerrillas are fierce, clever and elusive. They appear; they strike; they vanish. The Japanese army holds the railway lines, the block-houses, the bridgeheads, the fortified posts and the walled towns they have taken. They have not enough troops to go outside these: nor is it worth their while. The guerrillas who capture this small post or cut that railway line, or who trap and destroy some unwary reconnoitring Japanese party, cannot be found. It is quite easy to massacre Chinese villagers in reprisal. But what is the good of that? As 'Mr. Dooley' said long ago: 'Flogging China is like flogging a jellyfish.' Thus the Japanese General Staff strictly confine their action to the military communications and their army front, and pin their comforting flags upon the maps at all these points to prove their victorious career.

What lies beyond the Japanese front? Once the Canton-Hankow railway has fallen into Japanese hands, as it soon may, the war will enter regions in which there are hardly any railways and only a limited number of modern roads. As the Japanese advance into these vast regions their military difficulties and the danger to the supply of their forces will steadily increase. The Chinese armies have shown themselves very skilful in escaping from any of the cities they have defended on a large scale. They slipped away safely from Hankow. They retired in good time, probably wisely, from Canton. Chiang Kai-shek has perceived the true strategy for China, and has proclaimed that the farther the war moves to the west, i.e. into the interior, the greater will be the hopes of a Chinese victory. The Japanese may well be repeating Napoleon's experiment of marching to a Moscow. The size of the country is enormous. The masses of the people are enormous. The poverty is bleak. The armies which have retreated after fighting are still powerful and tolerably well equipped. The central government of China has retreated more than 500 miles to Chungking, which is also Chiang Kai-shek's headquarters. The intelligentsia the university life of modern and progressive China, finds a resting-place even farther west in Chengtu. There is no reason why China should not carry on and maintain its resistance indefinitely, if only the Chinese preserve the spirit of national unity and stand faithfully by their great leader, Chiang Kai-shek.

Supplies have become more difficult. The Japanese seizure of Canton has cut the supply-stream which entered China through Hong Kong. But the old Russian silk road through Turkestan still discharges its weekly tonnage of munitions from the heart of Asia, and the railway through French-China, Tongking, also carries a considerable traffic, unless Monsieur Bonnet, in his policy of 'appeasement,' allows it to be closed. Many nations sell arms to China—the United States, the Germans, and the Italians. The common front against Bolshevism does not apply where profit is concerned. Only the English sell no arms to China. They need them all at home.

Meanwhile in Japan, in the Land of Lost Illusions, once the favourite hope of the English-speaking world, the strain of this long, obstinate and ever-expanding war grows as the months roll by. The island empire is gripped by a harsh military despotism, which now seeks to clothe itself with Nazi-Fascist trappings, just as fifty years ago the liberal forces in Japan decked themselves in the plumes of Western civilisation. The whole population is bent beneath the burden of taxes; the task of maintaining well over 1,000,000 men beyond the seas, with all the expensive apparatus of modern war, falls heavily upon the Government. Japan, in order to carry on this ever-widening conflict, in addition to having to build and maintain a great Navy, has to import very large quantities of the raw materials of war industry. In oil and petrol she lives from hand to mouth; rubber is short; the reserves of many other war metals are exiguous. All have to be bought across the exchange. Credit has dried up, and the exporting capacity falls far short of the necessary import. The gold reserve has fallen to barely a quarter of what it was when the assault upon China began.

One must ask, 'Where will both these combatants, China and Japan, be a year from now, or two years from now, if the Chinese hold together and follow Chiang Kai-shek and his wise strategy?' It would seem to a detached observer that China has only to endure to save her soul. All the time the Russian Siberian Army, more than a million strong, watches and broods on the frontiers of Manchukuo. At any moment they may make a diversion such as occurred six weeks ago, and draw a hundred thousand Japanese troops hurriedly to the north; at any moment they may lean heavily forward upon the covering army of Japan. The United States, with no serious preoccupation at home, watch a conflict in which important American interests are involved—to say nothing of right and wrong. Nevertheless, the ever-growing naval strength of the American Republic must be a gnawing anxiety in the minds of the War Lords of Japan.

We avert our eyes from the cruelties, from the endless wanton waste and ruin which this invasion of China carries in its train. Immense distances of land or ocean cast their veils upon horrid, lamentable scenes. Yet sometimes the comfortable feather heads in their feather beds in New York, Paris and London might give a passing thought to the tremendous drama and tragedy which, if it reaches an evil conclusion, will have darkened the world for their children and for a generation yet unborn.

THE MORROW OF MUNICH
NOVEMBER 17, 1938

Everyone must recognise that the Prime Minister is pursuing a policy of a most decided character and of capital importance. He has his own strong view about what to do, and about what is going to happen. He has his own standard of values; he has his own angle of vision. He believes that he can make a good settlement for Europe and for the British Empire by coming to terms with Herr Hitler and Signor Mussolini. No one impugns his motives. No one doubts his conviction or his courage. Besides all this, he has the power to do what he thinks best. Those who take a different view, both of the principles of our foreign policy and of the facts and probabilities with which our country has to deal, are bound to recognise that we have no power at all to prevent him, by the resources and methods which are at his disposal, from taking the course in which he sincerely believes. He is willing to take the responsibility; he has the right to take the responsibility; and we are going to learn, in a comparatively short time, what he proposes should happen to us.

The Prime Minister is persuaded that Herr Hitler seeks no further territorial expansion upon the Continent of Europe; that the mastering and absorption of the Republic of Czechoslovakia has satiated the appetite of the German Nazi regime. It may be that he wishes to induce the Conservative party to return to Germany the mandated territories in British possession, or what are judged to be their full equivalent. He believes that this act of restoration will bring about prolonged, good and secure relations between Great Britain and Germany. He believes further that these good relations can be achieved without weakening in any way the fundamental ties of self-preservation which bind us to the French Republic, which ties, it is common ground between us all, must be preserved. Mr. Chamberlain is convinced that all this will lead to general agreement; to the appeasement of the discontented Powers, and to a lasting peace.

But all lies in the regions of hope and speculation. A whole set of contrary possibilities must be held in mind. He may ask us to submit to things which we cannot endure; he may be forced to ask us to submit to things which we cannot endure. Or again, the other side in this difficult negotiation may not act in the same spirit of goodwill and good faith as animates the Prime Minister. What we have to give, what we are made to give, may cost us dear, but it may not be enough. It may involve great injury and humbling to the British Empire, but it may not stay or even divert for more than a few months, if that, the march of events upon the Continent. By this time next year we shall know whether the Prime Minister's view of Herr Hitler and the German Nazi party is right or wrong. By this time next year we shall know whether the policy of appeasement has appeased, or whether it has only stimulated a more ferocious appetite. All we can do in the meanwhile is to gather together forces of resistance and defence, so that if the Prime Minister should unhappily be wrong, or misled, or deceived, we can at the worst keep body and soul together.

But these issues, although painful and important, are dwarfed by the dangers of what is called disarmament. What does that mean? Everyone would like to see it. Everyone would rejoice if the resources of all the great nations of the world could be turned into channels more fruitful to the mass of the peoples. But surely we have to take care that what is called disarmament does not in fact mean leaving Britain where she can be blackmailed out of her skin. I fear that seductive proposals will be thrust upon us, perhaps at very short notice. We shall be told that the Germans have agreed to abolish poison gas, which perhaps they never meant to use, unless they should change their minds, or until something happened which entitled them to say: 'Here is a new fact which supersedes all existing agreements.' And, after all, war is a new fact which many jurists hold automatically obliterates all previous agreements. Such an assurance would be a comfort which might easily prove a snare.

I should be very much in favour of a convention, for what it is worth, which scheduled large areas in every country in which aircraft would not intentionally cast their bombs, but I should be very sorry to see such an agreement our sole defence, because, as I have said, the weather may change very suddenly. We may be also told that the long-distance bombing aeroplane should be abolished, which would, in fact, mean that we could not reach Berlin but that Germany could very easily, with medium aircraft, reach London.

But above all, I fear a proposal that we should abandon the right to have an Air Force, in Mr. Baldwin's words, at least 'equal to that of any Power within striking distance of these shores.' I fear the kind of argument which will say, if Germany consents to be only a third as strong as Britain on the seas, is it not reasonable that Britain should consent to be only a half, or a third, or some fraction, of the strength of Germany in the air? To agree to that would be to betray the life and independence of the British nation. All these matters must weigh heavily with us while we are awaiting the results of the Prime Minister's impending negotiations with Herr Hitler. And the Government would do well to speak with more plainness upon these issues and give reassurance to the country, in so far as they are in a position to do so. It is not unlikely that we are moving towards a General Election in the coming year. It may be that Herr Hitler would desire that a General Election should take place in this country before he consents to serious negotiations. He would like to be sure that the Government with which he is to bargain will in fact be able to deliver the goods. From his recent speeches it might almost seem that he was anxious to bring about this election, or influence its course, by branding certain parties and persons, and suggesting that if the electors used their votes in a certain sense it would be the worse for them. One cannot tell.

If there is an election in the near future it will be a very strange and unhappy one. It is not so much a question who wins or loses, but what happens to the country. I have never seen it divided as it is to-day. The division does not follow exactly the regular groupings of party, but it cuts very deep, and will sever many ties and friendships. At Flodden Field the English and Scots armies had reversed their positions; they stood with their faces towards home and their backs to the enemy's country They fought just as hard all the same. But this is the kind of position into which we may very soon be drawn. One side will accuse its opponents of being warmongers; and Herr Hitler, from across the North Sea, will vehemently endorse this proposition. The other parties will no doubt make such answers as occur to them. And evidently there would be some answers that might be made. But where should we all be, whoever won, at the end of it? Nothing is more certain, whatever the result might be, than that an election at the present time would leave all parties in a very unusual and uncomfortable position, and the nation split from end to end.

And what is to happen meanwhile to rearmament? How are we to regain our strength and position in the world? We cannot possibly have any effective effort towards the revival of British strength unless we have both the Tory party and the trade unions working hand in hand with general political approval. Only in this way can the weapons we so sorely need be manufactured on the vast scale necessary. Such an election, however it went, would bar all prospects of any sturdy and hearty co-operation for at least another precious fleeting year.

FRANCE AND ENGLAND
DECEMBER 1, 1938

Speculation has been rife about the purpose and the results of the visit of the Prime Minister and Lord Halifax to Paris last week. In the grey aftermath of Munich, it was certainly necessary that the Ministers at the head of both countries should take stock of their position and of their mutual relations. An immense change has occurred in the balances of Europe; and far-reaching reactions are also in progress in the public minds of both the Western democracies. Great Britain is profoundly divided upon foreign policy. Political controversy is lively and will become more severe. In France the impact of September's grim event has struck all the more deeply because it has been borne in silence. The Chamber endorsed Messieurs Daladier and Bonnet's action almost unanimously, one single member of the Right, Monsieur de Kerilis, alone voting with the Communists against it. But every section of French society has been shaken to its foundations.

The bloodless conquest and virtual absorption of Czechoslovakia by Nazi Germany has transformed the military position of France. All her system of Alliances in Eastern Europe has collapsed and can never be reconstituted, except, perhaps, after a lapse of years and in an entirely different form. Hitherto France and Great Britain have had the feeling that they were stronger than Germany. Henceforward a different order prevails. We have seen what Herr Hitler has been able to accomplish in spite of his weakness. We have now to learn how he will use his strength. If Munich and other triumphs were gained in the green wood, what will be done in the dry? The statesmen of Great Britain and France have written, or will write, their names upon pieces of paper which Hitler willingly signs; but no one in either country feels any more security from such pious and vague affirmations of goodwill than the nations of the world felt about the Kellogg Pact, to which all subscribed.

It must be frankly admitted that the friends of France in England have sustained an impression of bewilderment. Even I, who for thirty years have steadfastly pursued in peace, in war, in after-war, the cause of Anglo-French solidarity, am now somewhat baffled. One does not know what the new France stands for, or amounts to, at the present time, or what internal changes lie ahead of the Third Republic. These changes may be drastic. I have no doubt that by one road or another they will end in a reassertion of the French will-to-live. No one who knows the inherent strength of France can believe the defeatist tales, which are spread so eagerly, that that great nation is willing to resign itself to the role of a minor Power. There must be, and there will be, a vehement revival on both sides of the Channel. But how it will come in France, and in what form, is a mystery of the future.

The outbreak of strikes and disorders, fomented by the parties of the Left, may have the effect of momentarily weakening France; but it would be a great mistake to regard them as a sign of morbid weakness. The principle which united the mass of the French people in resistance to the dictatorships of the totalitarian Powers has been rudely shaken. The Socialist and Communist workmen who obeyed a few weeks ago the mobilisation orders with devotion and punctuality, are no longer held to their duty by the theme of resistance to foreign tyranny. They do not quite understand what high world-object they are now to toil for. If it is merely to be an appeasement of Nazi and Fascist Dictators by concessions to their demands and submission to their wills, why should the hours of work be lengthened? The sun shines on a fair land; leisure is sweet to the working masses. Undoubtedly science and machinery could to-day give an easier and broader life for all, but for this external menace which casts its shadow across so many lands. Is Nazi aggression to be resisted, or are the Western democracies to sit by with folded hands and watch resignedly the formidable events which impend in the centre and east of Europe? We remember the sardonic war-time joke about the optimist and the pessimist. The optimist was the man who did not mind what happened, so long as it did not happen to him. The pessimist was the man who lived with the optimist. Is this, then, to describe our joint or respective futures?

It is now known that, during the late crisis, Herr Hitler concentrated three-quarters of his armies against Czechoslovakia, and left on the French frontier, to guard his uncompleted defences, a force far inferior to the French army.[1] Everything we have learned of those days shows the solid strength and quality of the French army. The sober confidence expressed in it by its chiefs was confirmed by everything that happened in the mobilisation. Although the German army is growing stronger month by month, and although Germany possesses double the man-power of France, it must not be forgotten that the French reserves of trained soldiers are at present far larger than those of Germany. It is only three years since conscription was reintroduced, in breach of Treaty engagements, throughout Germany. There are, therefore, only three annual quotas of trained Reservists. These quotas are no doubt numerically equal to five or six annual quotas of French Reservists. But France has twenty quotas of men who have been trained; and for all of these there are well-established and matured formations. Besides this, the shortage of officers in Germany is grievous, and cannot be speedily repaired. Either Herr Hitler must be a desperate gambler, or he must have felt pretty sure that he would be let alone to work his will on the Czech Republic.

As these facts soak into the French nation, they are bound to stir deep feelings. No one who has studied the history of France since 1870 can doubt that a fire is smouldering; but no one can say how and where it will manifest itself. Too little attention has been paid to the remarkable speech of the Comte de Paris, in which he condemned the capitulation

---

[1] Actually the Germans mustered 42 Divisions, of which 30 were massed against Czechoslovakia, 4 were in reserve, and only 8 remained to guard the German frontier from Switzerland to Luxemburg. Against these 8 the French superiority was enormous, and the French General Staff declared their confidence in the result, provided that Czechoslovakia could hold out for a fortnight.

of Munich. This speech should recall to their duty certain elements of the Right who have allowed their alienation from the Republic to lead them to take a poorer view of the strength of their country than is warranted by the circumstances. The reasons why France does not present herself in her full strength at the present time are not to be found among the working masses, who are also the soldiers of France, but in certain strata of the middle-class and the well-to-do. Something of this kind can also be seen in Great Britain.

The two great peoples whose fortunes are interwoven should search their hearts. It is certain that they have only to rouse themselves in their true strength, and in the spirit of old days, to put themselves in a position of security amid present dangers. They still have the power to command and safeguard their future, with which are intertwined the liberties gained for all the world by the long forging of the British Parliamentary system, and the swift, hard lessons of the French Revolution. Above all, it is indispensable that renewed exertions and sacrifices should be made by the British and French peoples, and that they should repel as a mortal thrust any manœuvre to separate them from each other.

NEW LIGHTS IN EASTERN EUROPE
DECEMBER 15, 1938

When Colonel Beck, the Polish Foreign Secretary, disciple and, to some extent, heir of Marshal Pilsudski, looks out upon the state of Eastern Europe on the raw morrow of Munich, he must feel rather uncomfortable. Otherwise he would surely not have made such haste to form a new contact with Soviet Russia, from whom, at one moment in the crisis only a few weeks ago, Poland had received a virtual ultimatum. It was no doubt very gratifying from the wreck of Czechoslovakia to acquire Teschen, about which there was a long story. But after the feast comes the bill. The bill is presented by the German landlord, who has nearly acquired the inn and adjacent property; it may be quite a heavy bill. The agitations which are now being fomented in the Polish Ukraine show that there are many large items in the account; among these may be mentioned Danzig and the Polish Corridor. Such is the bill that may be presented in the near future by Nazi Germany to Colonel Beck. But perhaps the Russian Soviet Union will come to his aid and help him not to pay it; but then again, perhaps not!

The Western democracies, France and Great Britain, have always had a very keen sentiment for Polish national independence. This sentiment has not been expressed in words alone. Napoleon made a memorable effort to reintegrate Poland. It was not till 1919 that the triumph of French and British bayonets made possible the undoing of the historic crime perpetrated by the three despotisms of Prussia, Austria and Russia more than a century and a half ago. I have always hailed the liberation of Poland from its tripartite bondage as one of the most inspiring consequences of the World War. The unsleeping, quenchless conception of national unity possessed by the Polish nation is one of the wonders of history, and that it should have reached fruition as a result of French and British sacrifices and victories was a grand event. No student of the past could but feel pain to see the newly reconstituted Poland in these last fateful months act with complete indifference both to the Powers who liberated her and to the cause of law and freedom in Europe. It was disappointing to those who had battered down the gates of a bastille, to find that the captive seemed to have forgotten nothing and learned nothing in his long incarceration. But after all disillusion is too often the fruit of experience.

All Eastern Europe spends this Christmas in deep fear. Against whom will the next blow be directed? Upon what countries, now independent and at peace, will the consequences of Munich fall? There is extreme tension in Rumania. We have lately received in England the visit of King Carol. The impression which he created in London was highly favourable; the British public had the feeling that here was a real man, a highly capable prince, facing extraordinary difficulties with resource and resolve. But

Rumania, with her oil and corn, with a host of recently acquired minorities in her midst, and with Hungary and its deep-seated grievance at her very doors, seems to be another country in danger at this unhappy time.

Beyond the two threatened countries, Poland and Rumania, lies the great mass of Russia, and farther to the south the powerful military Republic of Turkey. Russia and Turkey, for centuries foes, have become good neighbours. Together they form a counterpoise for Europe, which might well be of invaluable service. Russia is a mystery and a riddle, which none may rede. The part Russia has played in the Far East deserves the respect of both Great Britain and the United States. What Russia can do or will do in Europe in the event or in the advent of her soil being invaded, no man can tell. He would indeed be foolish to write it down as negligible.

But Turkey is another stabilising force, much smaller, but more definite in its character. The death of Mustapha Kemal, the saviour of Turkey in the war, and the guide and rebuilder of the Turkish nation since the war, was a loss most grievous and untimely both to the Ottoman people and to Europe. The tears which men and women of all classes shed upon his bier were a fitting tribute to the life work of a man at once the hero, the champion, and the father of modern Turkey. During his long dictatorship a policy of admirable restraint and goodwill created, for the first time in history, most friendly relations with Greece. The terrible injuries which the two races wrought each other after the Great War have been effaced by time and good sense. The disentangling of the populations was a feat of active statesmanship which has no parallel. The prediction that the Turks would not be able to get on without the presence of a certain number of Greeks as doctors, chemists, bankers, moneylenders, and handymen in their villages, has been happily falsified. Turkish capacity has been found equal to the task of providing a complete domestic economy.

How admirable also has been the achievement of the Greeks, who have managed to find room and subsistence in their by no means rich and fertile country for nearly 2,000,000 newcomers repatriated from Turkish lands. Both Greece and Turkey are animated by the friendliest sentiments towards Great Britain. There is not the slightest divergence of interest between the leading Mediterranean Naval Power and these two guardians of the Ægean. It appears to be an object of high consequence to Great Britain to foster and encourage the growth of prosperity, credit and trade, both in Turkey and in Greece. The loan of £16,000,000 which Mr. Chamberlain so prudently made earlier in the year, has been a substantial advantage to Turkey, and has been warmly acknowledged by the Turkish Government. It is to be hoped that means will be found to foster the Greek trade and otherwise to assist the people with whom British connections have been so long and so agreeable, and upon whose throne there now sits an able constitutional king, long resident in England.

Greece, Turkey and Rumania together can exert a highly beneficial influence in Bulgaria. A great step forward was made in Balkan politics when at the Salonika Conference Bulgaria definitely rejoined her sister States in the Balkan Peninsula. All these countries will be safe and prosperous if they act together and weld themselves into a strong block of peaceful but well-armed States. If they let themselves be divided and set one against another by German ambitions, or if they allow themselves to be infected by Nazi doctrines, Pandora's box of evils will once again have been prised open, and there is hardly any limit to the miseries which lie before them.

It may well be that the fate of Czechoslovakia, whilst it exposes the whole of Eastern and Southern Europe to further unmeasured dangers, will at the same time raise new forces of self-preservation in all the countries affected. No process could be more welcome to the Western democracies, or more likely to engage their interest and goodwill.

THE SPANISH ULCER
DECEMBER 30, 1938

Is it not about time there was peace in Spain? And is this not the moment when all who care for Spain should attempt it? Of course the interest of Great Britain lies in the settlement by agreement of this hideous Civil War. It has even become a major interest of the British Empire. Not only is the Spanish quarrel a hot stove near a powder magazine, but British political action would become more coherent once the addiction of classes and parties to one side or the other in Spain had passed away.

The bulk of the Conservatives admire General Franco; all the forces of the Left are ardent for the Republic. The difference between the Duchess of Atholl and the Scottish Tories in the Perth by-election began about Spain. The dominant element in those parts regarded her vehement sympathy for the Spanish Government as a proof that she was almost ready to carry Bolshevism into Britain, to confiscate their property, pollute their churches and, if necessary, cut their throats. Nothing has strengthened the Prime Minister's hold upon well-to-do society more remarkably than the belief that he is friendly to General Franco and the Nationalist cause in Spain. But these sentiments on either side may be pushed beyond the bounds of British interest. It would seem that to-day the British Empire would run far less risk from the victory of the Spanish Government than from that of General Franco.

I have always been deterred from espousing the cause of either side in Spain by the dread of what would happen to whichever side was vanquished. The spectacle of either a Franco Spain or a Negrin Spain, with the beaten half of the Spanish nation trampled underfoot, has always seemed to me so dark and cruel that, not being a Spaniard, I will not become a partisan. But it must be admitted that if at this moment the Spanish Government were victorious they would be so anxious to live on friendly terms with Great Britain, they would find so much sympathy among the British people for them, that we should probably be able to dissuade them from the vengeance which would have attended their triumph earlier in the struggle. On the other hand, if Franco won, his Nazi backers would drive him to the same kind of brutal suppressions as are practised in the Totalitarian States.

The victory of the Spanish Republicans would, therefore, not only be a strategic security for British Imperial communications through the Mediterranean, but gentler and reconciling forces would play a larger part. Britain would have great influence with the Spanish Republic. Nazi Germany would hold, or try to hold, Franco by the scruff of the neck. The character of the Spanish Government has changed remarkably since the first months of the Civil War. The monstrous incapacity to preserve order, which was the main justification for the military revolt, has been succeeded in a struggle for life by an iron discipline. Whereas in most conflicts of this character the more extreme forces have continually gained more power and become more violent, the reverse process has happened at Barcelona and Valencia. There Liberal and Moderate influences have waxed and the Anarchist and Communist doctrinaires and assassins are being brought monthly under the healthy restraint of military service enjoined by dire need.

Whereas at the beginning General Franco seemed to stand for a civilised and unified Spain, his enforced reliance upon German and Italian help has reinvested the Spanish Republic to a large extent with the national title deeds. Both sides have become conscious of the reproach of being anti-Spanish. Their propaganda now scrutinises with increasing attention the elements of foreign aid in the opposite ranks. General Franco is heartily ashamed of being so dependent on Germans and Italians. His advocates point with justice to the many Russian and Marxist international personalities who figure in the staffs of the Republican Army. The Spanish Government shows itself extremely sensitive on this point. The gathering together and dismissal of the International Brigades in the height of battle was an act of faith of which all Spaniards have taken note.

On Franco's side the unpopularity of the none the less indispensable Italian contingents and of the highly competent Nazi agents, staff officers, artillerists, and aviators is causing increasing tension. The expulsion from the Spanish Peninsula of all foreigners who have meddled in the domestic quarrel is the deep desire of the Spanish nation as a whole and certainly it is from a British point of view a solid and durable object. On all counts, therefore, strategic, humanitarian, and moral, Great Britain, if forced to choose, should to-day welcome the victory of whichever side in Spain is least dependent upon foreigners. But why should we have to choose? And why should Spaniards have to choose? Have they not an overpowering common interest in a true peace, in a lasting reunion based upon the independence, the integrity, and the restoration of their native land?

And here let us look back through the war clouds and across the corpses which cumber the battlefields and lie at the foot of so many prison walls. Nothing is more certain than that Spain never willed this thing. A ghastly misunderstanding, due to faults and excesses which might well have been controlled in the bosom of a stronger State, opened the flood-gates of hell upon a proud people, who, with their gifts and virtues, are an inseparable part of the European family. People forget that Franco was a leading General of the Spanish Constitutional Republic. Several weeks before the outbreak, in a remarkable letter published in the British Press, he warned the Government of the dangers which the rising tide of anarchy and the weakness of the Executive would bring upon the country. The breakdown of the political and Parliamentary game where the ball was pitched to and fro into the mire led the military chiefs, supported by all the social forces of old Spain, to make one of those 'pronunciamentos' for which there are many precedents, some of them highly beneficial, in modern Spanish history. The military coup d'état misfired. The Government disintegrated into the bloody fury of the mob. Thousands of executions swept the Spanish people into the deep, dark, bitter swirling waters.

Once ranged against each other their virtues of constancy and courage, as well as their undue insensibility to human pain, aggravated their plight. A long, ferocious, and obstinate war is devastating the homeland. Each side has catalogues of atrocities to unfold against the other. On each side many thousands of men and women have vowed themselves to their last breath to avenge some dear one, father, husband, brother, child, slaughtered—too often in cold blood. A sinister logic of retaliation has reigned. But where is it to stop? To-day, after more than two years of murderous fighting, no one can say who will win. All can be sure, however, that Spain will lose.

The debts can never be paid. Not here in this world, at least, can justice be exacted by either side. They can combine together by their fury only to win the fatal prizes of death and ruin for all. Franco's victory must be followed by a fierce struggle between the brave religious forces of old Spain, the romantic, valiant Requetes on the one hand and the German-backed Phalangists, to whom the noble tragic name of the young De Rivera has become a worship on the other. Here again a future only of rend and tear! But look across the lines. The Anarchists and Communists, held at present in a hard grip of self-preservation, will in the moment of success resume their struggle with each other and with the Republican Government. The triumph then of either Party, however complete, will merely turn one bloody page in order to deface another.

But has not Spain need of all her sons? Does not her ancient greatness call from the past for the help of all true men and true women in the land? The stubborn, unflinching Republican infantry who held the trenches around Madrid and across the Ebro, the dauntless Catalans with their long history, the unlucky, ill-guided and bewildered Basques, the heroic cadets, unconquerable in the Alcazar, the patriot Generals of the old army, their officers and faithful men—all have a common principle which should overpower the scent of newly-shed blood. Why should the ideals of religion and monarchy be incompatible with those of freedom and democracy? All flow together generously in our island. Why should they not mingle harmoniously in the Spanish Peninsula?

Now is the time! Now, while the issue still hangs in the balance. Now while the fronts are locked in winter, now before the huge shadow of European antagonisms further darkens the scene, now let the Spaniards come together and by a sublime act of oblivion save the land they love so well.

THE ANGLO-GERMAN NAVAL AGREEMENT JANUARY 12, 1939

There is much talk about the Anglo-German Naval Agreement now that the Germans have announced their intention of building to a hundred per cent. parity with British submarine tonnage. There is no doubt that Germany has a right to do this under the Treaty. The question arises whether the British Government of 1935 acted rightly or wrongly in making the agreement. The official view in Whitehall is that it was a masterstroke of policy, the first great step in the process of 'appeasement,' and an example to prove to all the world how easy it is to have working arrangements between democratic Parliamentary nations and Totalitarian dictatorships. It is not possible to judge such matters without looking back to their origins. We have to remind ourselves of the situation in the summer of 1935. The process is not pleasant, because it shows us how hideously our affairs have worsened since then.

In May 1935, Herr Hitler announced his intention of breaking the Treaty of Versailles by restarting universal military conscription in Germany. Most of his generals and advisers were shy about this, and warned him that the former allies would never allow him to take such a step. But as it turned out, he knew better than they. So he took the plunge. The result was the conference at Stresa, where Britain, France and Italy presented a common front against the Nazi repudiation of solemn engagements. This was the last act in foreign policy of Ramsay MacDonald, and without any doubt it was his best. The Council of the League of Nations was convened. It formally condemned what is called, in modern jargon, the unilateral breach of treaties. Thus not only were the three former allies all arrayed together, but the whole international and moral authority then represented by the League of Nations supported them. There was a combined opposition of force and of law to treaty-breaking, which Germany, then practically unarmed, could certainly not have overcome.

However, on June 18 the Anglo-German Naval Agreement was signed, and Europe was astonished to learn that the British Government had made a private bargain for themselves about naval strength with Nazi Germany which completely stultified the agreement of the three allied Powers at Stresa, and made the latest declaration of the Council of the League of Nations ridiculous. British Ministers had, it seemed, condoned the breaking of treaties about naval strength at the very moment when they were urging the smaller powers of Europe to make a combined protest against the breaking of the military clauses. This was a heavy blow at all international co-operation in support of public law. The Scandinavian powers had been represented at Geneva; they had joined in the protest against German army conscription. They now found themselves left high and dry, and the interests of Scandinavia and the Baltic were profoundly affected. It became certain that the Germans would soon re-establish their old and vital command of the Baltic. The whole outlook of Scandinavia was changed.

Signor Mussolini had his designs upon Abyssinia. He might well have been prepared to lay these aside for the sake of a large and faithful combination of the three great former allied powers. But as he saw the British Government ready to make private arrangements in what they deemed their interest, he felt that he might look after himself. If the currency of international good faith was to be debased in this manner, why should not the Italian mint be set to work too? From this among other causes a whole train of evils rapidly flowed.

One can understand the temptation of the German proposal to the British Admiralty. Before the War we maintained by great exertions a superiority of sixteen to ten in capital ships and two to one in cruisers and small craft. Now here was an offer from Germany to accept a ratio of only one-third of British Naval tonnage, and consequently to resign, on paper at any rate, all claim to the sovereignty of the oceans. When it was pointed out in Parliament by me that the building by the Germans of a new navy one-third the tonnage of the then antiquated British Fleet would entail the complete rebuilding of the British Fleet, the Admiralty remained quite cool. They welcomed the German construction as a spur and pace-maker, which would procure the necessary funds from the British Government. Thus the Agreement passed smoothly through the House of Commons, and all protests and warnings were unavailing.

Let us now survey the position of 1935 from Herr Hitler's point of view. He was concerned above all things with restarting universal military service in Germany. He had already worked up in secret a considerable force, but without a large conscript army he could not carry the policy of German expansion forward. Therefore, it was sagacious of him to make a concession to Great Britain about the Navy which would set her easy, which would break her step with the rest of Europe, and would help handspike the League of Nations. But did he even in the naval sphere give up anything that he wanted, or could do in the immediate future? Under the Versailles Treaty he had at that time hardly any navy at all. To have the right to build up to one-third of the British tonnage would absorb all the energies which Germany could spare from rearmament on land, or in the air, for a good many years to come. The German resources in skilled labour, in suitable plants and in high-grade war materials, have never been unlimited. The Air Force came first, then the new conscript army, and the navy could only be third. There was no chance of her overtaking Britain, and when Britain began to rebuild her Fleet in earnest, this became more obvious than ever. But still, if Germany had one-third of the British tonnage, she would secure the naval command of the Baltic. Thus to make the agreement gave Hitler immense advantages and cost him nothing.

Moreover, if when Germany has succeeded in building one-third of the British Fleet, she wishes to build more, how easy to say that the situation has changed, that the American building or Russian building has produced factors unforeseen in 1935, and to ask for a half, two-thirds, or even equality, as has already been done in respect of U-boats. History will long admire Herr Hitler's shrewdness, and wonder at the simplicity of those with whom he dealt.

We are now confronted with the situation as it exists to-day. There is no fear of Germany overtaking Great Britain on the sea. The immense fleets now under construction in the British dockyards leave Germany running along far behind. It will take her all her time to achieve even a third of the total British tonnage. The U-boats, in which she will soon have superior numbers and even tonnage, to the Royal Navy, would be a serious inconvenience and injury to British commerce in case of war. But the methods of dealing with submersible craft have been developed out of all measure, and provided the British flotillas and antisubmarine craft are multiplied on high priority and a large scale, there is no reason to believe that the U-boat will be a decisive weapon. Great Britain has incurred an avoidable danger, but a danger, nevertheless, with which she can undoubtedly cope, though with loss and suffering. Now that the Baltic is gone; the League of Nations is broken, and Italy estranged, it would seem to be a mistake to hold up the Anglo-German Agreement, having regard to its setting and its consequences, as a model of the kind of arrangements we should seek to make in time to come.

But a great danger still remains; we may be presented in the future with new proposals by Germany for so-called 'disarmament.' The Nazi negotiators will say that if Germany is willing to accept a British Navy three times their tonnage, surely Great Britain will accept a German air force twice or three times the British strength.[1] Thus the follies we have committed with one hand may be made the excuse for another set of far more deadly follies with the other. It would be wiser for Great Britain to let the Anglo-German Naval Agreement lapse and let Nazi Germany build whatever navy she can, rather than that we should accept any limiting ratio in the air in breach of Mr. Baldwin's pledge to Parliament of air parity.

Ministers who agreed to bind the British island to a permanent inferiority to Germany in the air would be guilty of a crime against the life of the Empire. It would even be advantageous that German energies and their limited supply of material should be expended upon a naval race which they cannot possibly win, rather than that they should be concentrated upon increasing their air menace to the freedom and the safety of Britain.

---

[1] Herr Hitler's one-sided denunciation of the Naval Agreement has relieved us from this.

MUSSOLINI'S CARES
JANUARY 30, 1939

Up till a few years ago many people in Britain admired the work which the extraordinary man Signor Mussolini had done for his country. He had brought it out of incipient anarchy into a position of dignity and order, which was admired even by those who regretted the suspension of Italian freedom. The English, although opposed to the Fascist idea, were glad to see Italy become a stronger nation, and in the sincerity of old friendship wished her well.

Since 1935 great changes have occurred. The conquest of Abyssinia, the violation of all pledges given to members of the League of Nations, the enforced retreat of the British Government from its Sanctions policy, have painfully altered the historic relations of the two peoples. The invasion of Spain by regular divisions of the Italian army, the repeated sinking of British ships by Italian aeroplanes, and at one time by Italian submarines thinly disguised by sale or loan to Franco, have made a profound impression upon the British working-classes; this has been worsened by the pretence of non-intervention maintained brazenly and persistently in defiance of truth and fact.

In March 1938, Mr. Neville Chamberlain made a vehement effort to forget the past and restore the old friendship. He forced Mr. Eden's resignation and became, in fact if not in form, his own Foreign Secretary. The Anglo-Italian Agreement was framed; and although the conditions about Spain prescribed by the British Government were not fulfilled, this agreement has now been ratified. In every respect it was favourable to Italy. Britain, which had taken the lead in imposing Sanctions to protect Abyssinia from aggression, now took the lead in recognising the Italian conquest, which has certainly not yet been completed. But neither a withdrawal of the Italian troops from Spain nor a revival of former goodwill has requited the Prime Minister's well-meant endeavours. His recent visit to Rome upon a somewhat chilly invitation produced nothing but polite recognition on both sides of wide differences of outlook and divergence of paths.

Meanwhile on the great field of Europe Germany has become the dominant, aggressive power. Austria has fallen; Czechoslovakia has been subjugated; German authority and German trade stride forward together down the Danube Valley. The steel-helmets of the German army glint upon the Brenner Pass. In the unequal partnership of the two Dictators, Hitler has gained everything, and Mussolini nothing. At the same time, the keeping of a large, wholly unproductive army in Abyssinia, without the slightest control of the country or chance of developing it, has imposed a grievous strain upon Italian finance and economy. The very large Italian forces maintained in Libya to-day are an aggravation.

But it is in Spain that Italian blood, money and munitions have been most seriously engaged. The Germans have contented themselves with sending specialists, technicians and aviators, together with masses of war material from their overflowing factories. Mussolini has actually done a large part of General Franco's fighting for him. Italian stocks of munitions of all kinds have been drawn upon heavily, and the burden upon the Italian people has become ever harder for them to bear. During the last year, for the first time, criticism has been rife in the ruling circles of Italian life and politics; and although the repeated submissions of the Western democracies to Dictatorial demands have veiled the movement of forces, there is no doubt that both Italy and her leader are to-day in a condition at once strained and fragile.

As a result of all these exertions and manœuvres Mussolini finds himself entirely in the hands of Hitler. His need to have some prize that can be exhibited to the Italian nation, to have some share in the immense gains gathered by Germany, has become imperious. But Hitler is the rich uncle who alone can help the loyal but improvident nephew through his difficulties. It must be admitted that the uncle is under obligations which must appeal alike to his good faith and his generosity. Will the uncle pay the bill, and can he fit its payment in with other heavy charges and projects? That is the question which exercises many minds to-day. It seems that from the British visit to Rome Mussolini learned that Mr. Neville Chamberlain had reached the limits of appeasement. The British Parliament is averse from making further one-sided concessions. In the approach of a General Election public opinion must be considered. Patience and readiness to respond to fair dealing are all that Great Britain can offer to the solution of Mussolini's problems.

Meanwhile, he has deliberately picked a quarrel with the French Republic. One has to look far and wide through the annals of Europe for such an apparently wanton provocation. Demands for Nice, Corsica and Tunis, obviously fomented by official authority, a campaign of calumny and insult in the Government-controlled Press, the denunciation of agreements hitherto deemed satisfactory, taunts and threats, are all the reward which France has reaped from her recognition of Italian sovereignty over Abyssinia. Here again Signor Mussolini comes to a full-stop; and it is of the utmost importance that he should not be misled, or mislead his countrymen.

The French, like the British, are anxious to live in peace. They have exposed themselves both to injury and mockery to prove that this is so. But it would be imprudent, and is indeed impossible, to disguise the fact that the French nation is now determined to resist by force of arms any attack, even the smallest, upon their territory. There is a new spirit of resolve in France; it animates all classes and parties. No delusion could be more dangerous to Mussolini than that, for instance, an attack upon Jibuti would be treated as a remote local incident upon which a conference might subsequently sit. It would be a major act of war involving the two leading Mediterranean Powers. Such a war might be immediately widened into a general catastrophe.

Is this what Signor Mussolini wants? Are his embarrassments at home so serious that only a world-wide explosion affords a means of escape? Do the Italian people realise that they might easily be drawn into a struggle which would either end in their defeat or in their rescue by Germany at a price fatal to their independence? There are also dangers connected with Spain which may lead to a disaster beyond the power of British goodwill to avert.

We must all devoutly hope that the Italian Dictator will count the cost before opening the flood-gates of carnage upon the world—and upon no part of the world more than the highly vulnerable country of which he has so long been the spirited and successful chief.

At this time a series of extremely encouraging statements upon future prospects in Europe and the speedy advent of a golden age were made by leading Ministers of the Crown. These authoritative pronouncements were largely accepted by the British press.

THE LULL IN EUROPE
FEBRUARY 9, 1939

There is, alas, insufficient justification for the ripples of optimism which have spread across the surface of British and European opinion since Herr Hitler's last speech. From every quarter comes the tale of heavy movements of German munitions and supplies through Prague, Vienna and Munich. The ordinary railway services are restricted while these great convoys pass. What is their destination? What is their purpose? The German army is maintaining with the Colours a far larger number of troops than even its own immense establishment requires. Many straws of technical information show the way the wind is blowing. There is no doubt that Signor Mussolini will soon focus upon France demands of a serious character, and although the German Nazi Government have by no means spurred him to this, Herr Hitler has declared that he will support him. Indeed, it is clear that the German Dictator could not afford to witness the downfall of his Italian colleague.

Everyone seems to be agreed that Nazi desires against the Ukraine are now relegated to a secondary and contingent stage in the programme of expansion. Hungary is in the grip of the Nazi system, and at any time all those grievous questions open between Hungary and Rumania can be made the subject of demands upon King Carol. The politics of Yugoslavia are difficult for outsiders to understand. This large, powerful, virile country, with its warlike population and inferior equipment, watches with acute anxiety the movements of the two Dictator Powers upon its borders. The sudden fall of the Stoyadinovitch regime is due to forces hard to measure. At the root of it, however, lies the question of national defence. So bitter is the discontent of the Croats with the present structure and system of the Yugoslav Government that it would not be possible to mobilise the soldiers of Croatia. These indeed, would fight with a good heart for the defence of their country, but once arms were placed in the hands of this sturdy and trained peasantry, it is more than probable they would be used for the purposes of establishing a federal Constitution for the Kingdom of the Serbs, Croats and Slovenes.

Evidently the need of basing the government of Prince Paul broadly upon the whole State has produced an internal spasm of resolve. Only by the ruling Serbs making common cause with the rest of the kingdom can its full strength, security and integrity be realised. Dr. Stoyadinovitch was markedly pro-German, and to some extent pro-Nazi, in his policy. He was one of those European statesmen who found in the Munich Agreement and the fate of Czechoslovakia a vindication of the course he had pursued. His government had always believed that France would abandon the Czechoslovak Republic, and on the morrow of that event his opponents who had wished to associate themselves with the interests of the Western democracies appeared utterly confounded.

We may judge, therefore, from his resignation that the stresses internal and external of Yugoslavia have reached a point where national self-preservation seems to be involved. It is idle to forecast the future course of events in these grim regions. One can only say that the stronger and more united are the three races who of their own free will became one State, the better for the peace of the Balkans and of the Danube Valley; and for larger causes as well.

A more immediate question is the attitude of France towards Italian claims in the Mediterranean. In this there was a fear that two voices would be heard. M. Daladier and the bulk of the French Cabinet have declared that they will not enter upon any conversations with Italy, even on minor points, while the outrageous Press campaign against France continues, and while demands for the cession of Tunis, Corsica and Nice are rife. M. Bonnet, however, had appeared to give a different impression; and it was difficult for people outside France to assess the mysterious elements of strength upon which the French Foreign Minister relied. The statement which he made on Tuesday to the Senate showed a complete solidarity in France.

The momentous declaration made by Mr. Chamberlain in the House of Commons on Monday that an act of aggression against France from any quarter would be equally resisted by Great Britain shows that the two Western democracies are resolved to act as one and stand together. Few can escape the feeling that the next few months will witness another confrontation and trial of strength and will-power between the rival forces in Europe. When Herr Hitler expressed his belief that a long period of peace lay ahead, it was no doubt in the expectation that matters would, after a time of tension, be adjusted to the satisfaction of the two Dictatorial Powers. Whether this will be so or not no man can predict. The assurances which Signor Mussolini has renewed that Italy seeks no territorial gains at the expense of Spain do not touch the military issue. The victory of General Franco may be followed by arrangements which, without altering sovereignty, give the effective use of all Spanish bases, both naval and air, to the two countries who have helped him so much. Such arrangements would, to all intents and purposes, be as detrimental to British and French interests as an actual transference of territory.

It would not, however, be right to look only upon the darker side. The remarkable action of President Roosevelt, undoubtedly sustained by the government and people of the United States, in letting it be widely known that not only American moral support but also practical aid in munitions and supplies will be accorded to the Western democracies should they become the victims of unprovoked aggression, is a potent stabilising force. It may well be that the preservation of European peace will be secured through his far-sighted and courageous policy. The spirit of resistance to Nazi encroachment has not been extinguished in Eastern and South-eastern Europe. Countries which before Munich were under the impression that they were being asked to confer favours on France and Great Britain, have now realised forcibly that it is their own lives which are endangered.

Here at home in England there has been a reconsolidation of national union. The attitude of the Government has stiffened, and some past differences are fading into history. Above all, there is a sense of gathering strength. The power and condition of the Royal Navy relatively to its possible tasks is unprecedented. The long-delayed flow of aircraft and munitions is now arriving. If redoubled exertions are made, a far greater measure of security may be procured for the civil population against air raids. While only astrologers and other merchants of superstition can declare the future, the day may yet come when the peaceful, law-respecting British nation may once again be able to pursue its journey without having to wait and listen on the wireless from week to week to the dictatorial orations from countries they defeated or succoured in the past.

HOPE IN SPAIN
FEBRUARY 23, 1939

Everyone must now desire a speedy settlement in Spain, and if the British and French Governments can help to bring this about they will deserve the thanks of all. They would certainly be entitled at this juncture to use the lever of Recognition to procure merciful treatment for the beaten side. Although General Miaja and the Madrid Army may perhaps be capable of maintaining a solid resistance for several months, they cannot prevent the ultimate victory of General Franco and the Nationalists. What then will be the use of a further cruel period of bloodshed, with Spaniards tearing the entrails of their Motherland?

Spaniards must come together. They must plan to live as one people in their broad peninsula. They must resume united contact with their history. They must regain their share in the economic expansion of the world. Who would benefit by a prolongation of this self-inflicted torture? Certainly no true friend of Spain. Virulent hatred arising from social stresses grew for a generation inside Spain. The vehicle of Parliamentary discussion could no longer carry the load; it broke down. An electric current became too strong for the cable; it fused. A society speechless with anger could only express itself by war. Spain has had its war. Some say a million lives have been lost in a population none too large for the historic land in which they dwell. None of those on either side, generals or Republicans, ever meant this hideous thing to come upon their country. It burst upon them with all the astounding force of an explosion. After that everyone had to choose his side, bend his head, and butt into the storm. There are moments in the story of every country when catastrophic frenzy may sweep all men off their feet.

Then comes the sword. Civil war is opened. The tolerances of life take flight; thousands fall in battle; thousands of others are shot against the wall, or basely murdered in the ditch. Feuds innumerable are lighted; scores are added up which can never be paid. But at length regular armies come into the field. Discipline, organisation grips in earnest both sides. They march, manœuvre, advance, retreat, with all the valour common to the leading races of mankind. But here are new structures of national life erected upon blood, sweat and tears, which are not dissimilar and therefore capable of being united. What milestone of advantage can be gained by going farther? Now is the time to stop.

An eminent Spaniard, Señor Madariaga, has uttered a suggestive warning to foreign enthusiasts and outside meddlers of all kinds. Let them be careful that they do not, in their airy detachment, prolong the agony of the Spanish people. Let them cease to regard Spain as a bullring in which the Fascist and Communist ideologies will be performing at Spanish expense. He, and probably ninety-nine Spaniards out of every hundred, ask that Spain should be left alone to wind up its quarrel in its own way. This is the Spanish attitude which now confronts the Western democracies as well as the Fascist-Nazi Powers. Upon that there are some remarks to be made.

At the beginning of the Spanish Civil War, which appeared at the first in the form of a military revolt against impending anarchy, we were suddenly surprised to find the French Government of M. Blum proposing Non-Intervention in a form which prevented the constituted Government of Spain from buying from abroad even the weapons which they had ordered before the outbreak, to pay for which they had ample funds. Such a policy required equal detachment and good faith from the Dictator States. These were not forthcoming; and an elaborate system of official humbug has been laboriously maintained. During the whole long period of the war, Germany and Italy have brazenly supported Franco not only with arms but with men. During the same period Russia and France have covertly furnished supplies to the Republicans. Britain only has stood aloof and tried to be impartial.

As long as the issue of the war hung in the balance, it would have been wrong for Britain to throw her weight on either side of the scale. Even a few months ago, when Catalonia, mountainous and separate, was still unconquered, the British recognition of Franco's Spain would have been an act of partisanship. Now all stands on a different footing, and the main interests of Britain must be considered. Those interests are nakedly apparent to the world. We seek a united, independent Spain, making the best of itself apart from Europe. For this purpose it is above all things important that no cruel retribution should be exacted from the vanquished. The interest of the British Empire is in fact identical with that of all Spain. Spanish peace, Spanish prosperity, Spanish independence, are all that we seek.

But for these we should be prepared to make exertions, incur expenses and run risks. The neutralisation of Spain from the contentions which are rife in the modern world is of equal interest for the British Empire and the French Republic. The two allied democracies should therefore move forward easily and naturally upon the path of Spanish peace and of general advantage. There is no additional danger, but rather the approach to a greater security, in pursuing that path with massive weight and resolve. To Spain we use the invocation of the great Pitt: 'Be one people.' For the outside world our policy should be 'Hands off Spain.'

It is impossible to forecast the course of events in Spain. General Franco's triumph opens to him only a vista of new difficulties. He cannot live by terror. Half a nation cannot exterminate or subjugate the other half. He must come to terms with the rest of his fellow-countrymen. It is in his profound interest to do so. I have several times reminded my readers that Franco was a Republican general who gave full warning to the Spanish Government of the political anarchy into which they were drifting. He now has the opportunity of becoming a great Spaniard of whom it may be written a hundred years hence: 'He united his country and rebuilt its greatness. Apart from that he reconciled the past with the present, and broadened the life of the working people while preserving the faith and structure of the Spanish nation.' Such an achievement would rank in history with the work of Ferdinand and Isabella and the glories of Charles V. The strong hands of Britain and France would aid him in this task.

There remains to be considered the grave question of whether this healing, compassionate and regenerative process will be obstructed by the two Dictators. One does not like to hear that they are opposed to the re-establishment of a constitutional and limited monarchy in Spain. It would seem that the placing of the supreme office in the Spanish State above the range of private ambition would give a stability invaluable to the work of Spanish reconstruction. It would afford a rallying summit upon which new loyalties might centre, and beneath which former political feuds might sink to an innocuous level, or even into oblivion. Naturally the British democracy, dwelling contentedly under an ancient monarchy, enjoying the fullest political liberty and having more food to eat each day in their homes than any nation in Europe, would be biased in favour of such a solution. It is certainly not one which we could obtrude upon Spain. We have our opinions and our long experience; but it is not for us to prescribe.

Whether Spain will be allowed to find its way back to sanity and health without foreign interference depends not upon us, nor upon France, but upon the general adjustment or outcome of the European crunch. Of this larger matter we shall presently become better informed.

IS IT PEACE?
MARCH 9, 1939

From every quarter come reports of the remarkable impression produced abroad by the British Defence Estimates for the new financial year. No less than £580,000,000 will be provided for the Air, the Navy and the Army. This follows upon a year in which £405,000,000 was actually spent. The great upward leap does not imply a new policy on the part of the Government. It is mainly the result of the enormous plants, which have been lengthily and laboriously erected, coming into operation, and of course of the cumulative effect of three very heavy naval programmes being simultaneously under construction. It cannot be doubted that unless some great change takes place in the world, all the figures projected for 1939 will grow much larger in 1940. That this extraordinary rearmament can be financed without any serious embarrassment to British credit, and even with a positive improvement in trade, is a proof of the wonderful economic strength of the British nation. A tribute is due to the control of the Exchequer during recent years, which has made such feats possible without undue strain or hardship.

It is certain that Italy can no longer compete effectively, or on the same scale, in this lamentable armaments race. Signor Mussolini's naval expenditure has never been more than a small fraction of the British, and is now barely a fifth. The Italian effort in the air has not only not expanded, but has already been definitely reduced. The drain of keeping three large armies overseas under war conditions in Abyssinia, Libya and Spain, has weakened the whole Italian military machine. It is a marvel how this process has been kept going so long. The patient, industrious, good-natured Italian people have made severe sacrifices to support the weight of a regime which gratifies their patriotic pride. The middle and wealthy classes have been sensibly impoverished. The need to purchase across the exchange so many of the costly materials of war production imposes constantly ever more obscure and delicate problems. It is certain that the coming year will register a marked decline in the relative strength at sea and in the air of Italy compared with Great Britain and the United States. Should trouble come, Germany would have to carry Italy upon her shoulders to a far greater extent than she carried the Austro-Hungarian Empire in the Great War. The peculiarly vulnerable character of the Italian Peninsula, and the impossibility of maintaining large Italian armies overseas once the command of the Mediterranean was denied, would make the discharge of the German task even more burdensome.

Let us then look to conditions in the mighty Reich, upon which the hopes and ambitions of the Axis Powers depend. A careful examination of German finance shows that the scale of expenditure, direct and indirect, upon armaments takes another forward step this year. It is calculated that for the year 1938–9 Germany will have provided more than the equivalent of £1,150,000,000 sterling. This follows upon expenditures which for the three previous years have never been far short of £1,000,000,000. When I mentioned for the first time at the beginning of 1936 the figure of £800,000,000 for the German arms expenditure it was generally considered fantastic. It was in fact an underestimate. But now the rate has risen still higher, and is computed to amount to nearly 26 per cent. of the entire German national income.

In rate of expenditure Germany is evidently under a strain far more severe than Great Britain. The proportion of the British national income to be devoted in the coming year to armaments is less than half the German proportion. It is true that the total German figure of £1,150,000,000 is also double the new British programme. But it must be remembered that the main charge upon the German military budget is for the Army, for which there is no comparable British expense. So far as the Navy and the Air are concerned, the amounts now at last being laid out in Great Britain must be very nearly equal to Germany in air expense, and are several times as large in naval expense.

What is the bearing of all these factors upon the question, which dwells with us from day to day, of the preservation of peace? Anyone can see that they cut both ways. On the one hand, the manifest intention and ability of the British Government to rearm upon the greatest scale has already gained a respect for British wishes and rights which was not previously apparent. On the other, it must be remembered that the large developments of rearmament in Britain lie in the future. The wide field is ploughed and sown. The crops are rich and promising, but they have not yet been gathered in. Whereas Germany, spending consistently for four successive years in the neighbourhood of an annual £1,000,000,000 has an immense accumulation of these evil harvests.

Mr. Chamberlain said the other day in the House of Commons that there was no public man or party in England who had ever contemplated what is called 'a preventive war' against any other country. The truth of this is evident when we consider what the expression 'a preventive war' means. The most common form in history is a war to forestall an opponent who is catching up in strength. When a country which has enjoyed a large superiority in strength sees its advantages diminishing, there is always the temptation to make a preventive war, or to bring matters to an issue while time remains. Our position is the exact opposite of this. We must, therefore, beware of supposing that the dangers inherent in the present European situation are removed by anything that has happened so far in the field of British national defence. On the contrary, the tendency upon the Continent is still towards a climax at no distant date. Whether that climax will take the form of war or of the measuring of strength without war is another question. But he would be a foolish optimist who closed his eyes to the underlying gravity of the months immediately before us.

We still await the formulation of demands upon the French Republic which Signor Mussolini is reported to intend. No solution of the German and Italian intervention in Spain has yet been reached. The military preparations not only of Italy but of France on the North-African shore are intensifying. It was surely not without serious information that President Roosevelt curtailed his cruise with the American fleet. The United States

Government are very accurately informed about Europe and study its problems from an angle of their own. It is certainly a time for the utmost vigilance and for unremitting effort.

The improvement in the East of Europe is, however, a most important stabilising force. A veritable wave of revulsion against possible Nazi aggression has swept all the countries from the Baltic to the Black Sea. The mutually defensive understanding reached between the principal Balkan Powers and Turkey affords a weighty guarantee of peace. The new Yugoslav Government, based upon effective reconciliation with the Croats, has recognised the identity of interests which it has with Rumania. Even Hungary has shown remarkable resilience. More favourable developments still have occurred in Poland. A strong sense of self-preservation seems to be awake in Eastern Europe. The fate of Czechoslovakia has not induced submission or despair.

Beyond all lies the great counterpoise of Soviet Russia. We may not be able to measure its present weight, but that it is ponderous and exerted in the maintenance of peace cannot be doubted. Mr. Chamberlain's visit to the Soviet Embassy in London betokens the new interest which Great Britain is taking in the possibilities of increased trade and co-operation with Russia. We may look, therefore, with hope to what is happening in the East of Europe, as well as to the growing strength across the Atlantic, as increasing guarantees against a breakdown of civilisation in this anxious year.

On the Ides of March, Herr Hitler, spurning his promises to Mr. Chamberlain at Munich, invaded, occupied and annexed the Czech Republic, taking its treasure, disbanding its army, and carting off its munitions and food. Thousands of Czechs were put in concentration camps, and an iron rule and censorship established.

Upon this Mr. Chamberlain decided to abandon the policy of appeasement and to try to form a Peace block of armed nations. British guarantees were sent to Poland and Rumania, and other negotiations set on foot.

THE CRUNCH
MARCH 24, 1939

A month ago in these columns I used the phrase 'the European crunch' because it seemed certain that some great trial of strength impended between Nazidom and its opponents. It was clear then that the German preparations portended another violent stroke. By the beginning of March the final arrangements had been made for industrial mobilisation and for turning over German factories to their alternative war production. At the same time a heavy movement of munitions and troops to the East was evident. The optimism in which those who could have had access to this information indulged, represented their wish but had no basis in known ascertainable facts. It is astonishing that any well-informed and thoughtful person could have believed that the spring would pass without a renewed act of aggression by the German Dictator.

The blow has been struck. Hitler, following exactly the doctrines of *Mein Kampf,* has broken every tie of good faith with the British and French statesmen who tried so hard to believe in him. The Munich Agreement which represented such great advantages for Germany has been brutally violated. Mr. Chamberlain has been ill-used and affronted. The entire apparatus of confidence and goodwill which was being sedulously constructed in Great Britain has been shattered into innumerable fragments. It can never again be mended while the present domination rules in Germany. This melancholy fact must be faced. A veritable revolution in feeling and opinion has occurred in Britain, and reverberates through all the self-governing Dominions. Indeed, a similar process has taken place spontaneously throughout the whole British Empire.

This mass conversion of those who had hitherto been hopeful took place within a single week, but not within a single day. It was not an explosion, but the kindling of a fire which rose steadily, hour by hour, to an intense furnace heat of inward conviction. Nothing is more impressive than the outward calm which has been preserved. It has hardly been thought necessary to argue the matter. Those who have seen in these events the melancholy fulfilment of their beliefs and warnings have not exulted. Those whose eyes are now opened, have not recanted: nor need they do so. Their aims were honourable. All are united in a resolve to meet the awful danger which threatens the civilisation of the world. There is a fatalistic feeling that events have inexorably shaped our path, and that we can do no other than follow it with steadfast perseverance. That path has become more arduous and hazardous than in September. The military strength of Nazidom has received an enormous reinforcement. The destruction of the well-organised, thoroughly-equipped Czech army, and the capture by Germany of all the arsenals, artillery and munitions of the murdered Republic, constitute a loss to the Western democracies of the first magnitude.

One can understand very readily how Hitler's mind has worked. He regarded Munich as an act of submission on the part of Britain and France under the threat of war. No one knew better than he the inherent weakness of his own position at that time. His generals and financial experts had warned him of the risks he ran. He felt that he knew the limits of the will-power of those against whom he was matched. He was sure that the sincere love of peace which inspired the British and French Governments would lead them to give way under pressure. He ascribed their action when they did so only to the basest motives. All their conscientious scruples about self-determination for the Sudeten-Germans were to him only the evidences of their lack of fighting quality. When what he had predicted to his circle was confirmed by the event, his confidence in his instinct and in his star bounded high.

'History,' [he had written in *Mein Kampf*] 'teaches us that nations which have once given way before the threat of arms without being forced to do so will accept the greatest humiliations and exactions rather than make a fresh appeal to force. He who has obtained such an advantage will, if he is clever, only make his fresh demands in small doses. When dealing with a nation which has lost all force of character owing to its having given way spontaneously, he will be entitled to expect that his fresh but piecemeal demands will not be considered worth resisting by the nation from which they are made.'

It must, therefore, have come to him as an ugly shock that Great Britain should have reacted so violently against his seizure of Czechoslovakia. He had assumed that the Munich Agreement implied the final ending of British and French resistance to his domination of Eastern Europe. He thought himself secure in giving full rein to his appetites and ambitions. If the great nations of the West would not fight for Czechoslovakia while she was strong, why should they concern themselves with her fate once she was entirely in his power? If they would not fight for Czechoslovakia, how much less would they fight, under more adverse conditions, for Rumania? A broad road down the Danube Valley to the Black Sea was open. The guardian bastion had been abandoned. Henceforth who would be so imprudent, and indeed, as it seemed to him, so illogical, as to bar his passage? One must admit that in his own fevered heart he had some grounds for being misled.

If the Nazi Dictator had the time to study English history he would see that on more than one famous occasion this island has lost great military advantages in Europe by its intense reluctance to be involved in Continental struggles, and has yet in the end led the way to victory. He had only to read the last two years of the reign of King William III and the opening years of Queen Anne to learn that an improvident unwillingness to enter a quarrel may be succeeded by unwearying and triumphant leadership in that same quarrel at a later and more difficult stage. How could Louis XIV believe that the England which had tamely watched his occupation of all the Belgian fortresses in 1701 would reach a long arm to strangle his armies on the Danube in 1704?

Hitler's disillusionment does not rest only upon the resurgence of will-power in the Western democracies. The whole attitude of Eastern Europe is hostile to Nazi aggression. Instead of being terrified by the fate of Czechoslovakia, Poland, Rumania, Turkey, Greece, Bulgaria, and by no means the least—Yugoslavia—have been roused to a lively sense of self-preservation. The Rumanian Monarchy has as its representative a man of masculine determination. The whole Rumanian people, in spite of the serious divisions of domestic politics, have rallied to the defence of their country. A strong regular army occupies the various defensive lines. Behind them both Turkey and Russia stretch forth friendly hands. The power and influence of Russia may well be underrated. The loyal attitude of the Soviets to the cause of peace, and their obvious interest in resisting the Nazi advance to the Black Sea, impart a feeling of encouragement to all the Eastern States now menaced by the maniacal dreams of Berlin.

The situation which confronts Hitler is therefore stern; and the question which now lies in suspense is how he and his circle will respond to it. It is certain that no tolerable relations will be possible for Germany with the outer world until Czechoslovakia has been liberated. There can be no question of Trade Pacts or cordiality while that crime still calls for justice and reparation. On the other hand, for a Dictator to recede and to disgorge is a step fraught with mortal danger. It is for this reason that the whole world position must be regarded as tense and grievous in the last degree.

One thing only is certain: the forces opposed to Nazidom are, in spite of what has happened, still by far the stronger. A period of suffering resulting from the air-slaughter of non-combatants may lie before us; but this, if borne with fortitude, will only seal the comradeship of many nations to save themselves and the future of mankind from a tyrant's grip.

On Good Friday 1939, Signor Mussolini invaded, and thereafter annexed, Albania. The resistance of the Albanians was beaten down by overwhelming force, and the seaports heavily bombarded.

MUSSOLINI'S CHOICE
APRIL 13, 1939

Speculation has been rife in many countries about whether Signor Mussolini will carry Italy into a world war on the German side. Most people think that after what has happened in the last fortnight this question has already been decided. The Anglo-Italian Agreement has been violated in the most barefaced manner. There is not one single point upon which faith has been kept.

Italy promised to reduce her army in Libya by 30,000 men. She has taken them away and then sent them back. Italy promised to withdraw her troops from Spain, at any rate when the civil war was over. The war is over and the troops are still there. She promised not to change the *status quo* in the Mediterranean, which included, and was understood to include, the Adriatic. She has now laid violent hands upon Albanian Independence. She promised that all major troop movements would be notified beforehand to the other high contracting party. All this has been contemptuously torn in pieces. As an additional piece of deceit, precise assurances were given by Count Ciano to the British Ambassador that no movement upon Albania was in contemplation. At that very moment the ships and troops were about to move upon their victim.

It is not possible to have a more complete instance of bad faith than has been shown. One may well ask whether a Government who have thus flouted and spurned a solemn agreement, newly contracted with a friendly Power, have not already made up their mind to carry their hostility to that Power to all lengths as occasion may require. Nevertheless, though faith may be broken interest remains. It was a maxim of the eighteenth century, mentioned by the great Duke of Marlborough—'Interest never lies.' And certainly Italian interests would be grievously injured in a war against Great Britain and France in the Mediterranean. There never was a country more completely sprawled than Italy at the present moment. Four separate Italian armies have left her shores and would be hopelessly cut off if the Italian Navy were beaten by the Anglo-French fleets. These fleets are incomparably more powerful than the Italian navy. Even if the Italian warships were all manned by Mussolinis, it is difficult to believe that they could keep the sea against the very heavy odds to which they would be exposed. Nothing that happened in the war and nothing we have learned since leads us to believe that man for man the Italian sailors are twice or three times as good as the British and French. Modesty compels resort to understatements of this character.

If a world war should be forced upon us all this year it might well be that the earliest decisions would be reached in the Mediterranean, and these decisions would bring consequential disasters upon the Italian armies in Abyssinia, Libya, Spain and Albania. There is a school of British strategists who hold that in a world struggle with Nazidom it would be a positive advantage to have Italy as an enemy. In this long vulnerable peninsula, with its lack of raw materials, they observe a theatre in which important victories could be gained. German troops—above all, German aviation—would become involved in the defence of Italy and so far as possible of Italy's overseas ventures.

This prospect cannot be at all pleasing to the Italian people. If the Nazi domination were successful in beating down the resistance of France and the British Empire, possibly assisted by the United States, there would, of course, be much loot to share. But Germany would be the tiger and Italy the minor attendant who had gone hunting with her. The Germans have a way, when they get into countries, of throwing their weight about. Even if the brightest hopes of the Berlin-Rome Axis were realised, Italy would be in fact, if not in name, a dependency of the Nazi power. But the fortunes of war might not take this course. The great nations of the West, whose existence would be at stake and whose allies in the East might gather under the pressure of events, might after all be successful. In that event Italy would not only have suffered and borne the brunt at the beginning, but at the end she would be upon the defeated side. Either way the Italian prospect does not seem inviting to any dispassionate eye.

There is every reason to believe that this is the view of the Italian people. The mass of them are not allowed to take any part in the shaping of their destinies. They are told only what it is thought good for them to hear. All free expression of opinion is sedulously prevented. But we are told that even in the Fascist Grand Council stern words have been used against the policy of dragging Italy into a Mediterranean war with Great Britain and France. One important leader is said to have declared that Italy must not be drawn into a war 'against the wish of the Church, of the King and of the people.' So far as we can tell, from the innumerable contacts which exist between British and Italian individuals, these sentiments are almost universal throughout Italy. It would be with genuine grief that the industrious and agreeable Italian population would find themselves condemned to a mortal struggle with the two democracies of the West. No doubt they are assured that the French and British are effete and decadent; that they are rotted with Bolshevism; that they are incapable of manly action. But this propaganda has not carried conviction with it, and to this moment it remains doubtful whether Signor Mussolini, if he had the will, would have the power to force the Italian people to this terrible plunge.

The breaking of agreements with Great Britain, which many people felt were not worth the paper on which they were written, is not necessarily a final test. The outrage upon Albania presents itself, like so many other episodes at these times, in an ambiguous guise. It may be that it is the first move in a German-Italian drive upon the Balkans, which must lead inevitably to general war. Certainly the movement of troops and munitions to Albania, far beyond what local needs require, would seem to support this sombre view. On the other hand, one can imagine Mussolini explaining that his Albanian excursion is a mere local incident. He made, he might say, demands upon France which he considered just, but which were bluntly refused. No Tunis, no Corsica, no Nice, without war with the Western Powers! 'Where else,' he might exclaim, 'could I go but to this Albania, which gives me something to show my people, after all their hardships, without bringing them into direct conflict with England and France?' It would indeed be rash to pronounce. All that is contended for in these pages is that no answer to it is yet forthcoming from the head of the Italian Government. But all must very soon become clear. The British and French Governments are believed to be about to give a guarantee to Greece and Turkey. Any attack upon the integrity or independence of Greece, which is nearest to danger, would precipitate the Mediterranean war and would no doubt be the signal for a far graver conflict in the north.

Although it is dangerous to prophesy in a positive sense, we may at least feel at the time of writing that the Berlin-Rome Axis stands upon a no more sacred foundation than does the Anglo-Italian Pact.

On April 16, President Roosevelt addressed a solemn inquiry to the two Dictators and Powers, about their intention towards the States on their borders. The answers received were not encouraging.

AFTER PRESIDENT ROOSEVELT'S MESSAGE
APRIL 20, 1939

It seems difficult to believe that the two Dictators will reject the fair and friendly offer extended to them from across the ocean by President Roosevelt. Yet up to the present moment there is no sign that they will accept it in the spirit in which it was made. Should we eventually have to recognise that it has been cast back in the teeth of the United States, it will be clear that the larger hopes of the world have received a very heavy blow. The two Dictators and their associates will have placed themselves and their associates in a class apart. They will have shown that their intentions are dark and malignant; that friendly processes are of no avail; and that civilisation must shortly withstand the onslaught of desperate men. Such rejection will prove even to the most doubting that the Nazi and Fascist Dictatorships have no confidence that their alleged grievances and evident ambitions could stand the test of faithful investigation.

If this should unhappily prove true, we must none the less regard the President's peace message as a weighty contribution to the cause of collective security. All the thirty States to whom he appealed, except those gripped by the Nazi terror, will be inclined to range themselves upon the side of peace and law. The recalcitrants will place themselves, to a large extent, in the dock. The process of building up a grand alliance of peace-seeking States against further aggression must receive a notable stimulus in Europe. The growing convictions of the people of the United States of America will be proportionately fortified. We may be certain that the United States will not intervene in any British or European quarrel. But they seem to be developing a very definite opinion of their own. At the time of writing we can but hope that Herr Hitler and Signor Mussolini, supported by their Ribbentrops and Cianos, will not allow this new ray of light to die without realising that it may not shine again.

Meanwhile our minds turn naturally upon the attitude of General Franco. There is no doubt that it is very different from that adopted by him in the September crisis. He then, much to the displeasure of Herr Hitler, declared himself resolved to be neutral. But at that time he had on his hands a life-and-death struggle with Republican Spain, and all his armies were extended on the long fronts of the Civil War. Now that all Republican resistance has been crushed, he may feel himself less held by local necessities, and at the same time more gripped in Nazi and Fascist hands. The British Conservative Right Wing, who have given him such passionate support, must now be the prey to many misgivings. There is no doubt that all kinds of potentially hostile preparations are being made opposite to Gibraltar. Reports which are not confirmed in official circles stream in of concentrations of troops and preparations of aerodromes behind the Pyrenees, and of submarine bases on the north coast of Spain.

We are certainly being fooled about the departure of the Italian troops. They were all to go at the latest when the war was over. Then they were to go by the middle of April; then, instead of going, large additional numbers of Italians were landed. But this, we were assured, was only for the victory parade and the triumphant entry into Madrid. Here, again, there are postponements. So joyous an event cannot apparently be hastened. It was fixed for May 2; it has now been postponed till May 15. Meanwhile the Italian Government are prodigal in their assurances that they will keep the word that they have passed to Mr. Chamberlain and the British Government. These assurances are, of course, not in themselves worth the breath that uttered them.

There is another respect in which our relations with General Franco are worse than in September. At that time Spanish Morocco was virtually undefended, and it would not have been difficult for a French or Anglo-French force to take possession of the heavy batteries erected on the African side. But now a large Spanish army of seasoned troops is available for their defence. We are told the Moorish troops are being repatriated to Morocco. This very natural operation does not touch the question of the part these troops will play when they have reached their homeland. In September last, or indeed as late as February British and French naval, military and air forces could have occupied the island of Minorca at the invitation of a friendly Spanish Republican Government. But now such an act would be justifiable only if some overt aggression had been committed by General Franco's Government; and by that time the operation might have become more difficult.

It is upon this foundation that we must study the proposed movement of a portion of the German fleet for healthful exercises on the coast of Spain. At first sight one would suppose that it was reassuring. If the Nazi Government can afford to send two of their pocket battleships and some cruisers, with flotillas of destroyers and submarines, far away from their home station in the Baltic, and place them in waters from which in certain circumstances return might be difficult—is this not, one asks oneself, a kind of tacit guarantee that there will be a longer breathing-space? On the other hand, the movement is capable of a sinister interpretation. We well remember how at the outset of the Great War the *Goeben* was risked in order to determine the action of the Turkish Government. The arrival of a German fleet at Cadiz or at Cartagena might well be intended to put the final screw on General Franco and drag the Spanish people into the cauldron of a world struggle. Alternatively, these pocket battleships would be well placed at Cadiz to strike at all the trade reaching the British Isles from the Atlantic. No doubt arrangements could be made by Great Britain to cope with this form of attack, but it is not one which is necessarily inappropriate to the conception by the Nazi and Fascist powers of what they call 'a lightning war.' The utmost vigilance should certainly be exercised by the British Admiralty, the men at the head of which hold our vital safety in their hands.

It would be a pity not to dwell upon the opposite factors which may determine General Franco's choice—if indeed he is allowed to choose. Spain has just emerged from a civil war which has rent the whole nation in twain. One side has triumphed by foreign aid, and the vanquished, at least half the nation, are for the moment crushed and impotent. The only plan for the Spanish people is to unite in rebuilding their shattered cities and devastated social life. This hope can only be realised by neutrality. In the Great War neutrality was very profitable to Spain. She became rich while others bled and were exhausted. A neutral Spain would be courted by all the combatants. The interest of Spain is to lead her own life and cultivate her own garden.

Should Spain be lured into what is for her the wild gamble of a world convulsion, it seems probable that she would be denied just that very period of recuperation of which she stands most in need. Unless immediate overwhelming victory rewarded the Totalitarian States, and Hitler with perhaps Mussolini at his tail became the master of the world, General Franco's Government would never be able to send another ship to sea, nor receive a salt-water cargo. They and their island possessions would be a target for powerful and indignant combatants. They would seem to condemn themselves to making a savage desert of Spain, roamed through by haggard tyrants, instead of enjoying, as they so easily can, a position of marked advantage and bargaining power. It must be hoped that these solid considerations of Spanish interests will prevail. But the possibilities remain either that General Franco is intoxicated by his success or that he is no longer a free agent to act in the true interests of his country. Should either of these results emerge, we must all prepare ourselves for a darker and more hazardous future.

At a moment like this everyone must sympathise with Mr. Chamberlain in his grievous responsibilities. No Prime Minister in modern times has had so much personal power to guide affairs. Everything that he has asked of the nation has been granted; and when he has not asked what many thought necessary, no steps have been taken to compel him. There never has been in England such a one-man Government as that under which we have dwelt for the last year. He has taken the whole burden upon himself, and we can only trust that he will not be found unequal to it.

THE RUSSIAN COUNTERPOISE
MAY 4, 1939

It seems only too probable that the glare of Nazi Germany is now to be turned on to Poland. Herr Hitler's speeches may or may not be a guide to his intentions, but the salient object of last Friday's performance was obviously to isolate Poland, to make the most plausible case against her, and to bring intensive pressure upon her. The German dictator seemed to suppose that he could make the Anglo-Polish Agreement inoperative by focusing his demands on Danzig and the Corridor. He apparently expects that those elements in Great Britain which used to exclaim, 'Who would fight for Czechoslovakia?' may now be induced to cry, 'Who would fight for Danzig and the Corridor?' He does not seem to be conscious of the immense change which has been wrought in British public opinion by his treacherous breach of the Munich Agreement, and the complete reversal of policy which this outrage brought about in the British Government, and especially in the Prime Minister.

The denunciation of the German-Polish non-aggression Pact of 1934 is an extremely serious and menacing step. That pact had been reaffirmed as recently as last January, when Herr von Ribbentrop visited Warsaw. Like the Anglo-German Naval Treaty, it was negotiated at the wish of Herr Hitler. Like the Naval Treaty, it gave marked advantages to Germany. Both agreements eased Germany's position while she was weak. The Naval Agreement amounted, in fact, to a condonation by Great Britain of a breach of the military clauses of the Treaty of Versailles, and thus stultified both the decisions of the Stresa front and those which the Council of the League were induced to take. The German-Polish Agreement enabled Nazi attention to be concentrated first upon Austria and later on upon Czechoslovakia, with ruinous results to those unhappy countries. It temporarily weakened the relations between France and Poland, and prevented any solidarity of interests growing up among the States of Eastern Europe. Now that it has served its purpose for Germany, it is cast away by one-sided action. Poland is implicitly informed that she is now in the zone of potential aggression.

This Nazi habit of illegally and faithlessly abolishing treaties without the assent of the other party, after having reaped all possible advantage from them, has rarely taken a more brazen form. Herr Hitler and Nazi Germany have virtually destroyed their power of making agreements of any kind to which validity can be attached. This melancholy realisation will long brood over European affairs. There is, of course, no need for Great Britain and France to be more Polish than the Poles. If Poland feels able to make adjustments in the Corridor and at Danzig which are satisfactory to both sides, no one will be more pleased than her Western allies. But there will be no disposition on their part to press Poland to make concessions damaging to her interests or security.

The questions at issue between Nazi Germany and the Western Powers are moral questions rather than geographical or territorial. The peace block of nations is being formed to resist further acts of aggression, and it is the character of the act and the pressure which accompanies it that constitutes the offence against peace. Although there have been phases of Polish policy in the last few years which have been painful to French and British opinion, general sympathy goes out to Poland in her new ordeal. One would hope that the history of Poland, marked by so many tragic vicissitudes, has now entered upon smoother paths. The monumental crime of the partition of the Partition of Poland has been repaired by the bayonets of the victorious Allies. Poland was liberated from her bondage of one hundred and fifty years and reunited under her ancient standards. No part of the Treaty of Versailles was more in keeping with the conscience of the civilised world than this great act of justice and vindication.

The Polish people knew how to keep alive during their long period of servitude and oppression the gleaming principle of national unity. Russia, Austria and Germany all found themselves during six generations preoccupied with 'the Polish problem.' The great Napoleon struck his blow for the liberation and reconstitution of Poland. The preservation and integrity of Poland must be regarded as a cause commanding the regard of all the world. There is every reason to believe that the Polish nation intend to fight for life and freedom. They have a fine army, of which now more than 1,000,000 men are mobilised. The Poles have always fought well, and an army which comprehends its cause is doubly strong.

But it must be vividly impressed upon the Government of Poland that the accession of Soviet Russia in good earnest to the peace bloc of nations may be decisive in preventing war, and will in any case be necessary for ultimate success. One understands readily the Polish policy of balancing between the German and the Russian neighbour, but from the moment when the Nazi malignity is plain, a definite association between Poland and Russia becomes indispensable.

These are days when acts of faith must be performed by Governments and peoples who are striving to resist the spread of Nazidom. The British Government, who have undertaken to go to war with Germany if Poland is the victim of aggression, have a right to ask the Polish leaders to study the problem of a Russian alliance with a sincere desire to bring it into lively and forceful action. We do not know at present what proposals have been made by the Russian Government to Great Britain and France. There is reason to believe that they are bold, logical and far-reaching. If so, it is of enormous consequence that they should be promptly dealt with. This is no time to dawdle. Peace may yet be saved by the assembly of superior forces against aggression. Grave risks have to be run by all the anti-Nazi countries if war is to be prevented.

Above all, time must not be lost. Ten or twelve days have already passed since the Russian offer was made. The British people, who have now, at the sacrifice of honoured, ingrained customs, accepted the principle of compulsory military service, have a right, in conjunction with the French Republic, to call upon Poland not to place obstacles in the way of a common cause. Not only must the full co-operation of Russia be accepted, but the three Baltic States, Lithuania, Latvia and Esthonia, must also be brought in to associate. To these three countries of warlike people, possessing together armies totalling perhaps twenty divisions of virile troops, a friendly Russia supplying munitions and other aid is essential.

There is no means of maintaining an Eastern front against Nazi aggression without the active aid of Russia. Russian interests are deeply concerned in preventing Herr Hitler's designs in Eastern Europe. It should still be possible to range all the States and peoples from the Baltic to the Black Sea in one solid front against a new outrage or invasion. Such a front, if established in good heart, and with resolute and efficient military arrangements, combined with the force of the Western Powers, may yet confront Hitler, Goering, Himmler, Ribbentrop, Goebbels and Co. with forces the German people would be reluctant to challenge.

THE ANGLO-TURKISH ALLIANCE
MAY 15, 1939

To understand the full significance of the Anglo-Turkish alliance, just declared, it is necessary to look back some way. In the autumn of 1911 Italy made an unprovoked attack upon the Turkish Province of Tripoli, now called Libya. An Italian fleet bombarded the coastal towns, and an Italian army established itself on the shore. The Young Turks were already in power at Constantinople, and a vigorous resistance was ordered. Enver Pasha, the hero of the Turkish revolution, went himself through Egypt to Libya in order to conduct the defence of the invaded Province. His colleague Djavid wrote to me at the Admiralty offering an alliance with Turkey, in return for protection against Italian aggression. The main dangers of the European situation made it impossible for the Liberal Government to take a hostile line against Italy, and thereby make effective her nominal adherence to the Triple Alliance. Upon this decision the Young Turks threw in their lot with Germany, with consequences which profoundly affected the course, though not the result, of the Great War.

But the attack of Italy upon the African possessions of Turkey set in train a series of events which culminated a little later in the combined onslaught of Greece, Serbia and Bulgaria upon what was believed to be the dying Turkish Empire; and the Young Turks, earnest in their task of national regeneration, ascribed to Italy in some measure the responsibility of the misfortunes that befell them.

Much water—and blood—has flowed since those days; but Turkey has always recognised Italy as her most uncomfortable neighbour in the Mediterranean. Now that the old antagonism of Russia and Turkey has passed away, Turkish sentiment still regards Italian ambitions as the most direct danger with which she is confronted.

The fact that Mr. Chamberlain should have made this Alliance with Turkey shows how unfavourably the British Cabinet have been impressed by the conduct of the Italian Dictator during the later years of his memorable career. With a foresight which deserves commendation, Mr. Chamberlain last year prepared the way by the grant of a ten million pounds loan to Turkey. This was warmly welcomed by the Turkish nation. The Alliance now contracted grew naturally out of mutual assistance and goodwill, and is a practical expression of the common interest of Great Britain and Turkey in the peace and freedom of the Eastern Mediterranean.

During the Great War Constantinople was saved mainly by the military conduct and energy of that ever-famous Turkish warrior, Mustapha Kemal. He it was who in the dark hours of defeat when all seemed hopeless rescued his native land from subjugation and partition. He it was who, with long-persistent statesmanship, rebuilt the strength of the Turkish homeland, and by a series of astonishing and revolutionary reforms modernized the institutions and, to a large extent, the civilisation of the Turkish race. The wonderful way in which the disentanglement and exchange of populations between Greece and Turkey was effected in the years following the Great War reflects the highest credit on the statesmanship of both countries. The relations of Turkey and Greece, like those between Turkey and Russia, have now become thoroughly harmonious. The historic feuds, with their frightful injuries given and received, which for centuries have afflicted these peoples, are now laid to rest. This achievement, in which the leaders of Greece and Russia have borne their part, must mainly be ascribed to the far-seeing steady wisdom of the great Ataturk, true Father of his country in war and peace.

The consequences of the Anglo-Turkish Alliance, which will no doubt be swiftly followed by a Franco-Turkish Alliance, can scarcely be over-rated. An immense and new stabilising force has become operative in the Mediterranean. A Nazi newspaper commenting upon this event declares that England has 'gained in peace what she could not win for all her efforts in the Great War.' This is true; and it may be hoped that the fact will have a sobering influence upon the German Dictator.

It was a maxim of the old Free-traders that 'All legitimate interests are in harmony.' This is certainly the case in the Balkans and in the Eastern Mediterranean. The British and French guarantees to Rumania against aggression by Nazidom could only be made effective if Turkey admits British warships and, if necessary, French and British troops to the Black Sea. The command of the Black Sea in British, Turkish and Russian hands, and the free passage of the Dardanelles to the ships of the associated and friendly Allied Powers, suits the interests of every State concerned. Effective protection and assistance— so far as she needs it, for the Turkish armies are strong and famous for their fighting quality—can be given to Turkey by the Western Democracies. The excellent relations between Turkey and Rumania add to the security of both countries. The contact and communication of the Western Allies with Russia through the Dardanelles and the Black Sea has been proved to be a vital need for the defence of the east of Europe in a war against German invasion. The wheat and trade of Southern Russia, as long as British and French sea-power rule in the Mediterranean, can flow freely out to the markets of the world, and whatever is necessary in munitions and the raw materials of war can be brought in return to the Russian Black Sea ports.

Both Turkey and Russia have a common interest in the independence and integrity of Rumania. A Nazi advance down the Danube valley through conquered Austria and intimidated Hungary would carry with it mortal danger both to Turkey and Russia. Already the Nazis have a powerful growing flotilla on the Danube. A Nazi capture of the mouths of the Danube would be speedily followed by the incursion into the Black Sea of numerous U-boats, transported in sections. If Russia and Turkey lost control of the Black Sea, any port on its shores might become the landing-base for the long-talked of German 'Drive to the East.' In fact there never was a more obvious unity of interests than that prevailing among the Black Sea Powers. Unless they stand together, measureless miseries must be again their lot.

All this has therefore come about naturally without being forced or fanned, and the two Western democracies have been well-advised to join themselves in a solemn and public manner to the Self-Preservation group of Black Sea Powers. No one can doubt that the peace of the whole world stands upon surer foundations as the result of an honourable, courageous and prudent act.

But there is one Black Sea Power of which I have made no mention. Bulgaria, the unlucky child of the Balkan family, is still adrift from the strong armed league of the East, and from the liberal nations of the West, as well as from Russia, against whom she turned in the Great War, but who fostered and aided her establishment as an independent State. Bulgaria took one false turn when after the first Balkan War of 1913 she presumed too much upon the brave services of her armies. She took another, even more fatal, wrong turning when at the end of 1915, King Ferdinand led her into the ranks of the Central Empires, and cast her fate upon the losing side.

A third opportunity is now open to Bulgaria, and we may be sure that both Rumania and Turkey have the strongest desire for her friendly comradeship. No doubt the scars and wounds of former conflicts have left behind them smarting memories. But this is also true of every State in the east of Europe. All in turn have suffered, and inflicted, the horrors of war upon the others. Now is the time to look forward, and to make good and loyal arrangements to safeguard Eastern Europe from another hideous series of devastations. It is certainly the duty of Rumania, who gained so greatly in territory from the victory of the Allies, and who is now in mortal danger, to join her good offices to those of Turkey and the Western Powers in bringing Bulgaria upon honourable terms into the ever-growing Peace Block. It would not be useful perhaps to suggest particular measures; but anyone can see that the union of Bulgaria with her neighbours would play perhaps a decisive part in warding off the curse of foreign invasion and internecine war from these fair lands and brave peoples who have already suffered too long.

EPILOGUE

Here then, in an hour when all is uncertain, but not uncheered by hope and resolve, this tale stops.

Great Britain stands in the midst, and even at the head of a great and growing company of states and nations, ready to confront and to endure what may befall. The shock may be sudden, or the strain may be long-drawn: but who can doubt that all will come right if we persevere to the end.

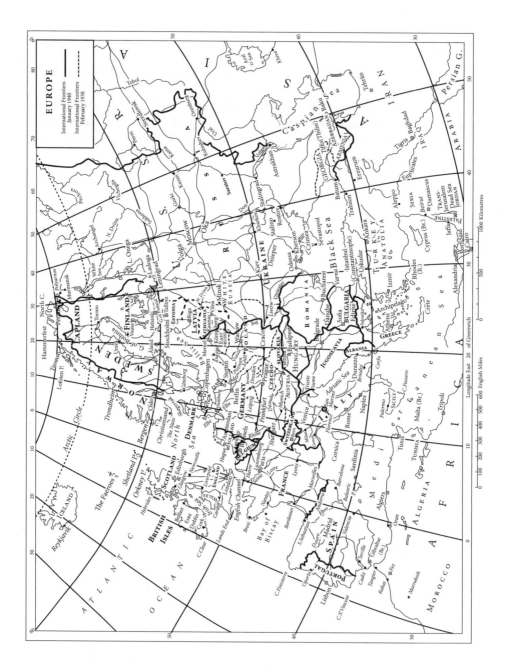